SIDETRACKED

The Betrayal and Murder of Anna Kithcart

RICHARD T. CAHILL JR.

WildBluePress.com

SIDETRACKED published by:

WILDBLUE PRESS
P.O. Box 102440
Denver, Colorado 80250

Publisher Disclaimer: Any opinions, statements of fact or fiction, descriptions, dialogue, and citations found in this book were provided by the author, and are solely those of the author. The publisher makes no claim as to their veracity or accuracy, and assumes no liability for the content.

Copyright 2017 by Richard T. Cahill Jr.

All rights reserved. No part of this book may be reproduced in any form or by any means without the prior written consent of the Publisher, excepting brief quotes used in reviews.

WILDBLUE PRESS is registered at the U.S. Patent and Trademark Offices.

ISBN 978-1-947290-28-0 Trade Paperback
ISBN 978-1-947290-27-3 eBook

Interior Formatting/Book Cover Design by Elijah Toten
www.totencreative.com

I dedicate this book to the memory of Anna Kithcart, a vibrant young woman whose life was ended far too soon.

SIDETRACKED

TABLE OF CONTENTS

Introduction	9
Chapter 1 – *A Racial Powder Keg*	11
Chapter 2 – *A Terrible Discovery*	18
Chapter 3 – *Annie's Last Day*	25
Chapter 4 – *The First Two Leads*	31
Chapter 5 – *The Circus Begins*	38
Chapter 6 – *The First Big Break*	48
Chapter 7 – *The Arrest*	56
Chapter 8 – *The Interrogation*	61
Chapter 9 – *The Interrogation Continues*	71
Chapter 10 – *Off to Court*	77
Chapter 11 – *Preliminary Hearing*	85
Chapter 12 – *Schleede Takes the Stand*	96
Chapter 13 – *Indictment, Bail, and a Protest March*	108
Chapter 14 – *Musical Attorneys*	120
Chapter 15 – *The Brawley Grand Jury Report*	128
Chapter 16 – *The Murder Trial Begins*	135
Chapter 17 – *A Blunder*	142
Chapter 18 – *Missed Opportunities*	153
Chapter 19 – *Dr. McNamara*	162
Chapter 20 – *Physical Evidence*	175
Chapter 21 – *Lippman Fights Back*	185
Chapter 22 – *Testimony From Family*	192
Chapter 23 – *The Dentists*	206

Chapter 24 – *The Pathologist*	**218**
Chapter 25 – *Blood, Hair, and Fibers*	**228**
Chapter 26 – *The Prosecution and Defense Rest*	**237**
Chapter 27 – *Summations*	**247**
Chapter 28 – *The Decision*	**259**
Chapter 29 – *Kiernan's Fate*	**268**
Chapter 30 – *Epilogue*	**271**
Photos	**281**
Acknowledgements	**299**
Endnotes	**303**

INTRODUCTION

"On that best portion of a good man's life; his little, nameless unremembered acts of kindness and of love."
William Wordsworth, 1798

THIS LINE BEST SUMMARIZES my memories of Annie Kithcart. In the late 1980s, she and I attended Kingston High School, though she was a year ahead of me. Annie was popular. I, on the other hand, was more of a geek. We were not friends. We were part of very different social cliques and thus did not substantially socialize. Being a small school, however, we ran into each other from time to time.

It was very common for popular students to mock and otherwise deride unpopular students. It was considered a *faux pas* for "cool" kids to be seen with a "not-so-cool" kid, unless they were insulting him or beating him up. Annie was different. Whenever I encountered her, she was always polite and pleasant. Never once did she ever insult me or put me down. She treated everyone she met with kindness. This was most certainly remembered by me, especially after her untimely death and the resulting media circus.

As the years passed, I became curious about what actually happened to her. I knew one man was convicted of the crime while another was charged with desecrating her corpse. I also clearly remembered Al Sharpton and his supporters calling my hometown a "Klan den." I knew little else other than that, as the media sensation grew, the one thing seemingly ignored was Annie herself.

I decided to research this case and learn the truth. I also felt it was time for Annie's story to be told.

In writing this book, it is my intention to present the events of the early morning hours of July 12, 1988, as they can best be determined. Some of the evidence is contradictory, and I have tried to present the most reasonable interpretations. I do present my own opinions at the very end of the book. They are based solely on the evidence, as I have no agenda concerning the guilt or innocence of the defendants charged in this case. Ultimately, I want readers to reach their own conclusions.

One conclusion is inescapable though. A very kind young woman was choked, beaten, and killed for no reason at all. It was a senseless waste of potential.

I hope I have done justice to her memory.

CHAPTER 1 – A RACIAL POWDER KEG

IN JULY 1988, WHEN a young woman named Anna Kithcart met her tragic fate, racial tension had been running high for months, if not years, in the state of New York. During the 1980s, several prominent cases of racially inspired violence led to public protests, marches and rallies, and raised the public profile of some lawyers and activists.

Perhaps the best-known occurred the year before, in 1987, when the alleged kidnapping and rape of a teenage African-American girl shined a national media spotlight on New York's troubles. Criminal accusations were lobbed at police and other white authority figures by advocates for the victim, who were accused themselves of exploiting the situation.

Tawana Brawley had been reported missing by her family in Wappingers Falls, a city in the Hudson Valley area, on November 24. The fifteen-year-old was found four days later, wrapped in a garbage bag with her clothes torn and burned, her body smeared with feces, and "KKK," "nigger," and "bitch" written on her body in charcoal.[1]

During transport to the hospital, ambulance technicians cut away the garbage bag and examined her. Tawana was largely unresponsive to smelling salts, though they discovered she had wads of cotton in her nose and ears. She resisted opening her eyes or straightening her legs.[2] Brawley was taken to a hospital where doctors determined that she had no signs of exposure, dehydration, or undernourishment. There were no drugs or alcohol in her system, and doctors found no evidence of physical injury.[3]

While doctors tended to their patient, police searched an apartment where Brawley had once lived, near where she was found. Inside the apartment, which was supposed to be empty, police discovered an electric heater on high that had tipped over and singed the rug. There were crackers on the floor and an empty carton of milk in the refrigerator. Scattered on the living room carpet were wads of cotton-like material and burned pieces of denim material. Inside the closet, police found a pair of white boots with some of the grey, cotton-like insulation removed. Also found was a pair of feces-smeared gloves.[4]

Police concluded that someone (likely Brawley) had been camping in the apartment for the previous few days.

Meanwhile, with the physical examinations completed, detectives wanted to question Brawley. At the specific request of her family, an African-American officer, Thomas Young, was brought to the hospital to take the girl's statement.[5]

Brawley initially refused to speak, but communicated by nodding her head, writing notes, and making physical gestures. In this manner, she told Officer Young that she had been taken to a wooded area and raped "a lot" by three people. One of them, she said, was a "white cop."[6] Later, when questioned by a doctor performing a rape kit examination, Brawley nodded when asked if she had been forced to perform oral sex. However, when asked about vaginal rape, she initially shook her head but then shrugged her shoulders.[7]

Not long after Tawana was released from the hospital, the press was contacted by her aunt, Juanita Broderick. Broderick also had called the FBI and Alton Maddox Jr., a prominent New York City attorney known for his work in racially charged cases.[8] In a hastily called press conference at the Brawley home, Broderick issued a statement of events that she said came from Tawana herself.

She told the press that Tawana said she had skipped school on Tuesday, November 24, and gone to the city of Newburgh.[9] Later, she took a bus to get home and was dropped off on Route 9D about a mile or so from her home. While walking north on Route 9D, a car with two white men in it pulled up. One of the men got out, grabbed Tawana by the hair, and pulled her into the car.

She screamed for the police, her aunt said, and the man hit her in the back of the head before yelling, "I am the police." They drove her to a wooded area where four or five more white men were waiting. Over the next four days, Tawana said she was sexually abused, defecated and urinated upon, and tortured. The men cut her hair, smeared feces on her, and wrote racial slurs on her body.

Tawana said she could remember nothing after that and had no idea how she got to the place where she was found.[10]

To add to the drama, Tawana's mother, Glenda Brawley, announced, "One was a white police officer who belongs to the KKK," while her stepfather, Ralph King, claimed the KKK was sending a message to them.[11]

When Tawana's story hit the media, the response was intense and immediate. Rallies were held in her support, and celebrities such as Bill Cosby raised money for a legal fund. Heavyweight boxer Mike Tyson gave Tawana a $30,000 Rolex watch.

The significant media hype did not really begin, however, until the Brawleys retained lawyers Alton H. Maddox Jr. and C. Vernon Mason, who brought with them a civil rights activist, the Reverend Al Sharpton.

These three African-American men had already gained significant notoriety in a case in Howard Beach, Queens, the year before, in which a group of white men attacked three black men who had walked into the predominantly white neighborhood after their car broke down. While fleeing from the assault, one of the victims was struck and killed by a passing car. Another was left badly beaten, but the third man fled the confrontation.

Three white men were initially arrested.

Sharpton organized a protest march of over a thousand people through the streets of Howard Beach while citizens shouted racial insults at them. Meanwhile, two of the victims hired Maddox and Mason to represent them. Maddox quickly accused the NYPD and the police commissioner of covering up facts in the case and secretly helping the defendants.[12]

Through their attorneys, the victims refused to work with the Queens County District Attorney's Office and demanded either a federal investigation or a special prosecutor. Governor Mario Cuomo eventually appointed a special prosecutor.[13]

When all was said and done, nine people were convicted on different charges related to the Howard Beach death.

However, at the time Sharpton and his associates entered the Brawley case, the Howard Beach matter had not yet been resolved and racial tensions were still running high. The Brawley case served only to turn up the heat.

When the Dutchess County District Attorney's Office convened a grand jury in January 1988, Brawley's family refused to cooperate. Governor Cuomo once again had to appoint a special prosecutor, selecting New York Attorney General Robert Abrams.

This did not alleviate the problem. The Brawleys still refused to cooperate. At a rally in Poughkeepsie, the county seat where the grand jury had been impaneled, Sharpton told more than eight hundred people that he wanted Maddox to prosecute the matter.

"Give Maddox the power, and we'll lock up all six men by six o'clock tomorrow," Sharpton roared. "Abrams' days are over. Cuomo, we'll retire you before we let you do this to Tawana."[14]

Maddox, who also was at the rally, added, "When we come to you, Governor Cuomo, we come to you with hate in our eyes. We come to you with hate in our hearts. We come to you with hate in our minds. We come to you with hate for all of the wicked things your people have done to us. We are not a happy people. You are not dealing with foot shufflers when you deal with us. No justice, no peace!"[15]

Cuomo refused to grant their wish, and Abrams began his own investigation and grand jury inquiry. There would be no cooperation from the Brawleys or from Sharpton, Maddox, or Mason. In fact, Tawana's mother, Glenda Brawley, sought sanctuary in a church to avoid a thirty-day jail sentence for ignoring a subpoena and refusing to testify before the grand jury.

During the months that the grand jury reviewed the case, protestors were regularly bussed in to Poughkeepsie by the advocates to chant and scream outside the courthouse in rallies often led by Sharpton.

Sharpton, Mason, and Maddox eventually offered up their own suspects and accused an assistant district attorney named Steven Pagones of being one of the rapists, suggesting they had evidence to prove it, but never providing it. They also accused Harry Crist Jr., a Fishkill police officer who had committed suicide a few days after the alleged attack on Brawley.

At a press conference on March 13, 1988, Maddox said, "Mr. Pagones was one of the attackers. He was one of the attackers, yes."

Shocked by the statement, a reporter yelled out, "Do you have evidence that supports this?"

"If I didn't have direct evidence, I wouldn't be sitting here saying that," Maddox answered. "We don't want to outline to Mr. Pagones what evidence we have. He's still a law enforcement official and is in a position to retaliate against the family."[16]

Later that same month, on March 31, Sharpton appeared on the "People Are Talking" talk show broadcast by Secaucus, New Jersey, television station WWOR. In response to a question from host Richard Bey, Sharpton made a similar allegation saying, "We stated openly that Steven Pagones, the assistant district attorney did it. His lawyers say he may or may not sue us. If we're lying, sue us, so we can go into court with you and prove you did it. I'll use your show to dare them to sue us – sue us right now. We are saying Steven Pagones did it. Now if Steven Pagones didn't do it, why isn't he suing us?" Pagones eventually won a defamation lawsuit against Sharpton for accusations he made in a television interview.[17][18]

These racially polarizing incidents continued into June while the attorney general presented witnesses and evidence to the Brawley grand jury. Then, on June 15, 1988, things began to turn against Tawana Brawley and her supporters.

Perry J. McKinnon, a top aide to Sharpton, charged in a television interview that the Brawley story was "a pack of lies." He further said he had been informed by other teens that the girl had attended two parties during the four days she alleged she had been kidnapped and sexually assaulted.

McKinnon said Sharpton, Maddox, and Mason had no evidence to support their wild claims and were using Brawley to build a political movement and incite rioting during the summer in New York.[19]

In a devastating turn, McKinnon charged, "The Tawana

Brawley story may be that there is no Tawana Brawley story. The real story is the political agenda of Sharpton, Maddox, and Mason."[20]

The New York attorney general called an immediate press conference. Abrams described McKinnon's interview as "explosive and astounding" and said it might mean that Brawley's advisers "have been consciously perpetrating a hoax."[21] The next day, Abrams called McKinnon as a witness before the grand jury.

As all of this controversy and racial tension swirled in Dutchess County, residents of Kingston (a small community, twenty-one miles north) were grateful that the racial and political circus had been largely contained to Poughkeepsie. Kingston residents had read the newspaper stories and watched television accounts, but the people of Poughkeepsie were experiencing it live and in person.

However, as the sun rose on the morning of Tuesday, July 12, 1988, all of that was about to change.

CHAPTER 2 - A TERRIBLE DISCOVERY

WHEN THE CITY OF Kingston, New York, was formed in 1872, the first public structure constructed was a large, three-story building used to care for the poor. Located on seventy-two acres near the intersection of Flatbush Avenue and East Chester Street with views of the Catskill Mountains to the west, the building was officially called the City Alms House, though most residents referred to it as the Poorhouse. It was shut down in the late 1940s and, by 1988, served as the Ulster County Department of Health.

In the woods behind the building, Joseph Kiernan awoke July 12 of that year just as the sun was beginning to appear. The night before, Kiernan had camped there after leaving his mother's home and walking nearly thirty minutes to the other side of town.[22] This was something he often did.[23]

After dressing, Kiernan broke camp, which consisted of picking up his blanket, shaking off the dirt and leaves, and folding it over his arm. He picked up his knapsack, put on his old fisherman's hat, and started walking through the woods.

Kiernan, a forty-two-year-old unemployed white man, had a history of mental illness and was well known to law enforcement officials. On different occasions, he had claimed to be an FBI agent, a CIA agent, and a member of Interpol. He also claimed to be pursued by the mob.[24]

He had not walked far when he reached the nearby railroad

tracks and train yard. These tracks had been in Kingston for over a hundred years. Initially used by the West Shore Railroad, the tracks now belonged to Conrail.

Kiernan continued following the tracks as they ran south past St. Mary's Cemetery and snaked through the city. When he reached the intersection of Smith Avenue in the midtown area of Kingston, he left the tracks and headed east toward his mother's home.

He decided to take a shortcut through the Board of Public Works storage yard. This brought him to the six-way intersection of Garden Street, Prince Street, East O'Reilly Street, and Hasbrouck Avenue.[25]

Running across the intersection was another set of railroad tracks. These had previously been used for freight and passenger service by the Ulster and Delaware Railroad. A popular way to travel west into the Catskill Mountains in the late 1800s, these tracks had been abandoned and neglected since 1976.

The remnants of the rail line went across the intersection and through a man-made channel running several hundred yards behind Kingston Hospital, exiting onto Foxhall Avenue. When the tracks were installed, the channel was dug through a hill to allow easy passage. Consequently, on each side of the tracks was a steep angled embankment about thirty-five feet in height. With no maintenance or upkeep for a dozen years, trees and brush had grown wild. As this was an area often used by drug addicts, derelicts, and heavy drinkers, the ground was strewn with trash and bottles.

Kiernan followed the tracks right into the channel. Forty or fifty yards in, something to Kiernan's left caught his attention. In his mind, he thought he saw "a love doll."[26] He cautiously approached.

Meanwhile, two nurses employed at Kingston Hospital, Debbie Stewart and Dottie Clarke, had parked their cars on Foxhall Avenue and were walking toward the hospital. It was about 6:35 a.m. Suddenly, both women saw Kiernan come running out of the channel behind the hospital. He was clearly agitated.[27]

Kiernan asked the women to call the police. He told them he had found a dead body or a mannequin on the tracks.[28] The nurses directed Kiernan to the nearest pay phone before walking together down the tracks to have a look for themselves.

They came upon the body of a young African-American woman lying near the tracks.[29] She was naked except for one shoe and a bra that had been pushed above her breasts.[30] They noted that the light-skinned woman's face was "blackish and deformed in the nose area."[31]

Being careful not to touch the body, the women returned to the hospital area and found Kiernan waiting for them. He explained that the pay phone they showed him was broken. Stewart and Clarke told Kiernan to wait where he was, and they went inside and called the police.[32]

While Kiernan and the two women were waiting for the police, a man named Matthew Felton walked into the woods by the hospital and also followed the tracks. He would later explain that he was on the way to his job and often used the tracks as a shortcut.[33]

When he encountered the body, he was scared and started to leave. Realizing that the young woman might still be alive, however, he went back and took a closer look. After he confirmed she was dead, Felton hurried off to the other side of the tracks.

As he was leaving, Felton saw two men near a local business called J&A Roofing. He got their attention and told them he had found a body. One of the two men was Robert Lunan, who had just taken a city bus to the corner of Foxhall Avenue and walked the rest of the way to work. When he got off the bus, he had seen a "bum" talking with a police officer. As he walked, two more police cars drove up. Until he heard Felton's tale, Lunan had thought maybe "the bum got mugged."[34]

Lunan and the other man (whose name was Jimmy) followed Felton, entered the channel from the East O'Reilly Street side, and found the body just as Felton had described it. They stared at the body for about a minute before a police officer responding to the nurses' call entered the scene from the Foxhall side. The three men decided not to stick around.

The officer was Maurice Vandemark, a second-generation Kingston police officer. His father, Curtis Vandemark, had been with the department for many years and was a detective. Maurice had been the first officer to arrive in response to the call from Debbie Stewart. As he drove his cruiser onto Foxhall Avenue, he saw Joseph Kiernan waving his arms. He pulled over, and Kiernan quickly told him what he had found. As two more police cars pulled up, Vandemark slowly started walking down the abandoned rail bed.

When Vandemark got to the scene itself, he saw the body on the ground and two men running away. (He never saw the third man.) He called for the men to halt and gave chase. Lunan, not wanting to be involved, kept running and got away, but Felton slowed and Vandemark quickly caught up.

As Vandemark questioned him, Felton reported what he had seen and insisted he had nothing to do with the woman's death. Vandemark cuffed him and brought him back to the scene. There, he turned Felton over to other police officers who were by then coming into the area. Felton was later brought to the police station to give a formal written statement.[35]

Vandemark and other responding officers secured the crime scene and called for backup. The small area would soon be overflowing with police officers and detectives.

At 7:25 a.m., Detective Richard Krom arrived. He had been called at home twenty minutes earlier and told that a body had been found on the old railroad tracks behind Kingston Hospital. When he arrived, he saw Officer Jim Grable guarding the entrance to the tracks from the Foxhall Avenue side.

After being allowed in, he walked about eighty yards before reaching the location of the body. Already on the scene were Vandemark, Officer Allen Saehloff, Officer Gary Longto, Sergeant James Brophy, Detective Thomas Scarey, Detective John Wallace, and Police Chief James Riggins.[36]

Krom noticed immediately that there were signs of a struggle. Leaves and earth had clearly been pushed around. To the right of the tracks on the inclined embankment, Krom saw the young victim. He immediately began taking notes.

She was young and appeared to be about twenty years old. Her complexion was light, and she had short, curly, brown hair. The woman was naked except for her left shoe and a bra that had been pulled up. The victim's head was on the high side of the incline, and she was lying on her back facing Kingston Hospital. Her left arm extended straight down away from her side, and the right arm was bent at the elbow and folded across the abdomen.[37]

There were deep lacerations on her forehead and blood on her face and in her hair. There was swelling around her left eye and abrasions and bruises on the right side of her neck. A piece of clear glass was imbedded in the neck just to the right of center. There was no blood from this wound, suggesting it had been done post-mortem. There were scrape marks on the thighs, shins, and buttocks, which Krom thought were consistent with the body being dragged [38]

Krom examined the woman's thighs and lower abdomen. What he observed there caused him to realize that this case was going to become a media nightmare. Clearly visible were the letters "KKK," scratched into the skin with a knife, piece of glass, or some other sharp object.³⁹

The potential involvement of the Ku Klux Klan or someone invoking their name meant that this case now had a possible racial motive. Given all of the racial chaos happening down in Poughkeepsie, it was now only a matter of time before Kingston would be engulfed.

Police Chief Riggins, upon learning of the KKK marks on the body, made it abundantly clear that any officer discussing this find with the media would answer to him. Riggins, though only recently promoted to chief, was highly respected by the rank and file. He ran a tight ship, and his orders were obeyed without question.

There is no reference whatsoever about the KKK marks in the initial handwritten notes from Detective Krom. Considering how thorough and detailed Krom usually was, this speaks volumes about the respect commanded by Riggins.⁴⁰

As the police waited for the county coroner, they carefully searched the path and area around the body for any evidence.

About eight or nine feet from the body was an old orange-colored washbasin that had previously been discarded by the hospital. There was blood on, in, and around the basin. Samples of the blood were secured, and the basin itself was taken as evidence.⁴¹

To the left of the body were two pieces of brick from which police recovered blood and a single hair. Blood was also recovered from a piece of Styrofoam and a small leaf, both of which were near the body.⁴²

In various locations, police took samples of dirt, and collected small change (thirty-seven cents near the body), some old and discarded clothes, and several empty alcoholic beverage bottles. The most significant of the bottles was a 40-ounce bottle of Colt 45, which would become important later in the investigation.

The police did not recover, however, any of the victim's clothing except for the shoe and bra left on the body. They concluded that the rest of her clothing was likely taken away by her killer.

Around 8:25 a.m., the body was removed by County Medical Examiner Harry McNamara, but not before Detective Krom secured the hands of the victim with plastic bags. This was to preserve any evidence that might have been under her fingernails. The various blood samples collected were given to McNamara to process.[43]

As they cleared the initial crime scene, the detectives and officers knew that it was only a matter of time before the press learned of the apparent racial aspects of the murder. Once that happened, all hell would break loose. The detectives knew that they had to focus on solving this murder as quickly as possible.[44]

CHAPTER 3 - ANNIE'S LAST DAY

AT THE SCENE OF the crime, several of the officers and detectives recognized the victim. She was nineteen-year-old Anna Kithcart.

The young woman known as Annie or "Kit" was well-known in the community as a friendly face who could be counted on in a crisis. She lived with her mother, Margaret Kithcart, in an apartment complex called Rondout Gardens in downtown Kingston. Her father, Eugene Kithcart, lived in the small town of Saugerties, fourteen miles north of Kingston, along with Gena, Annie's sister. At the time of the murder, Annie had not seen her father in nearly two months.[45]

Race is an issue that inflames communities, sometimes up to and even beyond the point of violence. Annie could have been a much-needed symbol for peaceful coexistence. She was the child of a biracial couple, a white mother and an African-American father. Her friends told reporters that her ethnic background presented extremely minor, if any, problems for her.[46]

In fact, she did not consider herself to be either black or white. One of her closest friends, Kristina Van Amburgh, recalled that Annie used to comment on her race by saying, "I'm both."[47] Van Amburgh said she had never known Annie to be a target of racist attacks. "Everybody loved her, and she loved everybody," her friend said. "Never, never did I see anything like that."

Annie was a vibrant conversationalist, and her outgoing personality extended not only to her friends but also to children in the neighborhood. She frequently played with the neighborhood kids and regularly bought them Popsicles, and would volunteer to baby-sit at her apartment complex without seeking payment.[48]

She was known to have a strong sense of fashion and was a fan of singer Michael Jackson. Friends and neighbors recounted the pride Annie felt when she purchased black patent leather "Michael Jackson" shoes that she had planned to break in at a local dance club.[49]

However, in recent months, Annie had become troubled. She had enjoyed partying and recreationally smoked marijuana since the eighth grade, though not heavily.[50] This changed in the five to six months before her death. A longtime friend, who described himself as a "childhood sweetheart," told reporters that she had become involved in the local drug scene and used cocaine, saying, "I know that she did coke because she was always asking for it."[51] Annie also had been spending time at Broadway East, an apartment complex known for drug sales and use.

In fact, when her father learned of her murder, he told the media that his daughter was a user and a victim of drugs. "I'm almost positive it was a drug rub," he said.[52]

Her mother was approached by a reporter and asked for a comment. She stared at him for a moment through eyes red and puffy from crying. Unable to find words, she slowly walked into her apartment and closed the door.[53]

As the media searched on the morning of July 12 for any scrap of information about Annie Kithcart, the Kingston Police Department was dividing the labor necessary to advance its investigation.

There were two significant things that needed to be done immediately. First, there had to be a neighborhood canvass.

Whenever a murder occurs, it is important to talk to anyone and everyone who lives in the area. Anything someone saw or heard might hold the key to solving the case.

The second job was to trace the steps of the victim on her final day of life. By finding out where Annie was the night before her body was found, the police would have more people to question and perhaps more clues to review.

Throughout the day her body was found, detectives talked to more than forty people who had seen or spoken with the victim on her final day. As a result, they developed a fairly good timeline.

Annie had spent the afternoon Monday with her friend Denise Noonan. They eventually went to a local city park and drank beer until a city police cruiser rolled up. Seeing they were underage, the officers made them pour out their drinks and leave the park.[54]

The women walked back to Annie's apartment and spent about an hour and a half hanging out and smoking weed.[55]

At about 9:00 p.m., they went for a walk. An hour into the walk, Denise and Annie saw a familiar blue 1985 Cougar driving toward them. It was being driven by a friend of theirs named Scott Mayer.

After the car pulled over and they talked for a few minutes, the women hopped into the car. They cruised around the midtown and downtown area of Kingston for the next hour making plans. Scott intended to meet a friend at a carnival on the other side of town later that night. He convinced the young women to join him.[56]

Before heading to the carnival, they rode up Broadway and pulled into a Convenient Mart about four blocks from the spot where Kiernan would emerge from the woods the next day announcing his grisly find.

After parking, Scott and Annie entered the store, while

Denise waited in the car. Scott went directly to the deli counter to get a sandwich. After being told that the deli portion of the store was already closed, Scott went back to the car and waited for Annie.[57]

A few minutes later, Annie came out of the store with a clerk close behind. Scott noticed she was hiding a 40-ounce bottle of Colt 45 under a towel she had been carrying. Seeing that the clerk was writing down his license plate, Scott panicked and pretended he didn't know Annie at all.[58]

After the clerk announced he was calling the cops and Annie heard Scott denying even knowing her, she took off running with the beer. She crossed Broadway and ran behind the Rondout Savings Bank building.[59]

Scott and Denise stayed in the store parking lot until the police arrived. They gave their statements and explained what happened. After the police left, Denise and Scott got back in the car and drove off.[60]

Meanwhile, after running behind the bank, Annie decided to temporarily ditch the beer. She wrapped it in her towel and hid it in the alley behind the bank. She then followed the alley until it exited to the street. She turned left and walked back to Broadway. Instead of turning left at Broadway, which would have taken her back to the Convenient Mart, she turned right and walked a block and a half until she reached the Royal Grill, a local bar.[61]

The Royal Grill was well known to the Kingston Police Department. Long the subject of complaints for selling to minors, the bar was also known as a location for the sale of narcotics. Not long after the Kithcart murder made headlines, the owner of the bar died of a heart attack and the bar was sold.

When Annie arrived at the bar, she saw Joe Misasi standing there. Joe and Annie knew each other from high school. They were not overly close, but, like most people, Joe liked

Annie and enjoyed speaking with her.

While they were talking, a man named Jeff Dawson drove up in his blue Firebird.[62] Annie immediately flagged him down. She told Jeff that she had beer stashed around the corner. She asked him to come with her and drink it. Jeff said he did not have time and quickly drove away. Ironically, Jeff did not have the time because he was late. He was the man Scott Mayer was planning to meet at the carnival.[63]

After Jeff left, Annie turned back to Joe Misasi and quickly convinced him to walk with her and retrieve the beer. They went back to the bank, and Misasi stood by the entrance to the alley while Annie went for the beer. A few minutes later, she returned with the beer still wrapped in her towel.[64]

Instead of going back to the Royal Grill, Annie and Joe crossed the street and walked down a side street, Jansen Avenue, that ran behind the bar. As they walked, Annie pointed out an alley that led to Broadway and came out right next to the bar. She suggested they drink the beer in the alley. Misasi refused, saying he had heard bad things about the alley. So, the two of them continued walking down Jansen Avenue until it ended at Foxhall Avenue.[65]

When they reached Foxhall Avenue, Annie pointed at the old railroad tracks running behind Kingston Hospital and suggested they drink the beer on the tracks. Misasi agreed. At approximately 11:30 p.m., Annie Kithcart started walking with him along the railroad tracks where her lifeless body would be found seven hours later.

When they had walked far enough that they could no longer see Foxhall Avenue, Annie sat down and opened the bottle. She and Misasi spent the next thirty minutes drinking and talking.[66]

While they drank, Annie asked Joe if she could borrow his shirt. When Misasi asked why, she admitted that she had stolen the beer and was certain the store clerk had given a description of her clothes to the police. Misasi declined, claiming the shirt belonged to someone else.[67]

When they were finished, Annie tossed away the bottle. Misasi heard it land, but it did not break. They walked back the way they came and then down Jansen Avenue until they were again at the alley that ran to Broadway and the Royal Grill. Annie suggested they go through the alley and continue drinking at the bar, but Misasi was not interested. He wanted to go home.[68]

Annie smiled at him and said, "Don't cut your hair. It looks good," before heading down the alley. Misasi waited until she was out of sight and then went home.

Somewhere between 12:15 a.m. and 12:30 a.m., Annie Kithcart came out of the other side of the alley and entered the Royal Grill.[69]

Over the next thirty to forty minutes, Annie was in and out of the bar several times. She asked a few different people to buy her a drink, but had no success. She eventually convinced a man at the bar to buy her a drink, but the bartender, Willie Davis, knew she was under twenty-one and refused.[70]

Annie left the bar around 12:45 a.m. and started walking down Broadway in the direction of her home. A witness reported seeing her walking alone on Broadway at around 1:00 a.m.[71] Annie's whereabouts could not be confirmed again until an hour and a half later.[72]

At around 2:30 a.m., Alonia Williams Jr. was standing in front of the Royal Grill talking with another man about selling a car when Annie Kithcart walked up to him and asked for a ride home. Williams told Annie to wait just a moment and resumed his conversation. When he looked back just a moment later, Annie was gone.[73] Williams was the last person known to see Annie Kithcart alive, other than her killer.

CHAPTER 4 – THE FIRST TWO LEADS

WHILE DETECTIVES WERE CONFIRMING the movements of Annie Kithcart on her final day of life, other members of the department were busy questioning Joseph Kiernan, the man who first found the body.

Detective Sergeant Thomas Scarey and Detective Wayne Freer started questioning Kiernan at around 10:30 a.m. that Tuesday. It was obvious that Kiernan was frightened and knew more than he was letting on.

They had already run a rap sheet that showed he had a limited criminal history. In January 1966, Kiernan was charged with burglary, though the charge was later abated and Kiernan was ordered confined in a state psychiatric hospital.[74]

Eight years later, in 1974, Kiernan was arrested for harassment and loitering, serving fifteen days in the county jail for the latter.[75] However, in the fourteen years since, he had either stayed clean or avoided being arrested.

The police had also partially confirmed Kiernan's statement that he had spent the night behind the old Alms House off Flatbush Avenue. Detectives Richard Krom and Michael Turck searched the woods behind the building and found a matted-down area just off the beaten path. There were a variety of cigarette packages there along with ten pages ripped from pornographic magazines.[76]

The detectives were certain Kiernan was hiding something

and suspected he might know something about the murder. Perhaps he saw something. Maybe he had even witnessed the murder.

Kiernan was willing to talk, but repeated over and over again that he had simply found the body. He denied killing Kithcart or cutting her. He maintained that he had not observed any of the "KKK" marks, something the detectives doubted.

Each time the detectives asked if he had touched the body, Kiernan became extremely agitated. He told the detectives that he thought he had found a "love doll," not a corpse. Once he pushed it with his foot, he knew it was a dead body and ran for help.

Not buying it, the detectives peppered Kiernan with questions, asking if he had killed or cut the young woman and demanding to know where the murder weapon was hidden. Kiernan denied every accusation and even agreed to take a lie detector test.[77]

Despite his loud denials, the detectives still felt that Kiernan was hiding something. As this was the first lead in the case, they decided to go ahead and schedule the lie detector test for the following afternoon.

The next morning brought a new lead. An employee of the Royal Grill named William Barksdale was walking through the alley next to the bar early Wednesday, July 13, when he saw a pile of clothes resting on a white bath towel. One end of the towel was partially folded over the clothes, and a long stick was protruding out from the bundle. Blood could be seen on the white towel. Barksdale wasted little time calling the police.

When Detectives Krom and Turck arrived at about 10:04 a.m., both ends of the alley were already taped off. The scene had been secured by Sergeant Barry Dunn and Officer Steven Spetalieri, the initial responding officers.

After waiting for police photographers to finish taking pictures of the entire alley, Krom examined the pile of clothing found about halfway down the alley toward the left side. To him, it looked like the clothing had been carried into the alley while wrapped in the towel. In addition to the blood on the towel, Krom noticed blood on the protruding stick. The stick was at least sixteen inches long and an inch and a half in diameter.[78]

Unwrapping the towel, Krom found a brown-and-gray striped terry-cloth top with a matching pair of terry-cloth pants that had been turned inside out. Both were stained with blood. He also found a white T-shirt and a pink pair of panties. There was blood on the panties as well.[79] These clothes would later be identified as the clothing Annie Kithcart was wearing the night she died.[80]

Also in the pile was a man's white muscle-type T-shirt. It was smeared with blood, and Krom believed it likely belonged to the murderer. Also found among the clothes were pieces of glass, hair, and leaves, as well as a few more sticks.[81]

Krom carefully collected everything, hoping the New York State Police lab would find some trace evidence off the muscle shirt to help identify the killer.

As Krom was collecting evidence, a television station's news van drove up and started taking video footage for the evening news. There were already a number of bystanders, but the news van drew even more. Additional officers had to be summoned to keep the growing crowd away from the scene.[82]

Like the initial crime scene where the body was found, the alley was strewn with trash and debris. Evidence technicians needed several hours to thoroughly comb the site. They did not finish their work until just after 1:30 p.m.

Around the time police finished with the second crime

scene, Joseph Kiernan was brought to the New York State Police barracks in the city of Middletown. Waiting for them was Thomas Salmon, a State Police investigator and trained polygraph operator.

Before being given the test, Kiernan was allowed to rest in a waiting room and was given coffee. Salmon took this time to advise Kiernan of his constitutional rights and make sure he understood that he did not have to take the test if he did not want to do so. Kiernan said he wanted to take the test and readily signed a waiver of his rights.[83]

As Kiernan rested and drank his coffee, the Kingston police officers gave Salmon the background of the case. This was necessary so he could construct proper questions for the test.

After about thirty minutes, Kiernan was escorted into the examination room. For the second time, he was read his Miranda rights before being connected to the machine's sensors.

A polygraph, or lie detector machine, measures and records data such as blood pressure, pulse, respiration, and skin conductivity while a person is asked and answers a series of questions. The general theory is that lying is a stressful act that causes physical changes in the body that the machine will record. A trained operator of the device is able to interpret the findings and determine if someone is being untruthful.

Although used by police in investigations (particularly in the 1980s), the results of a polygraph are not considered admissible evidence in court. In fact, the U.S. Supreme Court would eventually rule in 1998 that results of a polygraph were not reliable and were "no more accurate than a coin flip."[84]

Whether reliable or not, it did not take Salmon very long to conclude that Kiernan was not being completely truthful. He asked the detectives to step into another room with him to talk and told them that the suspect was telling the truth when he said he had not killed Annie Kithcart. He was not the murderer.

However, Kiernan was not being truthful when he said he never touched the body. His responses were so inconsistent that Salmon suggested to the detectives that Kiernan could have been involved with the crime even though he did not commit the murder.[85]

When the men returned to the exam room, Kiernan became agitated and immediately blurted out, "You know I didn't kill her!"

Freer looked at him for a moment before replying, "Let's talk about the cutting, then."

"I don't ever remember cutting her," Kiernan interrupted. "I didn't kill her."

Salmon stepped toward Kiernan and said, "You are not telling the entire truth."

"And it wasn't in just one spot," Freer added.

Kiernan just looked at the men for a moment before mumbling, "I found her. That's all. I didn't touch the body."

"You said you touched her leg and kicked her," Freer reminded him.

"Yeah," Kiernan replied. "I thought she was a love doll."

At this point, the detectives decided to focus on whether Kiernan had touched or moved the body. This was the one area of questioning that seemed to make their suspect extremely uncomfortable.

Salmon reminded Kiernan that scientific tests would prove if he ever touched the body in any way. "Just tell us the truth," he added.

"You're going to think I'm a ghoul," Kiernan answered.

When nobody replied, he continued. "You know ... necrophilia."

There was a palpable silence that seemed to last forever. Finally, Detective Freer said, "If that's all you did, just tell us the truth."

Kiernan let out a long breath before talking again. "I ate her. That's all I did," Kiernan told the stunned detectives. "Not longer than a minute or two."[86]

To their credit, despite hearing this staggering and frankly disgusting admission that he had performed oral sex on the corpse, the detectives followed up by asking, "Kiernan, when you were down there, didn't you see the KKK cuts on her legs?"

"No," Kiernan shouted.

"You had to," Detective Scarey shouted back. "What was it? Racial slurs?"

"I won't tell," Kiernan yelled before adding, almost as an afterthought. "I don't remember."

The detectives decided to wrap things up when Kiernan suddenly bellowed, "Look, you make up a statement as to what was there, and I'll sign it."

The detectives told him they would only put down what he said and were not interested in any stories. Kiernan had nothing more to say.

The detectives brought Kiernan back to the Kingston police station and put him in their holding cell. When the men reported the incredible admissions to Detective Lieutenant Paul Watzka, he looked over and yelled out, "Hey, Kiernan! Did you really do that?"

"Yeah," Kiernan replied.

"And what was that like?" Watzka asked disgustedly, not really expecting or desiring an answer.

Without missing a beat, Kiernan answered, "Like cold pizza."[87]

CHAPTER 5 - THE CIRCUS BEGINS

ALTHOUGH THE DISTRICT ATTORNEY'S Office and the Kingston Police Department had tried to keep the apparent racial aspects of the killing secret, rumors were rapidly swirling around the city.

Reporters for television station WTZA had interviewed Robert Lunan, the man chased by Officer Vandemark at the scene. He described the scene to them including seeing the letters "KKK" cut into the victim's legs. Reporters from the station had been calling for two days trying to get confirmation from police.[88]

Reporters from the *Daily Freeman*, Kingston's local newspaper, had heard these stories as well. They were busy checking with every source they had in the department hoping to be able to break the story.

Michael Kavanagh was not new to prosecuting crimes or dealing with the media. He was first elected Ulster County district attorney ten years earlier. Prior to that, he worked as an assistant district attorney in New York City for four years. He was well-respected in the community as a tough but very savvy enforcer of the law.

He knew it was only a matter of time before one of the media sources made the decision to report the racial angle without waiting for police confirmation. If that happened, allegations of a cover-up would dog his investigation and eventual prosecution. Kavanagh was not going to allow this.

So, on Thursday morning, July 14, Kavanagh met with the family of Annie Kithcart. With him were his chief assistant, Don Williams, and Police Chief James Riggins.[89]

Kavanagh revealed to the family the circumstances of Annie's death, the KKK marks scratched into her legs and abdomen, and Joseph Kiernan's admission of a sick desecration of her body. As Annie's family tried to comprehend these horrors, Kavanagh told them that he had to reveal this information to the public. It was the responsible thing to do, he explained, so that the public would know that all possible motives and causes of death were being pursued. Kavanagh pledged the full resources of his office and the Kingston Police Department. They would find the killer and put him away.[90]

Annie's family left the meeting stunned. They were already heartbroken knowing that the fun-loving young woman they loved dearly had been taken from them, but now they knew details not only of how she died, but also of things done to her body before and after her death. Worse, local television and newspapers were going to make all of this public information.

While the Kithcarts were heading home trying to understand life's cruel treatment of Annie, Joseph Kiernan was being arraigned in City Court on the other side of town.

Based on his confession, police charged Kiernan with sexual misconduct under Section 130.20 of the New York Penal Law Code. Subdivision three of this statute, though rarely cited, expressly prohibits sexual conduct with a dead body.

Kiernan was represented at the arraignment by David Clegg, an assistant public defender. He quickly waived a reading of the specific charge, entered a plea of not guilty on his client's behalf, and requested bail.

Waiving the reading of the charge was wise legal strategy. Clegg knew that the media would report the charge of sexual misconduct with a corpse, but having the judge read the specific and explicit details was not going to help his client. Frankly, the judge was probably pleased to not have to do so either.

City Court Judge Mike Bruhn set bail in the amount of $10,000 and remanded Kiernan to the Ulster County Jail. As Kiernan was being taken out of the courthouse to the waiting police van, members of the media, who had anonymously been tipped to the proceedings, shouted questions.

Kiernan did not miss his opportunity. "I'm innocent," he shouted dramatically. "They are not giving the details of the case."[91]

The sheriff's deputies quickly stuffed Kiernan into the van but not before he yelled out again in a wild voice, "It's connected to the Brawley case!"[92]

While reporters were returning to their desks to write about Kiernan's histrionics, District Attorney Kavanagh was busy putting together a release announcing a press conference. The document, written entirely in capital letters read:

THIS OFFICE HAS BEEN WORKING WITH THE KINGSTON POLICE DEPARTMENT INVESTIGATING THE CIRCUMSTANCES SURROUNDING THE MURDER OF ANNA KITHCART.

THE PURPOSE OF THIS PRESS CONFERENCE IS TO ANNOUNCE THAT THE INVESTIGATION IS CONTINUING AND THAT BECAUSE OF EVIDENCE UNCOVERED AT THE SCENE, ONE INVESTIGATIVE LEAD WHICH WE ARE NOW PURSUING IS THAT THIS GIRL'S MURDER MAY HAVE BEEN RACIALLY MOTIVATED.

SPECIFICALLY, WHEN THE DECEASED'S BODY WAS RECOVERED, THE LETTERS "KKK" WERE

FOUND SCRATCHED ON VARIOUS PARTS OF HER BODY.

BECAUSE OF THIS FINDING, WE HAVE REQUESTED AND HAVE RECEIVED ASSURANCES OF ASSISTANCE IN THIS MATTER FROM THE FEDERAL BUREAU OF INVESTIGATION AND FROM THE STATE ATTORNEY GENERAL'S OFFICE.

THIS IS BUT ONE OF SEVERAL INVESTIGATIVE LEADS NOW BEING ACTIVELY PURSUED.[93]

Later that afternoon, shortly before the scheduled press conference, Kavanagh met with his chief assistant to discuss the findings of the autopsy and other pieces of evidence to be discussed with the media.

Since the Ulster County coroner was not a pathologist and thus did not perform full autopsies, Kithcart's body was taken to the city of Syracuse the evening after it was found to be examined by Dr. Eric Mitchell, the Onondaga County coroner. Mitchell had been the coroner since 1983. His credentials were impressive. After graduating from the State University of New York Upstate Medical University in 1976, he completed a specialty program in anatomical and clinical pathology followed by on-the-job training as an assistant to the state chief medical examiner in Chapel Hill, North Carolina. Prior to taking his job in Syracuse, he served as a medical examiner in Miami, Florida, for two years.[94]

Although the official report and lab analysis of such evidence as blood, fingernail scrapings, and stomach contents were not yet available, the coroner had been able to give Chief Assistant District Attorney Williams a preliminary report over the phone.

Based on his review, Mitchell found evidence of manual strangulation and blunt force trauma to the head. The victim had suffered severe blows to her head and had fractures to her skull and one of her eye sockets. There was no sign of rape or forcible sex.

There was bruising to the back of her head as well as her neck and left arm. The bruises on the neck and arm appeared be from a round or rectangular object. Scraping marks on the rear of the legs indicated the victim had been dragged a short distance.

The letters carved into the legs and abdomen had been done with a sharp instrument. The act of carving started while the victim was still alive but was completed shortly after her death.

As to cause of death, it was Mitchell's initial opinion that death was caused either by manual strangulation or blunt force trauma to the head. He could not be more specific or definitive. He also estimated the time of death had been two to four hours prior to the discovery of the body.[95]

Once the press was assembled Thursday afternoon, Kavanagh and Chief Riggins made a brief presentation that varied little from the written release. The reporters were ready, however, with questions. One of the first questions dealt with the allegation from Kiernan that the murder was connected to Tawana Brawley.

"There is no evidence that can link the two," Kavanagh said. "If it exists, I have not seen it, but you can certainly draw certain parallels." As examples, Kavanagh cited the KKK reference, geographical area, and the race of the victim.[96]

When the reporters pressed the issue, Kavanagh said, "There is no evidence that the people alleged to have attacked Brawley were involved in Kithcart's death."[97]

Undaunted, a reporter asked if it was at all troubling that Kingston had a murder case so similar to the Brawley controversy in Poughkeepsie.

"It is like a nightmare come true," Kavanagh replied.[98]

"What other leads are you following?" someone yelled out.

"One investigative lead which we are now pursuing is that the girl's murder may have been racially motivated," Kavanagh answered. "Racial motivation is obviously a legitimate lead." The prosecutor deftly declined to mention any other current leads.[99]

Not wanting to suggest that the murder was a racial killing, Kavanagh added, "We do not know that the killing was racially motivated. If it was racially inspired, that's a horrible development."[100]

Kavanagh assured those assembled that he had already been conferring with the New York Attorney General's Office, since that office was now in charge of the Brawley investigation. If any evidence surfaced to connect the two crimes, it would be disclosed.

"Why did the police withhold the KKK marks from the press?" a clearly annoyed reporter asked.

Hearing a verbal attack against his department, Chief Riggins jumped in to answer the question. He explained that it was withheld to allow detectives to do their jobs and interview as many witnesses as they could before widespread media attention.

"I think that if we had announced this from the onset, we would have had every nut in town calling us up," Riggins said firmly.[101]

Before any follow-up questions, Kavanagh quickly added, "We did not want anyone to make the claim that we were withholding this for any illegitimate purpose."[102]

For the next twenty minutes or so, the press asked about autopsy findings, possible suspects, and so forth, trying to get more information before their deadlines. Although Kavanagh reported the preliminary findings of the autopsy, he revealed nothing about other suspects or areas of investigation. He had addressed the areas he felt were important and was experienced enough to keep his remaining cards close to the vest.

The only additional things offered came from Chief Riggins. He mentioned as part of the autopsy findings that a bite mark had been found on the victim's neck. Also, in response to a question about Joseph Kiernan, Riggins said, "He has not been 100 percent eliminated as a suspect."[103]

When the press conference was concluded, Kavanagh felt it had gone well. However, the media frenzy was just beginning.

"Slaying Could Be Racial" and "Case Like a Nightmare Come True" were the headlines the next day on the front page of Kingston's newspaper, the *Daily Freeman*.[104] The articles detailed the findings revealed at the press conference and the possible racial motive of the as-yet unknown killer.

Several members of the local black community were quoted on the question of racism in Kingston.

Everette Hodge, who had been active for twenty-eight years in the local chapter of the NAACP, did not discount the possibility of illegal drugs being involved but also said, "It was probably coupled with racism. A lot of people resent black kids and white kids going together. And it's not getting better. We're right in the heart of racism. It's not diminishing at all."[105]

The Reverend James Childs, a local pastor, noted, "There's no question that racism is flourishing throughout." He opted to withhold further comment until more details on the crime were uncovered.[106]

The papers even interviewed Annie Kithcart's uncle, Larry Kithcart, who served as executive director of the Ulster County Community Action Committee. He refused to discuss the murder, but said that he had never heard of any Klan activity in the area.[107]

It was not just the local paper reporting on this story. With the public revelation that Kithcart's body had been defaced with the initials of the Ku Klux Klan, the story became a national one. *The New York Times*, *Los Angeles Times*, *Washington Post*, Associated Press, and United Press International all ran stories and questioned whether the murder might be connected with Tawana Brawley's reported attack about twenty-one miles to the south.

At the time of the press conference Thursday in Kingston, the Reverend Al Sharpton was at a church in Brooklyn with Glenda Brawley, Tawana's mother, who had taken sanctuary there after she refused to testify before the special grand jury in her daughter's case. The previous month, a judge had held Mrs. Brawley in contempt and sentenced her to thirty days in jail, but officers opted not to enter the church to arrest her.[108]

Informed of Kavanagh's statements and asked about the possible racial motive in the Kithcart murder, Sharpton said, "This merely adds credence to what I have been saying all along … in that general area there is a racist cult group still operating."[109]

Sharpton further alleged that he had received a phone call from Kithcart's family and would meet with family members to discuss her murder.[110] (He would later say that it was actually the Brawley family who asked him to investigate the Kithcart murder.[111]) He said he and his associates planned to come to Kingston right away.

Upon hearing from the feisty reverend, reporters immediately contacted District Attorney Kavanagh to see if he had any comment about Sharpton coming to Kingston.

"I am not going to make any of the mistakes that were made

across the river," Kavanagh said, referring to the Brawley investigation in Poughkeepsie. "They are racial racketeers. They are more interested in promoting racial division than harmony. If they do anything in an attempt to obstruct this office or the Kingston Police Department that violates any law, they do so at their own peril and will be prosecuted."[112]

By that Friday afternoon, Sharpton and Alton Maddox arrived in Kingston at the Ulster County Jail. Maddox was wearing a suit and tie, and looked every bit the lawyer. He walked to the visitors desk and asked to see Joseph Kiernan.

Sharpton on the other hand did not look like an attorney visiting a client. The flamboyant activist was dressed in a purple running suit. He was wearing a gold chain, and the top of the running suit was open enough to show a large round medallion dangling from the chain.

The men were brought to the visiting area and spent over an hour interviewing Kiernan. When they emerged, about seventy-five journalists were waiting for them outside the main door. Sharpton and Maddox walked up to them and wasted little time going on the attack.

"It is possible Mr. Kiernan is being set up as a fall guy," Maddox began. "Kingston is filled up with racists."[113]

"This place is a Klan den," Sharpton added. "This is what Tawana got caught up in. This might be a pattern that is happening throughout this valley."[114]

Pausing for dramatic effect, he continued. "Several whites have told us there is Klan activity in the Hudson Valley area."[115]

Sharpton and Maddox announced that they not only intended to help the Public Defender's Office represent Kiernan, but they also planned to conduct their own investigation into the murder.

They alleged that the Kingston Police Department could not

fairly and properly investigate the beating and strangulation death.

They told the assembled press that Kiernan had information on both the Kithcart and Brawley cases, but they refused to give any details.[116]

"We understand that local people cannot be independent," Maddox said. "We plan to find out exactly what happened."[117]

Sharpton this time advised the press that he and his associates had been asked by the Brawley family, not the Kithcart family, to get to the bottom of the young woman's murder because of the possibility of "a gang running around" committing acts of violence.[118]

After finishing their inflammatory remarks, Sharpton and Maddox were starting to leave, when one of the reporters shouted out, "What do you think of the DA calling you a racial racketeer?"

The question clearly annoyed Sharpton, and he turned to face the reporter. "DA Kavanagh or anyone else can make any statement he wants," Sharpton roared. "I'm coming back, and I'm bringing everybody with me. We're going to lean on you until you bust. If you hear some bristling in the trees outside your house, it's not a cat. It's me."[119]

With that, Sharpton and Maddox went to a waiting car and left.

CHAPTER 6 – THE FIRST BIG BREAK

ANNIE KITHCART'S FUNERAL HAD originally been scheduled for eleven o'clock on the Saturday morning after her death. However, the family quietly held the funeral three hours earlier. Having been besieged by the media, the family wanted privacy in their hour of sadness. It was hard enough laying their beloved Annie to rest. Having reporters sticking cameras and microphones in their faces and asking how they felt would have been simply too much to bear.

Many of Annie's friends and acquaintances who showed up at 11:00 a.m. were upset when they learned the funeral and burial had already taken place.

Annie's life had been cut short at the age of nineteen at the hands of a brutal murderer and her corpse violated. Her reputation and memory had been sullied by a media more focused on her drug use in the months prior to her death than on her numerous positive qualities. Now, many of Annie's friends lost the chance to say their final farewells.

They tried to understand why the Kithcart family wanted privacy, but felt burning frustration at the sudden, brutal, and unexpected loss of their friend, coupled with the lack of closure and hints of racism spread by those seemingly more interested in their public persona than with Annie.

Later that afternoon, Kingston police caught their first big break in the case.

Lieutenant Douglas Gaston and Detective Wayne Freer

had been busy all day. They had heard though their street sources that someone had been bragging about committing the murder. They were determined to find out if there was anything to the talk.

After speaking with numerous people over a period of nearly seven hours, they traced the rumor back to a woman named Gloria Washington who lived on Jansen Avenue, less than five minutes from the site of murder.[120]

When the police arrived at the address that Saturday, Washington was home. Though she was initially unwilling to talk, the detectives eventually convinced her to tell her story. She at first said she would not give any names, but told the detectives that a friend had told her that he and his girlfriend had given another man a ride home to Brewster Street on Tuesday. On the way, this man bragged that he had killed a girl and washed the blood off in a neighbor's swimming pool. The next day, her friend had his girlfriend make an anonymous call to the police.[121]

For several minutes, Gaston and Freer questioned Washington trying to get names to go with the story. Finally, she said she would call the person who told the story. If he gave her permission, she would reveal all of the names.

She walked to the other side of the room and picked up the phone. After a very brief conversation, she hung up and turned to the detectives.

"The people who told me were Todd Schleede and his girlfriend," she admitted. "The man who bragged about the killing was Jeff Dawson."[122]

Now that they had names of a possible witness and perhaps even the killer, Freer and Gaston went directly to the police station to speak to Lieutenant Detective Paul Watzka, the head of detectives.

When Watzka heard the detectives' report, he knew this was

a strong lead because this was not the first time the name Jeff Dawson had come up in the investigation. In fact, there now were two people with that same name, men who were cousins, connected to the case. The younger of the two had given police a statement that he had seen Annie in front of the Royal Grill on Monday night when he pulled up in his blue Firebird.[123]

The other Jeff Dawson, who lived on Brewster Street, had been looked at earlier in the week as a suspect. Interestingly, he became a potential suspect the day after the body was found when an unknown woman called the police from a public phone booth in Port Ewen, a small hamlet about a mile south of Kingston. The woman said, "The girl that was killed, Annie Kithcart, Jeff Dawson did it," and hung up.[124]

This Jeff Dawson was well-known to the police. He had a long criminal record, including two prior felonies, and was on parole for a burglary conviction in 1984.

After the anonymous call Wednesday, police officers were sent to Dawson's home, but he was not there. About an hour later, Dawson and his wife walked into the police station saying they had heard the police were looking for them. They were ready to give a statement.

Dawson was questioned by Detectives Mike Jubie and Junious Harris. He admitted that he had been at the Royal Grill on the evening of the murder, but he said he had not seen Annie Kithcart. He and his wife left around 8:30 p.m. and went home. About three hours later, Dawson said, he ran out of cigarettes and went to Cheap Charlies, a little store next to the Royal Grill.

After getting his cigarettes, he went into the bar again and played a game of Pac-Man. When the game was over, he went home. He and his wife stayed at home the rest of the evening. After telling this to the detectives, Dawson also offered to take a lie detector test.[125]

Dawson's wife, Rose, was questioned in another room by Officer Stephen Spetalieri. She confirmed her husband's story completely.[126]

The couple's statements were typed up, and they were asked to sign them. Rose did so willingly. When Detective Harris gave the statement to Jeff, he hesitated, saying, "The last time I signed anything I went to jail. I think I should talk to a lawyer first."[127]

Harris gave Dawson a phone book, pointed him toward the phone in the room, and stepped out. A few minutes later, Harris returned. Dawson said his lawyer had told him not to sign the statement. When Detective Harris asked who the lawyer was, Dawson said he could not recall.[128]

With nothing to hold him on except an anonymous call, Dawson and his wife were allowed to go home. The police had already received another anonymous call claiming that the killers were Jamaican drug dealers. Such anonymous tips are common and often prove worthless.

Now, however, Watzka had another tip pointing to Dawson. This time, they had a name that might just be the original anonymous caller. Watzka turned to Detective Freer and Officer Spetalieri and ordered, "Go pick up Schleede and his girl."

Todd Schleede was no stranger to law enforcement. He had previously been convicted of the felonies of burglary and criminal sale of a controlled substance. He had done prison time and was still on parole. He was also suspected of being involved in a string of recent robberies. He was living with his girlfriend, Penelope "Penny" DeGroat, in Ulster Park, about six miles south of Kingston.

When Freer and Spetalieri arrived at their door that Saturday, neither Schleede nor DeGroat seemed surprised. They confirmed Gloria Washington's story and agreed to accompany the officers back to the station. Once there, they told an astonishing story.

On the evening before the murder, Schleede and DeGroat went into the Royal Grill at about 10:30 p.m. They saw Jeff Dawson playing Pac-Man. The three decided to go back to Schleede and DeGroat's place in Ulster Park and get drunk. On the way, they picked up a fourth person named Mark Washington.[129]

The men stayed in Ulster Park for about an hour and a half drinking. Jeff Dawson drank straight vodka while the others drank beer. Around 12:30 a.m., Schleede drove Dawson and Washington back to Kingston. He dropped them off on Jansen Avenue, near the alley running between Cheap Charlies and the Royal Grill before returning home. He did not see Dawson again that night.[130]

The next day, Tuesday, around 3:00 p.m., Schleede drove back to Kingston. Penny DeGroat was with him. While driving down Broadway near the old Kingston City Hall building,[131] which was right next to Kingston Hospital and the wooded area where Kithcart's body had been found, they saw Jeff Dawson walking. Schleede beeped his horn, and Dawson came over.[132]

After talking for a few minutes, Schleede agreed to give Dawson a ride. He hopped in the back seat with his feet up and across the seat. Schleede felt that Dawson seemed anxious and "hyped up."[133]

"Man, you ain't gonna believe what I have to tell you," Dawson said. "I have something bug to tell you."

As Dawson said this, Schleede turned the car off Broadway and down Foxhall Avenue. When he did, he saw several police cars and officers standing near the entrance to the old railroad bed. Ignoring what Dawson had just said, Schleede muttered out loud, "What the hell is going on?"

"They might be looking for me," Dawson answered.

Without saying another word, Dawson slid down in the seat to avoid being seen by the police.[134]

Since Schleede was aware of Dawson's criminal past, he actually didn't think too much of his friend's actions or statements. He just figured Dawson had scored some money.[135]

He continued to drive his friend around until they eventually arrived at Dawson's home. The two men got out, leaving DeGroat in the car. As they walked toward the house, Dawson put his arm around Schleede and spoke to him quietly.

"The reason those cops were back there is because I murdered someone last night," he said.

"Who was it?" Schleede asked.

"Do you know that bitch Annie Kithcart?" Dawson asked.

Schleede knew her. Dawson then gave some details of the crime. He said he had used a chokehold on the girl, and he even demonstrated his technique.

"I rolled up her clothes and threw them somewhere behind the bar," Dawson continued, "I was going to put them in a plastic bag, but I didn't have one."[136]

Dawson laughed nervously. As he did, Schleede noticed a small bruise under one of his eyes. He could not recall which eye. Dawson then pointed to a house and told Schleede that he had used his neighbor's pool that same night to wash off the blood.[137]

Schleede could not believe what he was hearing. He and Dawson had both committed crimes of theft, but murder was something completely different. He was still trying to process everything when Dawson suggested they go back to Schleede's place and have a cookout.

Schleede was stunned. This guy had just told him about viciously killing a woman and washing her blood off in a pool. Now, as if nothing had happened, he wanted to barbecue hamburgers and hotdogs. Schleede stammered for a moment before collecting himself and saying, "I can't right now. I have to go to my mother's house. I'll be back in an hour." Without another word, he went back to his car and drove off.[138]

Penny could see something was bothering her boyfriend when he got back in the car. He was clearly scared and upset.

"Jeff just told me the sickest thing," he croaked.

"Well, tell me," Penny said excitedly.

"I can't. You'll really bug."

"Well, tell me for Christ's sake," she demanded.

Todd then relayed the conversation to his girlfriend. After hearing the grisly story, she asked, "Why would Jeff tell you that?"

"I don't know," he answered.[139]

After discussing the matter for the rest of the day and barely sleeping that night, the couple agreed to make the anonymous call to the police the next day. DeGroat said she made the call herself.[140]

When Schleede finished relating his account of events, Officer Spetalieri realized that he was in a bit of a quandary. Although Schleede was willing to talk and sign a statement, his testimony might not be worth much. Like their suspect, Schleede had a long criminal history and was on parole. Dawson's felonies were all burglaries. Schleede had a burglary conviction too, but had also been busted for selling drugs. He was not the most credible witness.

For all Spetalieri knew, Schleede could be the killer and was concocting this wild story to frame Dawson. Yet, he found himself actually believing him. It was just crazy enough to be true.

Detective Turck was in the next room questioning Penny

DeGroat. Spetalieri knocked on the door and called for him. He wanted to know what she had said. Turck said she hadn't heard the conversation between Dawson and her boyfriend outside the car. However, she was able to confirm everything Schleede said about Dawson's statements in the car. The two stories were consistent.

Turck and Spetalieri went to their boss to determine the next step. After discussing the matter with Lieutenant Watzka, it was agreed that the only way they could use Schleede as a witness would be if Dawson's statements were on tape.

All three returned to the interrogation room where Schleede waited patiently. They asked him if he would wear a wire and try to get his friend to repeat his confession. Schleede readily agreed.[141]

After fitting him with the recording device and testing it, the police assembled their arrest team and drove to Brewster Street hoping to get the confirmation they needed.[142]

CHAPTER 7 – THE ARREST

JEFF DAWSON AND HIS wife lived in the upstairs apartment of a multi-family home on the corner of Brewster and Levan Streets. It was less than three blocks from the Royal Grill.

On the Saturday evening after the murder, July 16, at around 11:00 p.m., several cars drove into Dawson's neighborhood. Todd Schleede and Penny DeGroat drove their own car and parked directly in front of Dawson's home.

The other cars were unmarked police cruisers. They took various positions, with Detective Turck and Officer Spetalieri parking on Levan Street so they could observe the front door of Dawson's home and the rear doors on Levan Street.[143]

Police had arranged the wire to have both a recorder and a receiver so they could hear and record conversations, but could also give Schleede instructions if he got into any trouble.[144]

As Schleede parked the car, he turned to DeGroat and commented that he needed a drink. Lieutenant Watzka heard this over the wire and replied, "And what kind, Wild Turkey?"

"I'll drink the strongest shit they got," Schleede responded. "A mug."

"Yukon Jack?" Watzka offered.

"One hundred percent rubbing alcohol," Schleede joked.[145]

With the moment of levity gone, Schleede returned to business. He beeped his horn to get Dawson's attention. He waited a few minutes, but nothing happened.

"I'm gonna walk up and knock on the door," Schleede said nervously, "'cause all the lights are out."[146]

Leaving DeGroat in the car, Schleede walked to the front door and pounded on it several times. There was no answer.

"There's nobody home," Schleede announced to the listening officers. "I'm gonna pull around the corner and park."[147]

Returning to his car, Schleede drove away and parked a block or so down the street so he could not be seen from the targeted house. He and DeGroat walked to Levan Street to the car manned by Turck and Spetalieri.

Turck rolled down the window and leaned out. "There's a light on in the front bedroom," he observed. "Pull up right in front and start laying on that horn."

"All right," Schleede answered, "and then what if he ain't home?"

"You get out on the sidewalk and yell his name," Turck said, a little exasperated. "I think a window's open in the front."[148]

Without another word, Schleede returned to his car. He drove around the corner and again parked in front of 42 Brewster. He opened the driver's door and leaned on the horn several times. "Hey, Jeff!!" Schleede shouted.

"Ahh, maybe they're sleeping," one of the officers said over the radio.

Schleede hit the horn again. "Motherfuckers around gonna call the cops saying I'm disturbing the peace," he said sarcastically.[149]

The officers were still laughing at Schleede's joke when they heard another voice come over the wire.

"Who you looking for?" the voice asked.

"Jeffrey," Schleede responded. "Where you been hiding?"[150]

Between the beeping and shouting, Schleede had finally gotten Dawson's attention. The members of the arrest team quieted down to listen to the men's conversation.

Schleede: Check it out, huh, you see all that shit in the paper, man?

Dawson: Yeah.

Schleede: All that crazy…Who put that KKK on that girl? That other kid, who did it, that other guy?

Dawson: Nah. They had me down at the police station for like seven, almost eight hours.

Schleede: Yeah.

Dawson: Come up here and inspect the house and shit.[151]

Seeing that Dawson was not giving anything more than one syllable answers about the murder itself, Schleede tried asking about it again.

Schleede: Damn, man. What happened over there?

Dawson: She started bugging out man, just bugging me, man. She fell and cut her head and shit. She had a big gash. She's dead. I knew she was, and that's when I took the knife. I decided to make it look like…like a psychopath did it."[152]

Schleede: Who put the fucking KKK, the white guy?

Dawson: Nah.[153]

As the two men continued to talk, a marked patrol car drove by. Whether this was another unit on patrol or an odd move planned by the arrest team is not documented.[154] Regardless, Dawson saw the police car and reacted right away,

"**Look** at that white and blue, man," Dawson said

angrily. "I told you them niggers be following me, man."[155]

Schleede was becoming very nervous. He had not been told that a marked police car was going to drive by. All he knew was that Dawson was getting upset. Schleede tried again to get back to the murder and get a confession.

Schleede: What happened to her, man? How did she fall down and hit her head and shit? Was she drunk?

Dawson: Yeah.

Schleede: Damn. Sharpton and all them motherfuckers coming around here.

Dawson: Yeah, I know it. Just seen him on the news tonight with Tawana Brawley. They all handcuffed together and shit. They gonna go down there with Jesse Jackson and start some shit up.

Schleede: Ain't nobody seen you back there with her?

Dawson: You tell me, man. I ain't even been out on Broadway. These fucking niggers. They be driving and come around here every half on the hour. I be sitting in the window with the lights out watching them.

Schleede realized that he was losing any chance to get Dawson to talk. He was completely focused on the police car that had driven by and did not seem interested in talking about Annie Kithcart. Schleede decided to try one last time.

"Damn," Schleede interjected, "then some fucking guy came along and had sex with her corpse."

Seeing no reaction from Dawson, Schleede continued, "Motherfucking crazy man. You didn't fuck her?"[156]

Dawson just shook his head. When he did speak a few seconds later, he was back to complaining about the police.

"They searched the house for rings and shit like that," he

said.

"She hit you in the eye?" Schleede interrupted. "You got a black…a bruise on it?"

"Yeah," Dawson answered before immediately changing the topic. "It's gonna fucking rain."[157]

It was obvious that Jeff Dawson was not going to say anything more about the murder.

Lieutenant Watzka, who was in charge of the operation, picked up his radio and called Detective Turck.

"Where's Dawson?" he asked.

"I see him," Turck answered. "He looks like he's about ready to go inside."

Watzka wasted little time in his reply. "Take him now."[158]

Schleede and Dawson were still talking when seven officers came up and ordered them to the ground. It had previously been discussed with Schleede that he and his girlfriend would be cuffed and arrested with Dawson to hide the fact that he was working for the police. So, when the police arrived, Schleede played along.

Schleede and DeGroat were both marched away while Dawson remained prone on the ground, his hands secured behind him. He said nothing as other officers went into his house and arrested his wife, Rose.

After a few minutes, Dawson heard someone else walking toward him. He glanced up and saw Detective Junious Harris standing over him. The detective reached into his shirt pocket and took out a small card.

"Jeffrey Dawson," Harris began, "you have the right to remain to silent…"[159]

CHAPTER 8 – THE INTERROGATION

WHILE HE WAS BEING taken downtown to police headquarters, Jeff Dawson told the officers he was willing to give a statement. So, less than thirty minutes after his arrest, he found himself in a dingy interview room with Detective Harris and Officer Spetalieri.

Spetalieri started the cassette recorder at 11:50 p.m. Saturday and spoke first. Since he already knew Dawson was willing to make a statement, he got right to the point.

"All right, Jeff, why don't you tell me now, go back and tell me how this whole thing got started."

"I left the house about eleven thirty, maybe eleven o'clock," Dawson began, reflecting on the events of five days before. "I was supposed to meet up with somebody and we was supposed to do a burglary, but, uh, the person didn't come."[160]

He stopped talking, as if waiting for another question. The only sound in the room for several long seconds was an old clock whose ticking seemed amplified by the silence. Hearing nothing else, Dawson took a deep breath and continued his story of what happened that night.

With his planned burglary foiled by his apparently unwilling accomplice, Dawson went into the Royal Grill. He did not see many people he knew, so he decided to play a game of Pac-Man.

After his game, he walked outside and saw Annie Kithcart. She was drunk, but came right up to him.

"Hey, buy me a drink?" she asked.

"No," Dawson replied. "I ain't got any money."

Annie was undaunted. "Come on, we can do something," she urged. "Let's rob a liquor store, so we can get drunk."

"Naw," Dawson answered. "I already have plans to do something."

Dawson walked away and started heading up Broadway. Kithcart followed him.

"Listen," she said perkily. "I'm down with whatever you want to do."

Dawson ignored her and turned down Foxhall Avenue. Reaching the entrance to the old railroad bed, he looked back and Kithcart was still following him. He quickly walked down the tracks and into the darkness.

Kithcart continued to follow him nonetheless. He could barely see her as the overgrown trees and brush blocked almost all light. He could hear her clearly though. All the while, she kept at him, saying, "Come on, let's do something. Let's get drunk."

Her constant badgering was getting on his nerves, and Dawson felt his anger growing. When he felt he could not stand it any longer, he turned and physically pushed her away.

Even this did not stop her. She continued to verbally barrage him. "Come on, why don't you want to do anything?"

Dawson pushed her away again. When he pushed her this time, she tripped on a log and fell flat on her back. She stopped moving.

At first, Dawson thought she was faking. "Stop playing. Get up," he shouted. "Let's stop playing."

When Kithcart did not move, Dawson bent down and checked her. He put his hand behind her head to pick her up.

His hand came back wet with blood.

In a panic, Dawson wiped his hand on his white shirt. His mind began to race. He was on parole. A young woman was hurt. Nobody would believe him. He bent down again to check if Annie had a pulse. As his own heart was nearly pounding through his chest, he simply could not tell if she was alive or dead.

He staggered away from the scene and a minute later came out the other side of the rail bed. He made his way to the abandoned Old City Hall Building and sat on the stone steps just thinking about what had just happened.

An hour or two later, Dawson said, he decided to go back to the rail bed and check on Annie. However, when he got back, things were not as he had left them. Since he had left, someone else must have come along. Annie had been stripped of her clothes. They were all in a small pile by her feet. Annie's face was covered in blood, and there were cuts all over her body.

Dawson collected her clothes and wrapped them in the towel she had been carrying. He kept walking and came out the other side on Foxhall Avenue. He quickly ran over to Jansen Avenue, which ran behind the buildings facing Broadway. He cut through the alley between Cheap Charlies and the Royal Grill, and stopped halfway down the alley. He took off his own shirt because it had blood on it and stuffed it into the balled-up towel with Annie's clothes. He then dropped the entire package there in the alley and headed to his apartment.

About ten minutes later, Dawson arrived home. Realizing that he still had blood on his hands and chest, he climbed his neighbor's fence, quietly slipped into their above-ground pool, and washed it off.

When the blood was sufficiently rinsed away, Dawson got out of the pool, climbed back over the fence, and tiptoed up the stairs to his apartment, being careful not to wake his wife.[161]

When Dawson finished recounting his tale, he just looked down at the table in front of him. Spetalieri and Harris glanced at each other. Dawson had just placed himself with Annie Kithcart at the scene of her murder. This was a significant admission, but the men also knew that a great deal of what they had just heard was contradicted by the evidence.

Spetalieri leaned in a little toward Dawson. "When you got back to the scene, you said her clothes were in a pile?" he asked.

"Yeah," Dawson answered quickly without looking up.

"You didn't take the clothes off of her?" Spetalieri asked.

"No."

"Did you see anybody else in the area?"

"Nobody."

"Did you check her pulse?" the officer asked.

Dawson nodded without saying a word.

"On her arm or neck?"

"Her hand," Dawson said. "I put my ear to her heart to see if it was beating. I couldn't tell because my heart was beating so loud, you know."[162]

Spetalieri decided to change tactics. "You and Annie have any sexual contact?"

He had expected an angry reaction, but Dawson just shook his head.

"None whatsoever?" he demanded accusingly, but Dawson did not reply.[163]

"All right," Spetalieri said. "Let me ask you another question. You think about this real good now. You picked up the clothes. You walked along Jansen Avenue and placed them in the alley alongside Cheap Charlies, right?"

"Yes."

"There was a nice sized stick, a small log, that was in there with those clothes with blood on it. What was that about?"

"I don't know," Dawson answered. "I just picked up the clothes and just put them in there."

Spetalieri shook his head dismissively. "You must have felt a stick that big. It was about eighteen inches long, the size of a man's forearm."

"I don't recall," Dawson said stubbornly. "That's all I know."[164]

Detective Harris decided to jump into the discussion. "Did you struggle with her at all?"

"No," Dawson said turning to face his accuser. "Except for when I pushed her."

"Do you remember if she had her jewelry on? Maybe a brooch on the outside of her outfit?" Harris questioned.

"I think she had a ring."

"But no brooch?"

"No," Dawson insisted.

"She definitely had it on," Harris said defiantly. "We can't find that. No idea what happened to it?"

Dawson looked down at the table, but said nothing.[165]

After a few seconds of painful silence, Spetalieri asked, "What was your mental state at the time? I mean just before you pushed her?"

"I don't know," Dawson said with annoyance in his voice. "She was just getting on my nerves and I was like, just get the fuck away from me."[166]

"Did you lose your temper maybe?" Spetalieri asked.

Dawson just sat there, so the officer continued. "How about if you were in a state of rage? You kind of blacked out for a second or two, or kind of forget something you did?"

"If I was drunk," Dawson replied, "but I know I wasn't drunk because I didn't have nothing to drink."

"So, you were sober? You were straight?"

"I was sober."

"Did you do any drugs or anything?"

"No, I don't smoke reefer."[167]

Once again, the ticking of the clock was only sound in the room. Each tick seemed to pound the very walls until Officer Spetalieri spoke again.

"Did you see the cuts on Annie's legs?"

"I just noticed there was blood on the front of her," Dawson said. "There was blood on the front of her."

"Now," Spetalieri continued, "you say you pushed her and she fell, and you felt blood underneath the back of her head?"

"Yes."

"How do you think blood got on the front of her?"

"I couldn't tell you," Dawson insisted. "I don't know."[168]

Harris and Spetalieri were starting to get frustrated. Their suspect continued to maintain that someone else committed the murder, but his story was very hard to swallow. Worse, he kept answering in a very soft voice. Nothing seeming to bother him.

"What do you think the likelihood is of someone else being back there in the darkness down there in the middle of the night?" Spetalieri challenged.

"It's possible," Dawson said, showing he was not about to back down. "I know I walk through the railroad tracks a lot, you know, to walk to uptown. And you know, I always run into people sitting around drinking."

"And you didn't see anybody back there? Hear anybody back there?"

Dawson did not reply, so Spetalieri went right on, "You say she was naked when you came back down?"

"Yup."

"The cuts on her body were pretty obvious. You really couldn't miss them."

Detective Harris cut in before Dawson could answer, "She was messed up, her face."

"Think back now," Spetalieri said, raising his voice. "Maybe she got you a little angry?"

"I can't remember," Dawson answered contemptuously.[169]

The officers just stared at Dawson, waiting for him to speak further, but he would not. He just kept staring down at the table.

"There's got to be a little more to this story," Spetalieri said starting in again. "Couple of things are missing here. Did you think about trying to put if off on somebody else?"

He paused for effect, but it seemed to have none. So, he just pushed on. "Maybe a way to come up with an alibi? Maybe go back down there and do something to the body that would make us go off in another direction and blame somebody else? If you did it in a state of fear, it would be understandable."

Dawson looked up and locked eyes with his accuser. He said nothing, but kept his gaze on him.

Spetalieri sensed an advantage. "You panicked. You didn't know what to do," he pressed. "Maybe come up with an idea. Put the KKK on her, and maybe throw the light somewhere else. Cause a little confusion."

Dawson just stared for a moment and then once again lowered his eyes.

"I want you to look at me," Spetalieri shouted. "I want you to think about this. You pushed her, she fell. You left her for two hours, never left the area. You go back down there. It's just starting to turn light. She's cut up. Now you tell me you don't see it. How could someone else go down there in the darkness and carve letters in her accurately in the pitch black? It doesn't make sense. Now, if you're going to tell me, you should tell me everything. The whole thing. There is no sense leaving anything out, Jeff."

Dawson just shrugged saying, "I just told you what I know."

"Still leaves a lot of unanswered questions," Spetalieri noted. "A lot of people are suffering behind these unanswered questions. Annie's family."

"Yeah, that's for sure," Harris added. "Her mother and father aren't going to be right for years behind all this junk, you know."

"Let's put all this behind us," Spetalieri continued. "I think you know a little more, Jeff."

With almost no emotion, Dawson said simply, "That's all I know."[170]

"I want to tell you something else, Jeff," Spetalieri pressed on. "There was a bite mark on the body that occurred before death. Scientific evidence tells us that."

If Dawson was concerned about this potential evidence, he did not show it. "So?" he smirked. "You want to take a print of my teeth?"

"No," the officer said rather disingenuously. "I'm asking you to fill in a couple of empty spaces for us."

"I just told you everything I know," Dawson said sitting up and glaring. "I don't know nothing about no bite marks, but if you want to take a print of my teeth, then do that."[171]

"Well, I'm worried about the cut marks," Spetalieri said, changing the subject yet again.

"I have no idea."

"Tried to put if off on the Klan?"

Dawson sat back in his chair, but did not take his gaze off Spetalieri.

"Do you realize the tension and pressure," the officer continued, "the racial stuff going on behind this? Bad feelings that are going back and forth?"

"I just told you everything I know," Dawson repeated. "I mean, all the crime I ever did was burglary. I'm not a violent guy."

"I am not saying you did anything intentionally. Maybe in a state of fear, panic as you put it," Spetalieri said. "But, did you put her in a choke hold, Jeffrey?"

"No."

"The girl was choked."[172]

Before Dawson could reply, there was a knock at the door. Harris went to the door and an officer handed him a folder containing the sworn statement the police had obtained from Todd Schleede. He took the folder, opened it, and pretended to read the contents. It was just a show for their suspect, since Harris already knew what Schleede had said.

Harris walked toward Dawson. "You told someone else about this, right Jeff?"

"I told Todd Schleede."

"What did you tell Todd Schleede?" Harris asked.

"I told him that I pushed her and she fell. I told him she was dead. Then I took her clothes and stuff and I dropped them off on the side of the bar."

It was exactly what he had indeed told Schleede earlier that evening in the taped recording, almost to the word.

"Did you move her, Jeff?"

"No. No, I didn't move her."

"Do you know how close I was to your conversation with Schleede half an hour ago?" Harris asked. "Do you have any idea how close I was?"

"No."

"Close enough to hear what you said, brother. Close enough to hear what you said about the Klan," Harris said accusingly. "You put the KKK on the girl to put if off on the Klan."[173]

CHAPTER 9 – THE INTERROGATION CONTINUES

DETECTIVE HARRIS WAS LYING about what he heard, but that is not an unusual tactic used by the police during interrogations. The law prohibits beating a confession out of a suspect, but permits psychological tricks and deception, including outright lying.

The U.S. Supreme Court has upheld the legality of police telling a suspect that his accomplice already confessed[174] or that incriminating evidence was found at a crime scene.[175] Although there are limits, for the most part, the police may feed a suspect falsehoods hoping to get a confession or perhaps an incriminating admission.

Dawson was not going for it. "No, I didn't," he shouted. "You're lying. I did not say nothing about the Klan."[176]

"You know she was a well-liked girl. She would never hurt anybody," Harris answered back. "Whole conversation you had with Todd, we know about it, Jeff. We know the whole story."

When Dawson just stared at him, the detective continued, "And it's not the first time, so you might as well level with us and get it over with so we can get the hell out of here."

Now Dawson was becoming upset. He sat upright, looked Harris directly in the eyes and said, "If it's on tape, you don't need to hear me say it, because I know I didn't say nothing about no Klan."

"You're right," Spetalieri chimed in. "We really don't."

"I know," Dawson said turning toward Spetalieri, "because I didn't say nothing about them."[177]

"Todd is in the next room. He's telling us everything."

"It's like that telephone game," Dawson interrupted. "The story gets longer and longer, and people add stuff to it. I told you what I know. You got it on tape. That's everything I know."

"I don't believe that," Spetalieri said. "I think you know more."[178]

Dawson just stared straight ahead, so Spetalieri had Dawson start from the top and tell him his entire story again. He did so and told almost the same version word for word.

When he was finished, Spetalieri loudly tapped his pencil against the wooden table to get Jeff's attention. "So," he started, "you've already got yourself in a position where you're responsible for this girl's death. You realize that?"

"Yes, I know," Dawson admitted without looking up.

"Look at me," Spetalieri yelled again pounding his pencil. "You're responsible for that girl's death."

"Yeah, that's for sure," Harris added.

"Cutting her up," Spetalieri continued, "trying to get out of it, or whatever is secondary. It really is."

"I tell you," Dawson said raising his voice. "I did not cut her."

"Then how did she get cut?" Spetalieri roared.

"I don't know," Dawson answered emphatically.

Harris leaned in closer. "You want to see some photos?"

"I don't care," Dawson answered in an almost defeated tone. "I just told you everything I know."

"No, you're not," Spetalieri replied. "You're telling me some of what you know, most of what you know, but not all of what you know."

Dawson did not answer. Once again, there was no sound except for the ticking clock. Though it lasted for only ten to fifteen seconds, it seemed like endless minutes.

Finally, Spetalieri broke the silence. "Jeff, we heard your conversation with Todd outside your house. We recorded your conversation with Todd. Now, you're in here telling us something completely different."

"Play the tape," Dawson said simply.

Ignoring him, Spetalieri said, "You're telling us something other than what you said in the street."

"Get the tape and listen to it," Dawson said again.

Pounding his fist on the table, Spetalieri shouted, "I'm not listening to it. I know what you said."

Taking a breath to compose himself, Spetalieri continued, "You said something up there in relation to that KKK on that girl's body and in relation to the Klan. Now, you can sit here and deny it."

Dawson vehemently shook his head, but the officer ignored it and kept on speaking. "You can sit here and shake your head and tell me otherwise until you're blue in the face, brother, but it's not going to change what you said a half-hour ago in the street when you thought you were a free man and when you thought no one was listening."

Dawson continued shaking his head.

"Now, you go ahead and shake your head," Spetalieri said, "because we are going to disprove that with your own words and your own voice."

"I tell you. I didn't say anything."

"OK. You might have thought you were quiet. You might

have whispered. But, let me tell you something. This is 1988, and we have equipment that could pick up a heartbeat at one hundred paces."

He did not bother to tell Dawson that the actual recording was so poor that they were going to send it to the State Police to see if they could enhance the quality. Sometimes, the truth gets in the way of a good confession.

"All you're doing, Jeff, is getting yourself in deeper. When you do get yourself in front of a judge or jury someday, you know what they're gonna think of you? They're gonna say this guy's a stone liar. That's what they're gonna say – a stone cold liar, a cold-blooded murderer, a liar. You know what they're gonna give you? Ha! You'll never see the light of day again, brother."[179]

If he was expecting a reaction, he did not get it. Dawson just stared straight ahead as if he could see something nobody else could.

"I realize you're on parole," Spetalieri said changing his tune to try to sound sympathetic. "You were frightened. You panicked. It was probably done unintentionally. But, nonetheless it happened. We can't go back and pretend it didn't happen. It went down. It's over with. So, why go ninety percent of the way with me?"

Seeing Dawson was no longer even looking at him, Spetalieri tapped his pencil on the table. "You listening?"[180]

Jeff looked up but showed little interest.

Spetalieri tried again. "If you have any compassion, if you have some common sense, I urge you tell us the whole truth. Let's get this whole thing over with. What you're telling me is a fairy tale."

"People are going to be a little more sympathetic if you cooperate," Harris added.

Since Dawson continued to refuse to respond further in any

way, the officers stopped the cassette recorder and took a break. Harris got Dawson some cigarettes, while Spetalieri got a copy of the statement they had obtained from Todd Schleede.

When both officers were back in the room, they turned the recorder back on.

"I looked at Todd's statement, "Spetalieri resumed. "Please tell us the whole truth. There's stuff in there you never told us about."

"May I see it?"

"No, I am afraid not."[81]

For the next thirty minutes, Harris and Spetalieri grilled Dawson trying to get him to add more to his story. But, Dawson stuck to his original statement and would not budge even an inch.

Banging his fist in frustration, Spetalieri blurted out, "Do you know the difference between murder and manslaughter, Jeff? It's fifteen years." He tapped his pencil again to each syllable as he repeated, "Fif-teen years."

In a very soft voice and without any real emotion, Dawson finally answered. "I was just out here on borrowed time. It makes no difference. I've been out here a year and a day. It's been some kind of experience."[182]

"If you didn't think anything of yourself and you were as hard as you're trying to make yourself out to be right now," Spetalieri countered, "you would have walked away from that girl. You would never have said anything to anyone in the world, and it would have gone unsolved forever."

Dawson had no reply, so Spetalieri continued. "But, you couldn't deal with it. You couldn't live with that. Because you do think something of yourself, you had to get it out. You told somebody you trusted. You told Todd."

The officer was not really expecting a reply, but Dawson

had one right away.

"I didn't tell somebody I trusted. I told somebody I knew would tell."

This caught Spetalieri and Harris off guard. They looked at one another for a minute before Spetalieri followed up.

"What's your reasoning behind that," he asked. "You wanted to get caught?"

"I just told you I thought about going home."

Not understanding this cryptic answer, the officer asked, "Where's home?"

"Where I been for the last sixteen years," Dawson replied. "Locked up."

"You think that shit hole is home?"

"Hey," Dawson said sounding offended, "that's where I grew up."

"That's not for a man," Spetalieri challenged. "Do you need someone to tell you when to eat? When to sleep? When to shit and when to piss?"[183]

When there was no answer, Harris, said, "You're gonna need someone in your corner, Jeff."

"That's right," Spetalieri joined. "Be a man. Don't flush yourself down the toilet."

After a moment, Dawson took a deep breath as if we were going to say something significant. Instead, he just whispered, "I'm tired."

"Aren't we all," Spetalieri shot back, "but we still got business, brother."

Dawson just shook his head. "I want to go to sleep."[184]

As it was obvious that their suspect was no longer willing to talk, Spetalieri turned off the recorder, and Harris escorted the prisoner back to his cell.

CHAPTER 10 - OFF TO COURT

THE FOLLOWING MORNING, POLICE wasted little time bringing Jeff Dawson to court. A felony complaint charging him with murder in the second degree was drafted and signed by Detective Junious Harris.

City Court Judge Mike Bruhn held a special Sunday court session to accommodate the arraignment. Chief Assistant District Attorney Donald Williams was present for the prosecution. Knowing ahead of time that Dawson did not have the financial ability to hire a lawyer, Judge Bruhn called David Clegg, the assistant public defender assigned to his court, up to the bench.

Before Clegg could reach the bench, Williams was on his feet objecting. "Your Honor, Mr. Clegg's office already represents Joseph Kiernan. We anticipate that Mr. Dawson is going to blame Kiernan for this crime. This creates a legal conflict."[185]

There was little question that Williams was correct. Kiernan was already accused of molesting the corpse, and any competent defense attorney was going to charge that the police only had the mentally ill man's word as to when he arrived at the scene and what he did or did not do when there. Certainly, it would be suggested to the jury that Kiernan was the real murderer and not Jeffrey Dawson.

The Public Defender's Office could not maintain Kiernan's innocence and then turn right around and accuse him of murder. It was a clear conflict of interest.

Unable to go any further with the arraignment, the judge entered a not guilty plea on the defendant's behalf, scheduled a second arraignment for the next morning, and remanded him to the county jail without bail.[186]

Bruhn also selected a prominent and well-respected local attorney named Jeremiah "Jerry" Flaherty to be the new defense counsel.[187]

Reporters lobbed numerous questions at Dawson as he was brought to a waiting police vehicle for his ride to the county jail. He did not respond to any of the questions or make eye contact with any of the reporters.

Later that day, however, reporters were able to get some of their questions answered when District Attorney Mike Kavanagh and Police Chief James Riggins held a press conference in front of the Ulster County Courthouse to announce the arrest of a suspect.

Whenever an arrest is made in a case receiving heavy media coverage, prosecutors and police usually hold press conferences to make the announcement. The purpose is two-fold. First, since county district attorneys are elected positions, it is always helpful to show the voters that the bad guy has been caught. But, perhaps more importantly, it allows the prosecution to set the narrative for the case. Often, the underlying theory of the case, such as the murderer was a disturbed loner, or a jealous lover, and so forth, are brought out for the first time at the press conference announcing the arrest.

In this case, Kavanagh had a more important reason. Thanks to Reverend Sharpton and his associates, many in the media and the public itself already considered this case to be an act of vicious racism perpetrated by an unknown anti-black group or cult. Many also felt it was related to the Brawley case down in Poughkeepsie.

Obviously, with the prosecution's contention that the murderer was Dawson, an African-American man, it seemed anti-black racism was not going to be part of its theory of the crime. With tensions riding so high throughout the Hudson Valley, it was important for Kavanagh to make clear to the media that this case had nothing to do with the Brawley matter, racism, or Klan activity.

After providing some background information to the reporters about Jeffrey Dawson, including his record of prior felony convictions, Kavanagh quickly turned his attention to the allegations previously made by Sharpton and Maddox.

"Our investigation certainly convinces us," Kavanagh said, "that this was not the product of any organized hate group."[188]

"The killing of Annie Kithcart was not racially motivated," Kavanagh pronounced. "As the result of an argument, Jeffrey Dawson strangled Annie Kithcart and hit her head with a cinder block." As for Dawson's motive, the district attorney was rather vague, saying "We don't know yet, but I suspect drug and alcohol consumption may have had something to do with the argument."[189]

"What about the KKK marks?" a reporter shouted out.

"That is still under investigation," Kavanagh answered, "but police believe that Kiernan likely scratched those marks into the victim's flesh."[190]

In support of this theory, Kavanagh revealed some interesting information provided by the New York Attorney General's Office.

When Attorney General Robert Abrams was assigned to investigate the Tawana Brawley case, he established a hotline for the public to offer information and a task force to deal with those tips.

Assistant Attorney General Timothy Giles had informed the

Kingston police that about four months prior to the Kithcart murder, Joseph Kiernan had contacted the hotline claiming to have information of importance.

Members of the task force had investigated. In fact, Kiernan had brought them to the person from whom he obtained his so-called information. The exact nature and value of the information was not publicly disclosed.[191]

The implication was clear. Kiernan had a history of mental illness, had involved himself in the racial quagmire of the Brawley investigation, and now had come upon a corpse that ended up with racial epitaphs carved into the flesh. The idea that Kiernan might have scratched the offensive letters on a dead mixed-race woman seemed very reasonable.

Chief Riggins stepped forward and announced that he and Detective Scarey had interviewed Kiernan for two and a half hours. During that conversation, Kiernan confessed that he had "carved up the body," but there were parts of his other answers that were inconsistent.[192]

"Right now," the chief added, "there is more than a distinct possibility that he did it, but we can't be sure."[193]

Riggins advised the reporters that they were waiting for additional medical evidence to see whether the scratches were made before or after death before reaching a final conclusion. Hair, blood, and saliva samples had been taken from Kiernan and an impression made of his teeth.

(Interestingly, no mention was made at the press conference that Kiernan could not possibly have made the bite mark found on the body. He only had two or three teeth in his entire lower jaw.)

What Riggins was basically saying was that, while Kiernan had admitted to a variety of things, his questionable mental state made it necessary to have other proof before anything he said could be accepted as fact.

The question "Why did Kiernan cut letters into the body?" rose up from the mass of assembled reporters.

"I don't have an idea," Kavanagh answered, taking the lead back from Chief Riggins. "He is a bizarre character. You're dealing with an unstable personality."

To nobody's great surprise, Kavanagh informed the press that, due to his psychiatric issues, the prosecution would not be calling Kiernan as a witness at trial.

Kavanagh further stirred the pot by saying, "While he made numerous admissions to the police, Mr. Dawson denied adamantly placing any of the marks on the body."[194]

As the press conference wrapped up, one of the reporters threw out a question about Al Sharpton.

"We still expect there will be an onslaught from Sharpton," Kavanagh said, stepping back to the microphone. "I know whatever we say they'll certainly take issue with."[195]

Hearing no additional questions, the district attorney turned and walked into the courthouse toward his office.

The "onslaught" mentioned by Kavanagh did not come. Reporters reached out to Sharpton for comment. He was unavailable, however. On the same day that Jeff Dawson was handcuffed and arrested, Sharpton was getting handcuffed in Brooklyn under quite different circumstances.

As nearly five hundred supporters stood outside a Brooklyn church and cheered them on, Sharpton and attorney C. Vernon Mason handcuffed themselves to Tawana Brawley, her mother, Glenda, and her aunt, Juanita, before boarding a bus to lead about fifty people to the Democratic National Convention in Atlanta, Georgia. Their intent was to protest the handling of Tawana's case by New York state authorities by picketing outside the hotel where Governor Mario Cuomo was staying during the convention.[196]

During their protests, they made national news when they

jammed a corridor in the Radisson Hotel and confronted New York delegates for civil rights activist Jesse Jackson. The delegates were forced to leave the hotel through another exit.[197]

Although Sharpton previously warned Mike Kavanagh that he was "coming back and bringing everybody with (him)," Sharpton never returned to Kingston or commented on the Kithcart case again.

The press was able to reach Alton Maddox in Atlanta. When told of the arrest in the Kithcart murder, he acknowledged that he did not have all of the facts about Dawson's arrest, but added ominously, "I would be very cautious. I believe it was a racially motivated crime. We may have a new fall guy here."[198]

Unlike his friend Sharpton, Alton Maddox would later return to Kingston and involve himself in the case, though not on behalf of Jeffrey Dawson.

Kavanagh and Riggins were not the only media event in town that day. WKNY, a local Kingston radio station, obtained an exclusive interview at the Ulster County Jail with Joseph Kiernan.

Kiernan's lawyer was present during the interview, but said little. He had met with his client prior to the interview, likely to try to talk him out of it. It is rarely a good idea for a defendant to talk with the media, especially since the prosecution will quickly obtain copies of anything he says. However, no matter how a defense attorney pleads, if a defendant wants to talk to the press, he can.

During the interview, Kiernan spoke rapidly and his sentences were disjointed, tending to jump from topic to topic. From the start, he strongly denied molesting Kithcart's body.

"I am absolutely innocent," Kiernan began. "I couldn't believe it was a body."

Asked to describe what happened, Kiernan continued, "I came through the alley and saw it. It looked like a love doll. I'd never seen a dead body before. I reached down and jiggled it. I touched it with my hand. The body was cold. I was only there a minute or two. I was very scared and went to report it."[199]

Asked if he had scrawled racial slurs on the girl's body, Kiernan vehemently denied it. "I didn't know what was scrawled there, because I didn't do it," he said. "I didn't know KKK was there. The police said I killed her. I'm innocent."

"I'm scared," Kiernan suddenly added.

"Why are you scared, Mr. Kiernan?"

"The Ku Klux Klan is going to kill me," Kiernan answered.

Before the reporter could pose another question, Kiernan rambled on in a stream of consciousness. "There are white supremacists in the Kingston police," he said. "One of them showed me a KKK ring."[200]

After that, Kiernan started mumbling incoherently. It was obvious the interview was at an end.

The next morning, Jeffrey Dawson was back in Kingston City Court. Although he was now dressed in a jail jumpsuit, he was decidedly more comfortable than he had been the day before. When Dawson was arrested, he was not wearing shoes or socks. As such, he had been brought to court the day before barefoot. Now, he was wearing proper foot attire, compliments of the county jail.

The proceedings went quickly. Jerry Flaherty entered a not guilty plea on his client's behalf, and Judge Mike Bruhn scheduled the preliminary hearing for Wednesday morning.

Under New York law, when a person is charged with a felony and being held in jail, he or she may demand a preliminary felony hearing. At such a hearing, the prosecution must produce enough evidence to establish reasonable cause to believe that the defendant has committed a felony. This hearing must be held within 120 hours from the arraignment or, in the event that a Saturday, Sunday, or legal holiday occurs during such custody, 144 hours from the arraignment. If the prosecution cannot produce sufficient evidence, the court must release the defendant.[201]

There are two exceptions to this rule. A preliminary hearing does not need to be held if the defendant is indicted by a grand jury or if the defendant chooses to waive the hearing.

Flaherty had no intention of waiving the hearing. It was too good an opportunity to cross-examine whatever witnesses the prosecutor produced.

So, unless the district attorney obtained an indictment, they would have to present what little evidence they already had. Since the scientific evidence would not likely be ready in time for presentation to the grand jury, Wednesday morning was going to be the first chance for Dawson to face his accuser, Todd Schleede.

CHAPTER 11 - PRELIMINARY HEARING

ON WEDNESDAY, JULY 20, at eleven o'clock in the morning, Judge Mike Bruhn took the bench and called the case of the *People of the State of New York v. Jeffrey A. Dawson*. As all parties approached the judge, the assembled members of the media began taking pictures and writing notes. (The judge had approved photography and video at the last court appearance.)

Both attorneys, however, expressed their objection to allowing it to continue. Assistant District Attorney Don Williams expressed his concern first.

"Your Honor," he began, "I have no objection to having the media here for the entire proceeding of the preliminary hearing, excluding the testimony of one prosecution witness who, quite frankly, has given information and has acted as a police informant for the duration of this particular case. As a result of that, I'm going to request that, during the course of his testimony, no photographs or no live camera be allowed to be operated in the courtroom."

Judge Bruhn turned to opposing counsel. "Mr. Flaherty," he asked, "do you have a position on either the taping in general or Mr. Williams' request for a specific exclusion?"

"Your Honor," Flaherty replied, "initially we had objected to anyone being in here. Apparently, this case has been tried in the paper on the prosecution's side. The only problem is, if evidence is offered today—and I don't know what the

People are going to offer today—that at a later date may be determined to not be competent or otherwise admissible evidence at trial, quite possibly the media could publish that and potential jurors may become aware of it."[202]

The judge contemplated the arguments for a moment. Before he could announce a decision, Flaherty began to speak again.

"It's probably at this point impossible to get a fair trial in this court anyway," he said, "fair in the sense of impartial jurors who have no opinions of the case, unless we find twelve people who do not have a TV or read the newspapers in the Mid-Hudson Valley. I think it may be too late."

This statement prompted an immediate reply from the assistant district attorney. "Your Honor, for the purpose of brevity, which sometimes is extremely difficult for Mr. Flaherty," he said snidely, "the prosecution will offer two witnesses. Today, the first witness will be Dr. Harry McNamara, who is the county medical examiner, who did a preliminary examination of Annie Kithcart. Clearly, there will be no suppression issue concerning what Dr. McNamara would be testifying about."

He paused for a moment to allow his words to take effect before continuing, "The second witness will be the informant, Todd Schleede. There may be an issue of suppression that Mr. Flaherty may raise subsequent to this proceeding. That is the only proof that will be offered at this preliminary hearing today."[203]

At this point, the judge put both hands up in front of him as a clear signal that he wanted no further arguments on the point.

"Mr. Flaherty, are you asking that the entire proceeding be closed?"

"Yes," the defense attorney replied.

"I'll deny that application," the judge ruled, "and I will grant Mr. Williams' request that there be no videotaping of the informant, no still pictures of the informant. The rest of the proceeding can be taped or still photos or whatever."

"Your Honor?" Williams asked. "There was also an application that any type of tape recording of the informant's testimony be excluded."

The judge quickly added that limitation to the proceeding as well.[204]

"Mr. Flaherty," the judge said, turning toward defense counsel, "the defendant is ready to proceed with the preliminary hearing?"

"Your Honor," Flaherty answered, "I'd ask that his handcuffs be removed so he can cooperate with me in defending him. You can't write when you have handcuffs on."

Dawson had been brought to the court wearing shackles around his ankles. There was a large chain around his waist and each hand was cuffed to the chain at his sides.

Williams stood at this request. "I have no objection to that, but obviously the concern is from the Sheriff's Department," he said pointing to the deputies who were guarding Dawson.

One of the deputies immediately addressed the court. "Give us an order, Judge, and we'll take them off."

"Please do," the judge replied politely.[205]

The deputy quickly removed the restraints, and Dawson rubbed his wrists, seemingly needing to restore blood flow and sensation in his hands.

With all of the pre-hearing motions and posturing apparently concluded, the judge turned to the assistant district attorney and said, "Do you want to call your first witness?"

"The People call Dr. Harry McNamara," he replied curtly.

The doctor took the stand. After being sworn in, the doctor

was asked to state his medical credentials. Before he could answer, Flaherty stood and advised the court that he was well aware of the doctor's credentials and would stipulate to them.

No longer needing to ask introductory questions, the prosecutor got right to the point. "Dr. McNamara," he asked, "on July 12th of 1988, did you have the opportunity to respond to the scene of a wooded path near Foxhall Avenue?"

"Yes, I did."

"Approximately what time was it that you responded to that location?"

"I received the call about seven a.m., and I was at the location at seven thirty a.m."

"When you arrived at that location, could you briefly describe the particular area that you responded to?"

"There's apparently an abandoned railroad track off Foxhall Avenue behind Kingston Hospital which is pretty heavily shaded on both sides with various vegetation. In order to proceed down there, there's a tremendous amount of trash, broken glass, you name it. I don't know the exact yardage, but as we proceeded down there, there was the body of a female, young female, somewhat inclined on the right side going down. All that she was dressed in was a shoe, a white shoe, moccasin, on one foot and a white bra which was up above her breasts."[206]

"Doctor," the prosecutor inquired, "was the body that you examined that morning later identified forensically?"

"Yes, it was."

"Who was it?"

"It was Anna Kithcart."[207]

Now that the identity of the victim had been announced, Williams moved on to the actual forensic examination.

"Could you tell us what, if anything, you noticed in the area of the head and neck of Annie Kithcart, specifically when dealing with your opinion as to cause of death?"

The doctor looked down at his notes, before answering. "She had three lacerations which broke through the skin on the forehead," he replied. "She had a piece of glass sticking out of the right side of the neck, and there was a marking on the abdomen and legs…"[208]

Williams, realizing the witness was about to discuss the KKK markings found on the body, immediately interrupted McNamara. He had no intention of those marks even being mentioned in that day's proceeding.

"Specifically, your observation dealing only with a cause of death," he instructed.

Jerry Flaherty flew out of his seat and objected. "Your Honor," the defense counsel protested. "He's trying to answer the question, and apparently we are having a problem that the People don't appreciate the answers."

Flaherty was experienced enough to know exactly what his adversary was doing. Williams was trying to present as little evidence as he could to win the hearing.

One of the reasons why defense attorneys often demand a preliminary hearing is to get the opportunity to see some of the evidence against their clients and to question whatever witnesses are produced. Flaherty wanted very badly to ask about the racial marks found on the body. It was clear, however, that the prosecutor intended to fight him every step of the way.

Judge Bruhn ended the dispute quickly by saying simply, "The objection is overruled."[209]

Returning to his direct examination, Williams asked the doctor about the findings related to the cause of death.

The doctor replied that he discovered hemorrhages on the

eyes, bruises around the neck, and fractures of the skull caused by an unknown blunt instrument. Additionally, there was a fracture in one of the bones of the throat and a hemorrhage in the area, which was indicative of strangulation.[210]

"Based upon your examinations," Williams asked, "have you reached an opinion within a reasonable degree of scientific certainty as to the cause of death?"

"Yes."

"Could you tell us what that opinion is?"

"A severe head injury plus strangulation."[211]

The prosecutor had the doctor state his further opinion that the injuries inflicted could not have been done accidentally before turning his witness over for cross-examination.

The purpose of the coroner's testimony was actually very limited. He was not called to prove that Jeffrey Dawson committed the murder. Rather, he was merely to testify that a murder had in fact occurred within the state of New York, which needed to be established before turning to the issue of naming the suspect.

Williams planned to have Todd Schleede testify that Dawson admitted to him that he committed the murder. Under New York law, a confession is not sufficient unless there is actual proof that a crime was committed.[212]

Put another way, if a person walks into a police station and signs a confession stating he robbed the First National Bank earlier that day, he cannot be convicted unless it can be established that the First National Bank was in fact robbed earlier that day.

In 1988, it was an open question whether or not a confession alone would be sufficient to meet the burden of proof for a preliminary hearing, as the statute only refers to a conviction. Williams was not taking any chances though.

Jerry Flaherty stood for his cross-examination of McNamara.

He knew that he would not be able to change the doctor's testimony. There was no doubt Annie Kithcart had been murdered. It was his job to pull as much information out of the witness as possible.

"Doctor," he began, "having examined the body in question here, could you tell us approximately what time the person died?"

"At the best, we can make a guess, somewhere between four and six hours from the time I examined her."

"So, are you saying between four and six o'clock in the morning was the time of death?"

"No," the doctor corrected. "I would say roughly between two and four."[213]

"When you examined the body," Flaherty asked, changing subjects, "had rigor mortis set in?"

"It was beginning rigor mortis when we got there in the morning."

"And where was it when it had set in?"

"I'm going to object," Williams announced, rising from his chair. "This is a preliminary hearing, Your Honor. Irrelevant."[214]

The judge sustained the objection.

A preliminary hearing is a limited procedure to determine if there is reasonable cause to find that the accused committed a felony in the state. As such, the prosecutor tries to limit cross-examination of witnesses to that issue. On the other hand, defense attorneys are supposed to press the envelope and get as much information about the case against their client as possible. The back and forth on this issue often permeates the entire proceeding.

Moving on, Flaherty asked the doctor if he would agree that the nature of the crime scene prevented an extensive examination of the neck area of the body. The doctor agreed.

"Do you know how the body was removed from the scene?"

Williams was on his feet quickly. "Same objection," he intoned. "How the body was removed from the scene is purely irrelevant to the issues at this preliminary hearing."

The judge sustained the objection. This time, however, Flaherty decided to contest the ruling.

"Your Honor, if I could be heard?"

"Go ahead," the judge replied.

"If the doctor didn't examine the neck area at the scene and now testifies as to how the neck area appeared at a later time and at a later place, I think it is very relevant as to what happened to the body in between that time period. How do we know these neck injuries did not occur at some other place, at some other time?"[215]

Flaherty's argument failed to convince the judge. So, he went back to his cross-examination, albeit to a different area of inquiry.

"Doctor, you have told the People on direct that you had an opinion that the cause of death was strangulation. Is that correct, sir?"

"There is an indication on inspection that there was a possible strangulation."[216]

"Doctor, you told us that the victim had several lacerations about the head. Is that correct?"

"Yes."

"And you told us that that was caused by some sort of blunt instrument. Is that correct?"

"That's correct."

"So, which is it?" Flaherty challenged, raising his voice slightly for effect. "Strangulation or the blow to the head from the blunt object?"

"It would only be conjecture," the doctor replied flatly.

"The strangulation," Flaherty pressed, "was it done by a foreign object?"

"I would assume it was either by hands or arm."[217]

"Could it have been an accident?"

"Strangulation?" the doctor asked. "No."

"The injuries to the neck could not have occurred by accident?" Flaherty asked in a slightly mocking tone.

"Asked and answered," noted the prosecutor. "I object."

"Sustained," said the judge.

"Now, sir," Flaherty asked, turning his attention back to the doctor. "You've told us that there was a fracture of one of the bones within the neck?"

"That's true."

"Which one?"

"I don't recall if it was the larynx. That was a telephone report."

Flaherty seemed surprised at this answer. "So, someone told you on the phone that there was a fracture of the larynx of the neck of this body. Is that correct?"

"That's correct."

"And based on that," Flaherty questioned, with an obvious tone of sarcasm on the last syllable, "you have given an opinion within a scientific certainty that this person died by means of strangulation?"

"That's correct," the doctor answered as Williams rose from his chair.

However, Flaherty immediately changed topics, and Williams started to retake his seat.

"You told us there were some markings on the abdomen, could you tell us what you meant by that, sir?"

Now, Williams was back up. "Objection," he said strongly. "I know the doctor testified there were markings. However, they are irrelevant to the cause of death."

Judge Bruhn shook his head. "Overruled."

"Could you tell us please?" Flaherty asked again.

"Well, there was a mark on the abdomen which looked possibly like a 'K' and marks on the upper…"

"I'm going to object at this point," Williams interrupted. "The doctor has answered the question and anything else would be surplusage. The question was in reference to the abdomen."[218]

"Your Honor," Flaherty offered, a hint of annoyance in his voice. "On the record, I am going to object to this continuance of the People telling the witness how to answer questions because that happened once or twice, both on direct and cross-examination. It's very difficult to elicit testimony from a person who is being told how to testify and, Judge, that's what…"

"Is that an objection?" Williams interjected sarcastically.

"Let him finish," the judge chided.

"We have to be out of here by nine o'clock tonight, Your Honor," Williams added.

Bruhn's head snapped back over to Williams. "There is no time limitation on this," he said very firmly.

Williams was an experienced prosecutor. He knew by the look on the judge's face and the tone of his voice that he had gone too far. He nodded his head slightly in a sign of respect to the bench and sat down without another word.

"I'll allow the doctor to answer the question as to what he observed on the abdomen," the judge said, putting emphasis on the last word. "Has it already been fully answered, doctor?"

"Yes."

The judge turned his attention back to Flaherty. "This is only a preliminary hearing," suggesting strongly that he should not ask about the marks on the thighs.

"I understand that, Your Honor."

"Any further questions?"

Flaherty had a lot of questions he wanted to ask, but he knew by the tone of the judge's last statement that he was not going to be allowed any more leeway. He had gotten as much as he was going to get from this witness.

"No, Your Honor," he said.

With that, McNamara was excused from the witness stand.

Reminding everyone in the gallery to put away their cameras and recorders, the judge instructed the prosecution to call their next witness.

Williams stood and announced in a clear voice, "The People call Todd Schleede."

CHAPTER 12 - SCHLEEDE TAKES THE STAND

AS HE TOOK THE stand, Todd Schleede was very nervous. He had been in court before, but always as the accused, not as a witness for the prosecution. It was also the first time he had seen his former friend since their recorded conversation four days earlier. He found it difficult to look Dawson in the eyes.

He was also physically uncomfortable. A day earlier, he had an accident and suffered a broken rib and an injured arm. His ribs were taped, and his arm hung in a sling.

"Mr. Schleede," Don Williams said sharply, causing Schleede's head to snap up. "Do you know the defendant, Jeffrey Dawson?"

"Yes, I do."

"Do you see him in the courtroom today?"

"Yes."

"Would you please point him out?"

Schleede turned to Dawson and pointed his finger at him. "Right here," he announced. "Next to Mr. Flaherty."[219]

Williams asked the court to take official notice that the witness had correctly identified the defendant. The judge so noted.

"Mr. Schleede," Williams said, turning back to his witness,

"on the afternoon of July 12th of 1988, did you see Jeffrey Dawson?"

"Yes, I did."

"Approximately what time was it that you saw him?"

"About three o'clock in the afternoon."

"Where?"

"Across from the high school by the Old City Hall."[220]

"Could you tell us what happened," the prosecutor asked, "what you did, when you saw Jeffrey Dawson that day?"

Schleede took a deep breath and retold the events. He discussed picking Dawson up in the car and how Jeff had slumped down in the back seat when he saw the police. He told the court that he had asked Jeff why he was hiding and that Dawson told him that the police might be looking for him.

"By the way," Williams interrupted, "when Dawson got into the car that day, could you describe his demeanor? Do you know what demeanor means?"

"Yes, he was hyped up."[221]

"What happened next?" the prosecutor asked.

"We continued over to his mother's house, and he kept telling me he had something bug to tell me."

Williams raised his hand for the witness to stop. "Something bug, B-U-G?" he spelled.

"Yes."

"Is that some sort of street word?"

"Something that I probably wouldn't believe," Schleede said by way of explanation, "something outrageous."[222]

"OK," Williams continued, "what happened after he told you that?"

Schleede testified that he had driven to his mother's home and that they then headed toward Dawson's home on Brewster Street.

This was not offering much, so Williams tried to prompt his witness to get to the point by saying, "And what happened next?"

"We continued to drive towards his house, and he told me he went swimming last night."

"Went swimming last night?" the prosecutor asked, repeating Schleede's words.

"Yes."

Williams was becoming annoyed. His witness was not getting to the point. But, like the experienced prosecutor he was, he did not allow himself to lose sight of the target or outwardly show his displeasure. He just formulated his next question to get the witness where he needed him to go.

"And when you got to the house, what happened?" he asked with a little more urgency.

"He told me to get out of the car," Schleede said finally getting to the point. "He put his arm around me and said he murdered somebody last night."

"He put his arm around you and said he murdered somebody last night," Williams said, restating his answer again.

"Yes."

"And what happened next?"

I asked him who, and he said, did I know that bitch Annie Kithcart." [223]

When Schleede stopped talking, Williams simply instructed, "Go ahead."

"Well," Schleede continued, "he was showing me some kind of hold." He then attempted to demonstrate.

Williams stopped and addressed the bench, "Your Honor, the record should reflect that Mr. Schleede is attempting to demonstrate something with his arm, and currently I believe he has a broken rib and his left arm is in a sling. I don't want to get involved in the demonstration, but I'm going to ask perhaps an officer of the court to assist Mr. Schleede in making this demonstration to the court."

Looking around the courtroom, the judge saw a detective in the back of the courtroom.

"Detective Scarey," the judge called out, "would you please assist us here?"

The detective came forward and stood next to Schleede.

"Now, Mr. Schleede," Williams said, "slowly, I want you to demonstrate to the court and the defendant exactly what he demonstrated to you that night."[224]

For the next few minutes, Schleede instructed the detective to move his arms until he ended in a position with one arm pointing toward the ceiling, fist clenched, and the other across the neck grabbing the other forearm.[225]

When the demonstration was finished, Detective Scarey was excused and he returned to the rear of the courtroom.

"What is that called, by the way?" Williams asked his witness.

"I guess it's a yoke hold," Schleede replied weakly.

Moving on, Williams asked, "What happened next after he showed you the yoke hold?"

Schleede told the court that Dawson pointed to his neighbor's pool and told him he used it that night to wash off the blood. He also said he had wrapped up the clothes and hidden them near the Royal Grill bar.[226]

Sensing he was on a roll, Williams asked, "Did he say whose clothing that was that he wrapped up?"

"No," Schleede replied, "he said, 'the clothes.'"

"Did he tell you anything else that he did at that time?"

"When he was telling me," Schleede answered, "he had started laughing about the whole thing."

"Did he tell you at all that day about returning to the scene?"

"No."

"Did he tell you anything beyond the hold that he did to Annie Kithcart?"

"No, he didn't."[227]

Disappointed at Schleede's inability to recall more, the prosecutor shifted his attention to the recorded conversation from the previous Saturday night.

"On the evening of July 16th of 1988, did you see the defendant, Dawson, again?"

"Yes, I did."

"Approximately what time was it that you saw him this time?"

"It was very close to midnight."[228]

Interestingly, Williams did not make any mention of the conversation being recorded or of Schleede wearing a wire. Instead, he just asked about the nature of the conversation.

"Tell us what you remember about the conversation," the prosecutor instructed.

"I asked him if he had been reading the papers and does he know what is going on," the witness replied. "And I asked him if he put the KKK on her, and he said no."

Williams had already listened to the recording and knew that any answer from Dawson to this question could not be heard.

"Did he say no?" he asked.

"He shook his head no."

"Go ahead," Williams continued. "Did he tell you anything else?"

"I asked what happened when I dropped him off that night," Schleede explained. "He said she fell down and hit her head, so he cut her up to make it look like a psycho did it."[229]

"Did he tell you anything about the clothing, if you can recall?" Williams was confusing the two conversations. Although Schleede had reported that Dawson discussed hiding the clothes during their first conversation next to the car, they never discussed it the night he wore the wire.

"No, I can't recall," Schleede answered. "I asked him did anybody see him go back there, and he said no." Schleede was now also mistakenly referring to the first conversation with Dawson.

"Back where?" Williams asked, a little confused by the last answer.

"I just said back there with her."

"Did he tell you where he did this to Annie Kithcart?"

"No," Schleede answered.

As Williams was looking at some papers deciding on his next question, the witness offered, unsolicited, "I asked him did he fuck her, and he said no."

Realizing that he had gotten more than enough from this witness to win the hearing and not knowing exactly what Schleede was liable to blurt out next, Williams looked up to the judge and said, "I have nothing further at this time, Your Honor."[230]

Jerry Flaherty approached the witness to begin his cross-examination.

"Good morning, Todd," he said politely. "How many years

do you know Jeffrey?"

"I guess over ten years."

"You have been pretty good friends?"

"On and off," the witness answered. "He wasn't always around."

"Sometimes you weren't around, and sometimes he wasn't around?" Flaherty asked, obviously hinting at both men's multiple stays in prison.

"Yes," Schleede said, clearly not getting the reference.[231]

For the next ten minutes, Flaherty went over every detail of Schleede's first conversation with his client after the murder. He knew it was very unlikely that he was going to make Schleede change his story, but by locking him down on the record, he would have ammunition at trial if he varied in any way on those details.[232]

He also had Schleede testify that his girlfriend, Penny DeGroat, was in the car when Dawson showed the choke hold he had used. In a very clever move, he asked Schleede what his position was in relation to the car during the demonstration. Schleede said he was sideways to the car and no more than three feet away.[233]

At a future trial, this testimony could be invaluable. DeGroat might not have been able to hear what was being said, but would have been hard pressed to not see someone three feet away showing off a choke hold. If she had not seen it, then he could use that to attack Schleede's credibility.

Flaherty then did nearly exactly the same thing regarding the recorded conversation, locking the witness into detail after detail. Flaherty knew he was not going to win the preliminary hearing, but he was going to get whatever he could for the eventual trial.[234]

After tediously going over fact after fact, Flaherty decided to bring out some of Schleede's background.

"Presently, you are on parole, is correct?"

"Yes."

"Could you tell the court what you were convicted of?"

"Criminal sale of a controlled substance."

"That's not the first time you were convicted of a felony. Tell the court your previous felony conviction," Flaherty ordered.

"Burglary charge."

"Sentenced to one to three years in state prison?"

"Yes."

Flaherty walked Schleede through his other interactions with the law, both felony and misdemeanor. The witness admitted every charge and sentence without hesitation.[235]

Quickly jumping to a new topic, Flaherty asked, "How is it you came to be wearing a wire for the Kingston Police Department on July 16th?"

"Well," Schleede replied, "I was brought down here, and I told them what I knew and I agreed to wear a wire."

"You did this gratuitously?"

"Excuse me?"

"You did this gratuitously?" the attorney repeated.

"I did it when?" Schleede answered foolishly.

Don Williams stood as some in court laughed quietly. Before he could object, Flaherty said, "He knew 'demeanor,' so I figured he knew 'gratuitously.'"

The judge signaled the attorneys to move along, so Flaherty amended his question asking, "You did this of your own free will?"

"Yes."

"And you got nothing in return?" Flaherty asked in a tone

clearly showing his disbelief.

"Right."[236]

Earlier, Schleede had testified that he had dropped Dawson off near the area of the Royal Grill on the night of the murder. Flaherty had the witness confirm this again.

"And you were all by yourself then?" he asked.

"Yes."

"Did you know Annie Kithcart?"

"Yes."

"Did you know her previous to July 11th?"

"Yes."[237]

Flaherty was smartly establishing that Schleede did not himself have an alibi for the night of the murder and that he was familiar with the victim. Neither would help at the hearing, but both facts could be helpful at trial.

Flaherty was finished. He had not damaged Schleede's credibility, but had obtained useful tools for trial.

Assistant District Attorney Don Williams announced that he had more questions for his witness. He had two points he wanted to cover.

"Mr. Schleede," he asked, "when you saw Jeffrey Dawson on the afternoon of July 12th of 1988, did you get a look at his face?"

"Yes."

"Did you notice anything unusual on his face on the evening of the 12th that you did not see on the evening of the 11th?"

"I noticed a bruise on his face," Schleede noted, "somewhere in the area of the face, by the eyes."[238]

The obvious implication of this testimony was that Dawson had gotten the bruise when Annie Kithcart struggled for her life.

Williams spent the next few minutes dealing with his second point, by having the witness testify that neither the Kingston Police Department nor the Ulster County District Attorney's Office threatened or pressured him, or promised him anything in return for his testimony. He was testifying of his own free will.[239]

With that, Todd Schleede stepped down from the witness stand and walked out of the courtroom.

As soon as the courtroom door closed, Williams stood and advised the court that no more witnesses would be offered.

"Your Honor," Flaherty interjected, "may I have a very slight recess to speak with the witness we'd like to call at this time and his attorney?"

Williams was ready for this request. "Your Honor, I believe there's a subpoena that has been issued. Perhaps a conference in chambers with the benefit of the Public Defender's Office would be necessary."[240]

The judge readily agreed and ordered a recess, leaving those in the courtroom wondering about the identity of the mystery witness.

When court resumed, David Clegg of the Public Defender's Office was seated next to Flaherty at the defense table. The judge wasted little time getting right to the point.

"Mr. Flaherty?" he asked.

"Your Honor," Flaherty said standing up, "we anticipated, pursuant to a subpoena issued, that Honorable [Judge] Vincent Bradley[241] signed yesterday, to have Mr. Kiernan testify today. Mr. Kiernan, not being a co-defendant in this matter but, according to the newspaper, had been arrested on a collateral matter to that which is before the court."

These words caught the attention of the reporters. Testimony by Joseph Kiernan would make great news. Their excitement was short-lived, however.

"Mr. Clegg is here today," Flaherty continued, "and it's my understanding that he represents Mr. Kiernan and he would have a statement to make."

Clegg stood to address the court. "I can confirm the fact that my client was subpoenaed by the defendant," he began, "I would represent to the court that I have advised my client that he should exercise his right under the Fifth Amendment not to testify. He will not testify today."

"Thank you," the judge said in reply.

"As such," Flaherty interjected, "I presume the People are not going to give Mr. Kiernan immunity?" This was a very weak attempt to get around the Fifth Amendment defense.

"He shouldn't be so presumptuous," Williams responded coldly.

"Well," Flaherty said, "the defense has no witnesses to call at this time."[242]

With the hearing now over, Judge Bruhn issued his ruling. "Based on the evidence that has been presented here this morning, I find that the People have sustained their burden for purposes of this hearing and the defendant will be held for action of the grand jury."[243]

Dawson was escorted out of the courtroom. He would remain in jail at least until his indictment and most likely until the trial itself.

As Dawson was being transported back to the county jail, Kiernan was just arriving. He was also to appear before Judge Bruhn that day on the question of bail. It had previously been set at $10,000, but the Public Defender's Office had asked for a hearing to seek a reduction.

When the case was called, Clegg asked the judge to consider releasing Kiernan into his brother's custody. "Ten thousand dollars far exceeds any amount he could possibly make," Clegg pleaded. "He's not a danger to the public. He's an indigent person."

Assistant District Attorney Joan Zooper, appearing for the prosecution, opposed the request, pointing out to the court that Kiernan was a vagrant with no known address.

"No, that's a lie," Kiernan interjected loudly. "I have an apartment."

"Mr. Kiernan," the judge asked, "have you ever lived with your brother before?"

"No, Your Honor," Kiernan replied.

"I have a concern, Mr. Clegg," the judge said turning to defense counsel, "that Mr. Kiernan's brother might not be able to exercise control over the defendant."

The judge denied the request for release, but cut the bail in half to $5,000. Kiernan would have to stay in custody until his family could collect the money.

Outside the courthouse, as Clegg was walking to his car, a reporter asked him if it was true that Alton Maddox, the New York City attorney involved in the Brawley case, was going to take over the defense from him.

"My client does not want to be represented by Mr. Maddox. He specifically told me that," Clegg replied. He took another step toward his car, stopped, and turned back to the reporter. With a smile, he said, "But who knows what tomorrow may bring?"[244]

CHAPTER 13 - INDICTMENT, BAIL, AND A PROTEST MARCH

TWO DAYS AFTER THE preliminary hearing, Alton Maddox returned to Kingston and held a press conference at the Ulster County Jail. Joseph Kiernan was also there.

Maddox advised the press that he was not representing Kiernan but wanted to help him by working to raise the $5,000 needed for bail.

"I'm really interested in justice," the attorney announced. "I do not believe that Kiernan is guilty of any crime regarding Miss Kithcart." Pausing for a moment, he added, "I think he is a hero."[245] Maddox did not choose to explain why he thought Kiernan was a "hero."

Maddox also called Jeff Dawson a scapegoat, though he admitted that he had never met him. He alleged a cover-up of the entire case and went so far as to accuse local law enforcement of involvement in the crime.

"Only law enforcement officials had the means and the opportunity," he charged, "to leave the body behind the hospital so it can be readily discovered."[246]

To support his outrageous claims, Maddox pointed to the police records showing an investigation into the theft of a quart of beer from the Convenient Mart on the night of the murder.

He also made reference to a newscast the previous week by

a New York City television station that incorrectly claimed that Annie Kithcart had been chased by the police the night of her murder.[247]

Maddox was insinuating that Kithcart had been chased and killed by the police because she had stolen beer, and her body moved to where it was later found. He offered no motive or proof to support his scandalous allegation. Just as he and his colleagues did in the Brawley case, Maddox was making unsubstantiated allegations against local police.

Informed by members of the assembled media that there were no reports of any suspects being chased by police anywhere in the city from 11:15 p.m. to the time Kithcart's body was found, Maddox callously replied that police reports "could have been tampered with."[248]

Reporters were furiously scribbling notes from his latest pronouncement when Maddox abruptly changed topics. He informed the press that Joseph Kiernan's birthday had been the day before and that he had a present for him.

Maddox produced a vanilla-frosted cake with the words "Happy Birthday Joseph" written in red icing and set it on the table in front of Kiernan.

Kiernan responded by standing up and said, "I'm a scapegoat of Mr. Kavanagh's career. I'm innocent."

After the press conference, Kiernan was allowed to eat some of his cake, but not until it was thoroughly checked for contraband.

The media representatives then contacted District Attorney Kavanagh, hoping for a comment in response to Maddox's claims. Kavanagh did not disappoint them.

"He is a racist," Kavanagh said of Maddox. "The truth is incidental to what he does. A real indication of his character is that he's bringing a birthday cake to someone who has admitted to sodomizing the corpse of a young black girl and who, I believe, defiled her body with the letters KKK."[249]

Later that day, the media heard from Jerry Flaherty, the attorney for Jeff Dawson. He announced that he had received "stunning" and "very positive" evidence that would help clear his client. The evidence did not lead to another suspect, however.[250]

Asked to elaborate, Flaherty said he had obtained the information from another one of his clients, but could not give details. He said he was ethically obligated to make sure that revealing the nature of the evidence would not violate his other client's right to attorney-client privilege.[251]

The attorney-client privilege is the right of a client to keep discussions and communications with his or her lawyer private. It is a legal right strongly enshrined in the American judicial system.

The U.S. Supreme Court, in an opinion written by Justice William Rehnquist, has stated that confidentiality of communications between client and attorney must be preserved so that clients feel free to make disclosures to their attorneys, who are then better able to provide candid advice and effective representation.[252]

Assistant District Attorney Don Williams, when contacted about this unknown but "stunning" evidence, responded by saying that he planned to submit eight to ten witnesses before the grand jury and obtain an indictment.

"If he has information that is useful to this case," the prosecutor added, "he should inform this office."[253]

True to his word, a week after the preliminary hearing, on Wednesday, July 27, Williams announced that the grand jury had voted to indict Jeffrey Dawson on a charge of murder in the second degree on two different legal theories. The first count of murder alleged that Dawson intentionally caused Kithcart's death.[254]

The second count of murder accused Dawson of recklessly engaging in conduct under circumstances evincing a depraved indifference to human life. This conduct created a grave risk of death to Anna Kithcart and in fact caused her death.[255]

This charge is commonly referred to as depraved indifference murder. Intentional murder is when death results from a specific or conscious intent to cause death. With depraved indifference murder, death results from an indifference to or disregard of the risks involved in the conduct of the defendant.[256]

Put another way, to be convicted under this statute, it has to be shown that a defendant did not just willingly take a grossly unreasonable risk to human life, but also that he did not care if someone died as a result.[257]

One of the big problems in the case against Jeff Dawson was a complete lack of motive. Police were unable to find any reason why Dawson would want to kill Annie Kithcart. They were not involved in a romantic relationship, and there was no known animosity between them.

In his recorded statements to the police and Todd Schleede, Dawson had never given any indication of hatred or dislike for the girl other than referring to her as a bitch. All of Dawson's statements held that he had pushed Kithcart causing her to fall and hit her head, suggesting to the police that Annie either died accidentally or was still alive when an unknown third party wandered by and killed her.

If a jury was to believe Dawson's account that Annie died accidentally, he would likely not be convicted of murder. Instead, he would be convicted of manslaughter, which would carry a maximum of fifteen years in prison, or of criminal negligent homicide, which would carry a maximum of four years in prison.[258]

In a media-charged case involving the brutal death of a

young woman, a prison sentence of four years would be seen as an abject failure by the District Attorney's Office. To avoid this potentially disappointing result, prosecutors added the depraved indifference charge.

One of the many theories held by the police was that Dawson accidentally injured Kithcart and then panicked. Believing she was already dead, even though she was actually just unconscious, Dawson smashed her face and tried to make the scene appear as if a psychopath had committed the crime. Police had the suspect on tape making this admission to Todd Schleede.

Prosecutors, by adding this second count, could now point out to a jury that if Kithcart had been knocked unconscious by accident, Dawson could have carried her to the emergency room at Kingston Hospital, only a few hundred yards away. Instead, without having confirmed that she was truly dead, Dawson smashed her skull and ended her life.

If Dawson had been less concerned about potentially going back to prison for a parole violation and more concerned with saving a human life, Annie Kithcart might not have died.

That was not the argument prosecutors wanted to make. They wanted to seek a guilty verdict for intentional murder. However, if the defendant testified and put out a claim of accidental death, they now had a response.

When advised by members of the press of the indictment, Jerry Flaherty had a quick response. "An indictment is just a piece of paper," the defense attorney said. "As the evidence, or lack of evidence, begins to unfold, the evidence will show that Mr. Dawson did not commit the crime of murder."[259]

The attorney did not stop there. He accused the prosecution of racing the case through the grand jury in just a few days in response to the intense media coverage and allegations of racism.

"Haste makes waste," Flaherty said cautioning that a slow and steady review of the case was needed.[260]

The next morning, Joseph Kiernan was back before Judge Bruhn in City Court. This time, however, he had new legal representation. Just minutes before the hearing was to begin that Thursday, Kiernan announced that Alton Maddox was now representing him.[261]

David Clegg, not knowing that his office had been removed from the case, was present for the proceeding along with Maddox. When the judge learned of this development, he asked the defendant to confirm his decision on the record. When he did so, Judge Bruhn discharged Clegg with the thanks of the court.

As the public defender left the courthouse, he was followed by an eager reporter. Asked for a comment, Clegg said simply, "I hope Kiernan will get the proper attention from Mr. Maddox and that it won't become a circus."[262]

Back in the courtroom, Alton Maddox offered his first statements to the court as Jeffrey Kiernan's attorney. He announced that his client had nothing to do with the murder of Anna Kithcart. (Since Kiernan was not charged in her killing, the statement was not relevant to the proceedings.)

Then, Maddox complained to the judge about the unfair attention his client was receiving from the media. "It would be a sad day in the annals of jurisprudence," he said, "for a man to be arrested by people who want to inflame racial tensions."[263]

This was interesting remark, coming from Maddox. Slightly less than a week earlier, while presenting the birthday cake to Kiernan, Maddox had accused police of a racially based cover-up saying that only law enforcement could have planted Kithcart's body where it was found.

A few weeks before that, he had said that the city of

Kingston was "filled up with racists"[264] while his friend and colleague Al Sharpton called the city "a Klan den."[265]

Now Alton Maddox was complaining that the racial tensions, which his own comments had helped stoke, were causing an unfair atmosphere for his client. It was the height of hypocrisy.

"I think I am missing the point of the statement you're making," replied the judge.

Maddox insisted his statement was about the evidence against his client, but Judge Bruhn politely disagreed.

Maddox immediately changed the subject and asked about a reduction in bail. After hearing arguments from both sides, the judge refused to lower the amount of bail, but did alter his prior decision by ruling that the $5,000 bail could be posted by an unsecured bond.[266] This meant that the amount of cash required was only $500, a much easier amount to raise.

Finally, as Kiernan's prior attorney had already filed a motion seeking to suppress Kiernan's statements as having been coerced and not voluntary, the judge adjourned the case until August 30 for an evidentiary hearing on the matter.

When the court proceeding was complete, Kiernan was taken to a waiting police vehicle feeling optimistic that he might be able to get out of jail soon. Meanwhile, his new attorney spoke with the media gathered just outside the courthouse.

Maddox expressed that he was deeply troubled by the charges against Kiernan, but hoped his client would get out of jail and have the charges against him dismissed.

As Maddox started to leave, a reporter asked how Kiernan had chosen him as his attorney. Maddox replied sarcastically, "I'm a practicing attorney in New York state. I reckon he looked me up in the Yellow Pages."[267]

On Friday morning, Jeff Dawson was arraigned on his indictment. In New York, arraignment on a felony complaint, as well as the preliminary hearing, is handled in local court. However, once a defendant is charged by a grand jury, he must be arraigned on the indictment in either County Court or Supreme Court.

Dawson was brought to County Court before Judge Francis "Frank" Vogt. Vogt had been on the bench for ten years. Before becoming a judge, he had been the Ulster County district attorney from 1970 to 1978. He was well-liked and highly respected in the legal community.

Jerry Flaherty entered a not guilty plea for his client and asked the judge to consider bail. Although bail may not be granted on a murder charge in local court, the County Court judge may do so.

As part of his case, Flaherty argued that the Ulster County Jail was so overcrowded that it would be unfair to send his client there.

"There are way too many people at the county jail," Flaherty argued. "There are people sleeping on the floor. It is an unhealthy situation."

Assistant District Attorney Don Williams was quick to respond. "The jail may be overcrowded," he said, "but jail conditions should not be taken into consideration when determining whether a person charged with a brutal murder should be released to the streets."

Judge Vogt waived off any further discussion. The judge said he felt he had no choice but to deny bail given the seriousness of the charge and the defendant's prior record.[268]

About ten minutes later, Dawson was on his way back to the county lock-up.

Although Dawson was unable to get released, Kiernan was more fortunate. Just before noon, he was released from the

Ulster County Jail after Alton Maddox posted a $5,000 unsecured bond as bail.

He walked into the sunshine wearing the same white T-shirt, navy blue pants, and canvas sneakers he wore during his last court appearance.

Someone had obviously tipped off the press because reporters were waiting for Kiernan. He initially ignored them before saying to nobody in particular, "Where's my lawyer?"[269]

Kiernan was carrying several books and a brown paper bag. A reporter asked him what was in the bag, but Kiernan just stood there, seemingly waiting for someone. After several minutes, he turned to the reporters to make a statement.

"It was pretty rough in there," he said, "but I am innocent. We have evidence that shows I didn't do this."[270]

Despite several questions, Kiernan had nothing more to say. A moment later, a red car pulled up, driven by a woman.

"There's my sister," Kiernan announced, getting into the car.

Reporters continued to shout questions at Kiernan and his sister. The woman seemed very uncomfortable, but said she was very happy her brother had been released before driving away.[271]

Two days later, a protest march was held by more than fifty people, many of them Annie Kithcart's friends. The event had been organized by Kristina Van Amburgh. Her intention was to draw attention to the impact of drug use on local youths, like her friend Annie.

Interviewed shortly before the event by a local reporter, Van Amburgh said, "I think we'll be showing that the youth is getting together to fight against drugs. This demonstration will be the first in a series of events to draw attention to the local drug problem."

Van Amburgh listed some ideas that she and other friends

of Annie Kithcart had discussed such as a local drug hotline and a proposal that city parks remain open until 10:00 p.m. with lighting and supervision to keep youths out of bars and away from the drug scene.[272]

When the parade began, marchers carried signs reading "Down With Drugs" and "Crack Down on Crack." They marched from Forsyth Park through the city before finishing at a parking lot across the street from the Royal Grill.[273]

The Royal Grill had been intentionally chosen as the ending point of the march for two reasons. First, the area around the bar was the last place Annie had been seen alive. Second, the bar had a public reputation for serving alcohol to minors and had been the subject of numerous drug-related complaints.[274]

To Annie's friends and some of her family members, the Royal Grill was very much a symbol of the drug and alcohol culture they believed caused Annie's death. They would get some solace when within three months of the march, the Royal Grill, after complaints with the State Liquor Authority and the sudden death of its owner from a heart attack, was closed and later sold.

Whether Annie's death was directly linked to drug and alcohol use, however, was far from clear. Though she had been drinking that evening, and there was a witness who claimed Annie had been trying to buy cocaine, there was no evidence that her killer's motive had anything to do with drugs or alcohol.

Indirectly, alcohol intoxication may have contributed to Annie going into the railroad bed where she died. Confused and devastated family members told reporters that Annie always hated the dark and slept with a nightlight on.[275] They did not believe she would have voluntarily walked into such a dark and deserted area, even with friends. Alcohol lowers inhibitions and often gives false courage. Perhaps that allowed her to walk somewhere she otherwise never would.

By all accounts, Annie Kithcart was a teenager who drank on weekends and had been experimenting with cocaine in the weeks and months before her death. There was no indication that she was an addict.

Many teenagers and young adults who experiment with alcohol or drugs reach a point where they have to make a decision. Will they keep drinking and taking drugs and potentially ruin their lives or will they walk away from it and get their lives on track?

Annie Kithcart had allowed drugs and alcohol to sidetrack her life. She had not seen some of her friends in a few months. A longtime friend, describing himself as a "childhood sweetheart," lamented that Annie had become involved in the drug scene.[276]

There were some signs that Annie was making efforts to get her life back on track. She held several jobs trying to save some money. She had not graduated from high school but had told people she was planning to continue her education and get a degree.[277]

Annie had many friends and no known enemies. She was kind and generous to children. She was independent, but more than willing to go out of her way for her friends. She had a great deal to offer and could have forged a very nice life for herself.

In all the hype over allegations of racism and questions of drug use, a very important fact seemed to have been sidetracked and ignored. A nineteen-year-old girl, who had her whole life in front her and who had family and friends who adored her, was gone. All of her potential was destroyed.

The sad reality was that, for whatever reason, she ended up in the darkness on the old railway tracks with the wrong person. In a matter of minutes, she was choked, beaten, and murdered, forever denying her the chance to make the decision.

The prosecutions of Jeff Dawson and Joseph Kiernan might result in convictions and long jail sentences. Even if they did, the painful reality was that Annie Kithcart was never coming back.

CHAPTER 14 - MUSICAL ATTORNEYS

ON AUGUST 8, JERRY Flaherty was given permission by the County Court judge to withdraw as Jeffrey Dawson's attorney.

Sixteen days earlier, he had announced that he had "stunning evidence." He had not disclosed the nature of the evidence because it involved a former client and he had to consider that individual's legal rights.

As it turned out, he was unable to get his former client's permission to use the information. Additionally, Flaherty realized that if this unknown evidence was used at trial, he himself might be called as a witness. If that happened, he would have to refuse to answer, citing attorney-client privilege.

This placed him in an impossible ethical situation. The only remedy for him was to seek to be replaced as defense counsel. As an experienced judge, Vogt understood the request and granted it. He further advised both sides that he would announce a new attorney for Dawson later in the week.

Approached by the media later that day, Flaherty declined to discuss the matter other than to say, "I regret getting off the case. No one should draw a negative inference from the move."[278] His intention in saying this was to make it clear that he was not abandoning a sinking ship. His reasons for withdrawing had nothing to do with Jeff Dawson's guilt or innocence.

So, what was the stunning evidence Flaherty had found that forced him to eventually withdraw from the case? To this day, Flaherty has maintained his professional ethics and refused to discuss it. However, records maintained by the Ulster County District Attorney's Office offer a likely answer involving Todd Schleede, the main prosecution witness.

Schleede had been arrested earlier in the year, on March 10, 1988, along with a man named Mark Washington, and both were charged with attempting to rob a Stewart's Shop in the town of Saugerties, about fifteen miles north of Kingston.[279]

Schleede was represented in that case by the Public Defender's Office, but Washington was represented by Jerry Flaherty.[280]

The arrest came about after a man named Terry Anderson, who was already on probation, was arrested and agreed to cooperate with the police. As part of his cooperation, he provided information about some robberies in the area.[281]

Anderson told the police that he had committed a robbery with Todd Schleede and Mark Washington. He also revealed that the Schleede and Washington were planning to commit another robbery. The target was the Stewart's Shop in Saugerties.

After getting details from Anderson, including descriptions of both men and of the cars they used, detectives arranged a stakeout with unmarked police cars hoping to catch the men in the act.[282]

On March 9, at about ten minutes to midnight, the investigators observed a car matching the description given by Anderson. The car went past the Stewart's Shop and entered a parking lot of a large plaza adjacent to the Stewart's parking lot.

As investigators watched with binoculars, two men got out of the car and headed toward Stewart's. Between the two lots was a small area of grass, brush, and trees. The men entered this area and went from tree to tree, ducking behind each one. They came out of the brush and started toward the store.

About a hundred feet from the store, the men stopped suddenly. They were within twenty feet of one of the undercover cars and apparently recognized the detective sitting inside. Without a word, the men turned and headed back toward the brush and their waiting vehicle on the other side. They hopped into the car and started to drive away.[283]

The police, realizing that their surveillance had been discovered, moved in. They pulled the car over just a couple of blocks away and arrested both occupants, Schleede and Washington. Detectives found a claw hammer and a length of clothesline type rope in Schleede's possession. In the car, they found two masks made from long-sleeved underwear or long johns.[284]

Both men were arraigned and remanded to the county jail on $50,000 bail. Police obtained a statement from Mark Washington that he had no idea Todd Schleede intended to rob the store. Once he realized the plan, he refused to participate.

Police did not believe this claim because they had noted that Washington had been leading the way toward the store.[285]

A few months later, all charges were dropped by the District Attorney's Office. Although Kavanagh believed that the men only gave up on their robbery plan because they spotted the police surveillance, they never got to the point where their conduct was an actual commission of a crime. As such, their conduct supported a defense of renunciation.[286]

Under New York law, when a person is charged with an attempted crime, he may present a defense that, under circumstances manifesting a voluntary and complete renunciation of his criminal purpose, he had abandoned his criminal effort and avoided the actual commission of the crime. This defense is called renunciation.[287]

Assuming this was the information that Flaherty was referring to, it becomes very clear why he could not use it and why it would be very damaging to the prosecution's case against Jeff Dawson.

Todd Schleede's record of convictions included burglary and selling drugs. There were no charges involving violence. However, robbery is considered a violent felony. Additionally, Schleede had a claw hammer in his possession, presumably to use as a weapon.

Moreover, it is reasonable to assume that Flaherty's client Mark Washington may have revealed the prior robbery mentioned by Anderson involving himself and Schleede.

This was information that he could use to destroy Todd Schleede's credibility on the witness stand. Schleede was presenting himself as someone on parole who reported Dawson's statements about the murder after having an attack of conscience. However, this new information could paint a picture of a man on a criminal rampage committing numerous crimes despite being on parole.

Further, while the charges related to the Stewart's Shop in Saugerties had been dropped due to renunciation, what about the other robbery allegedly committed by Schleede, Washington, and Anderson? Had it been investigated, or had the prosecution agreed not to do so in order to maintain their main witness in a murder case?

In front of a jury, allegations and accusations like these would be dynamite. In addition to destroying Schleede's credibility, it might also cause a jury to more readily accept the idea that Schleede himself might be the murderer.

The problem, however, was that Schleede would just deny it when he testified. The prosecution and Schleede had already denied any deals at the preliminary hearing and would certainly continue to do so.

Flaherty needed a witness to provide support to such allegations. That witness would have to be Mark Washington, Flaherty's former client. But Washington could not testify without potentially subjecting himself to a prison sentence.

He could not get on the witness stand and testify under oath that he committed a robbery with Schleede and Anderson. If he did, the moment he stepped down, police officers would be waiting with handcuffs and a jail cell. All they would need would be any witness who said that a robbery as described by Washington had indeed occurred. There would be more than enough evidence when combined with the sworn testimony to put Washington in prison for a long stretch.

Flaherty himself could not testify to this information. If his client had revealed to his attorney that the robbery did occur and Flaherty tried to testify about it, he would be breaking attorney-client privilege. He would assuredly have been disbarred and forever prohibited from practicing law.

It was, as the attorney had told the media, evidence that was "very positive" for Jeff Dawson, but it did not point to another suspect.

Consequently, Flaherty was in a no-win situation. He had information that could assist his current client, but he had no way to effectively use it without violating the rights of his prior client. He thus did the only thing he ethically could do. He withdrew from the case.

A week later, Judge Vogt appointed Alan Zweibel to represent Dawson. Zweibel was a 1969 graduate of New York University, and had graduated from New York Law School in 1973. Before starting to practice in the Hudson Valley, he was a staff attorney with the New York City Legal Aide

Society's criminal division.

Zweibel was not in court when the assignment was made. Judge Vogt told Dawson that his new attorney was just beginning a short vacation, but would be in contact with him as soon as he returned. The judge also announced that he would give the new attorney whatever reasonable time he required to get up to speed and make pretrial motions.[288]

Two weeks later, Joseph Kiernan was back in the news. On Tuesday, August 30, he was brought to City Court. His case was scheduled for a Huntley hearing, a pretrial suppression hearing used to determine whether statements or confessions of a defendant were made voluntarily and can be used at trial.[289]

Unfortunately, while Kiernan himself and the prosecution were present, defense counsel was not. Alton Maddox called the court around 9:00 a.m. to advise that he was still in court in Brooklyn, but would try to make it in time for the 10:00 a.m. hearing.

Not surprisingly, since Brooklyn is a two-and-a-half-hour car ride, Maddox did not make the hearing. Judge Bruhn rescheduled the matter for September 27 and threatened legal sanctions if defense counsel was not present then.[290]

Outside the courthouse, Kiernan spoke with the media while waiting for a ride. He was much more relaxed than at previous court appearances. He was clean-shaven and dressed in blue slacks, a flannel shirt, and blue canvas sneakers.[291]

"I'm innocent," Kiernan said to nobody in particular. "I never touched the body. It was already in bad shape. It looked horrible."[292]

As he waited, Kiernan told the reporters that he was a contract employee of the CIA and that he was undercover at the time of his arrest. "I may have gone too far with my cover," he said. "I grew my hair too long."[293]

A few moments later, Kiernan's ride arrived. As he got into the car, he looked back to the reporters saying, "Every time I come back to my hometown, I get into trouble."[294]

On September 15, Zweibel heard Jeff Dawson on the radio giving an interview from the county jail. In this interview, Dawson complained that his new attorney was too close to District Attorney Mike Kavanagh to be a fair lawyer for him. Zweibel went directly to the jail to speak with his client, but to no avail. Dawson wanted nothing to do with him.[295]

So, less than a month after being appointed as Dawson's lawyer, Zweibel filed a motion asking the court to discharge him due to a breakdown in the attorney-client relationship.

Judge Vogt decided to have all parties in court to discuss the situation. Zweibel informed the court that the only association he had with Kavanagh was a professional one.

"We have exhibited to each other the proper adversarial attitudes," Zweibel said. "He's one side of the case, and I'm the other."[296]

Dawson maintained strongly that he did not feel Zweibel should be his lawyer. He told the judge that, at their first attorney-client meeting, Zweibel recommended that he take a plea bargain for fifteen years to avoid a sentence of twenty-five years to life for murder and save the district attorney a lot of time.

"I don't feel that's the type of lawyer to represent me," Dawson said. "He just doesn't believe me."[297]

Judge Vogt granted Zweibel's request and discharged him from the case. He then told Dawson that he was going to appoint one more lawyer for him, but had no intention of going through this process again. He was not going to play musical lawyers. The next attorney was going to handle this case or Dawson would represent himself.

About a week later, Vogt appointed Barry Lippman to

represent Dawson. Lippman graduated from New York University in 1961 and obtained his law degree in 1969 from St. John's University in Queens. He had tried a variety of criminal cases in Ulster County, though was not as well-known as Flaherty or Zweibel despite having practiced law for a longer period of time.

On the same day that Zweibel was being removed from Dawson's case in County Court, Joseph Kiernan was back in City Court before Judge Mike Bruhn for his Huntley hearing. Once again, however, Alton Maddox failed to appear and the case was again adjourned. Just prior to the hearing, Maddox had called the District Attorney's Office to advise them that he was handling a trial in a higher court and could not attend.

Although Judge Bruhn had expressed annoyance at the previous adjournment, he did not do so this time.

"If he's on trial in some higher court, the lower courts have to take a back seat," Bruhn said. "It's no big deal."[298]

Despite his genial comments, Bruhn's frustration with the controversial defense attorney was growing. Over the next few months, Alton Maddox would do his best to fan the flames.

CHAPTER 15 - THE BRAWLEY GRAND JURY REPORT

FROM THE MOMENT THAT the details of the Kithcart murder became public, the Reverend Al Sharpton and his colleagues had tried to connect the case to the Tawana Brawley investigation. They claimed repeatedly that a racist cult of some kind was operating throughout New York's Hudson Valley, though they provided no proof.

With the arrest of Jeffrey Dawson, a black man, their claims became considerably less credible. Sharpton had not returned to Kingston, choosing instead to focus his attention on the Brawley case and the Democratic National Convention. Although he generated favorable headlines for a speech he gave at the convention, the coverage of Sharpton's involvement in the Brawley case was about to become decidedly negative.

On October 6, New York Attorney General Robert Abrams called a press conference at the State Armory in Poughkeepsie. Over a hundred reporters were in attendance when Abrams, surrounded by members of law enforcement who had worked the Brawley case, stepped to the podium. He was dressed in a dark suit that contrasted with his crisp white shirt and striped tie.[299]

Waving a copy of the 170-page report issued by the grand jury assigned to investigate the Tawana Brawley matter, Abrams addressed the assembled media in a manner much more animated than anyone had ever seen the normally sedate attorney.[300]

"Based upon all of the evidence that has been presented to the grand jury," Abrams said, reading verbatim from the report, "we conclude that Tawana Brawley was not the

victim of a forcible sexual assault by multiple assailants over a four-day period. There is no evidence that any sexual assault occurred."[301]

Abrams carefully noted that the report of the grand jury was based upon a complete and thorough investigation including 6,000 pages of testimony from 180 witnesses, as well as 250 exhibits of evidence.[302]

The report noted that there was no forensic evidence of any kind to support claims of an abduction or sexual assault. The grand jury concluded that Brawley's condition when found had been self-inflicted. The evidence strongly suggested that she had smeared the dog feces and written the racial slurs on her own body.[303]

"We have the facts," Abrams continued. "We have solved the case. The allegations she made are false."[304]

Next, Abrams switched to the subject of Assistant District Attorney Steven Pagones and the late Fishkill Police Officer Harry Crist. Pagones and Crist had both been repeatedly accused by Sharpton and Maddox of being two of the men who supposedly assaulted Brawley. Reading from the grand jury report, Abrams told the reporters that there was no evidence that in any way connected Pagones or Crist to any incident involving Tawana Brawley.

Having advised the media of the grand jury's conclusions, Abrams turned to the topic he really wanted to discuss. For months, he had been ridiculed, mocked, and insulted. Now, he was finally going to unload his frustration, anger, and venom on his tormenters: Al Sharpton, C. Vernon Mason, and Alton Maddox, the three Brawley advisers.

"Their outrageous acts have increased the atmosphere of tension between the races throughout this nation," Abrams lashed out. The incensed attorney further charged that, because of the three men's irresponsible behavior and allegations, a legitimate victim of racial violence in the future might not be taken seriously.[305]

He was not content to simply levy verbal charges. Abrams produced a ten-page letter he had written to the grievance committee for the 2nd and 11th Judicial Districts in Brooklyn and the disciplinary committee of the First Judicial Department in Manhattan. In this letter, he asked both bodies to investigate Mason and Maddox.[306]

As Maddox and Mason both were attorneys admitted to practice in New York, their behavior when handling legal matters was governed by the state's rules of legal ethics. One of the most basic rules of ethical behavior is that, in representing a client, a lawyer "shall not knowingly make a false statement of law or fact." Put simply, an attorney may not lie.[307]

In the ten-page document, Abrams accused Maddox and Mason of repeatedly lying during their handling of the Brawley case. These lies included wild accusations made by one or both of the attorneys that:

1 Steven Pagones and Harry Crist Jr., a Town of Fishkill police officer, were two of Brawley's attackers.

2 Law enforcement authorities, including the district attorney and the attorney general, knew the identities of those who assaulted Brawley, but covered it up.

3 Governor Mario Cuomo appointed the attorney general to cover up a crime and exonerate the suspects.

4 Officials in Dutchess County, the FBI, and the U.S.

Attorney's Office in the Southern District were in cahoots with mobsters.

5   The ambulance attendants who transported Ms. Brawley to the hospital on November 28, 1987, "wanted her to die."

6   Governor Cuomo tried to set up Al Sharpton for physical assassination.

7   The attorney general engaged in sexual acts in front of a picture of Brawley.[308]

Another important ethical rule is that, in representing a client, a lawyer shall not counsel or assist a client in conduct that the lawyer knows to be illegal or fraudulent.[309]

In his letter of complaint, Abrams wrote, "Mr. Maddox and Mr. Mason counseled their client Glenda Brawley, Tawana's mother, to refuse a lawful mandate to testify before the Grand Jury, and thereafter actively assisted Mrs. Brawley to evade arrest for criminal contempt. By counseling and assisting Mrs. Brawley in conduct they knew to be illegal, I believe Mr. Maddox and Mr. Mason violated Disciplinary Rule 7-102 (A)(7)."[310]

By sending his letter, Abrams was seeking to get both men disbarred and end their legal careers.[311]

"One is hard pressed to imagine," Abrams wrote, "statements more scurrilous and in flagrant disregard for the truth or more deserving of disciplinary scrutiny than those that have been made by Mr. Maddox and Mr. Mason during the course of their representation of the Brawley family."[312]

If Alton Maddox was worried about these ethical complaints, he did not show any signs of it when reached by the press for comment. Instead, Maddox went on the attack against not only Robert Abrams, but also the grand jury.

"What should we expect from twenty-one whites from Dutchess County?" he asked sarcastically. "We know that the district attorney of the state has singled us out for prosecution because of the fact that we had the temerity to stand up to the state in the absence of any black leadership in the state."[313]

Al Sharpton, who was in Chicago planning to attend a convention of the Nation of Islam, a religious group headed by Louis Farrakhan Sr., took a similarly aggressive stance. He alleged that the grand jury report was the work of "incompetent prosecutors, incompetent liars, and incompetent cover-up men."[314] Sharpton made it clear that he was not going to back down on his support for Brawley or his belief in her claims.

"Tawana Brawley was raped and sodomized," he thundered. "We knew it then, and we know it now. We believe it, and we can prove it." He refused to provide any details to back that up, however.[315]

Five days later, another press conference on the Brawley case was held in Poughkeepsie. This time, the event was at a Holiday Inn and was hosted by Steven Pagones, the embattled Dutchess County prosecutor.

Pagones read calmly from a prepared statement. He announced that his lawyers were preparing a multimillion-dollar lawsuit against Tawana Brawley, Al Sharpton, and attorneys Maddox and Mason for slander and libel. He expected the suit would be filed in about a month.[316]

Pagones referred to attacking remarks from Sharpton, Maddox, and Mason as "blatant, disgusting, and deplorable lies." He further accused the three of making the past six months a living hell for the parents and friends of the late Harry Crist.[317]

He also said he, too, would file a complaint against Maddox and Mason similar to the one filed by New York Attorney General Robert Abrams. Pagones said he felt both attorneys should be disbarred for their lies and false statements.[318]

He was nearly finished with his remarks when he was interrupted by a booming voice that cried out, "Your accuser is here!"

Pagones looked up as heads turned to see the source of the interruption. There, standing just outside the doorway of the conference room, was Al Sharpton.

"I'm here, Pagones!" Sharpton shouted again. "Your accuser is here. Why don't you give me the papers?"

"Excuse me," Pagones fired back. "I'm holding a press conference here."

However, members of the press were already turning their cameras away from Pagones and toward Sharpton. Now the center of attention, Sharpton started to step forward.

Suddenly, with almost comical timing, an employee of the hotel slammed the conference door shut, preventing Sharpton from entering the room. He then stood in front of the door holding it closed with both hands. He would stay that way for the balance of the event.[319]

Once Sharpton stopped trying to force his way into the room, Pagones tried to continue his statement. He had great difficulty doing so as tears started filling his eyes. This was supposed to be his moment of triumph. The grand jury cleared him and told the world that he had been wrongfully accused. Now, Sharpton had stolen his moment of vindication from him. Even now, the flamboyant reverend would not leave him alone.

"It has affected every aspect of my life, my health, my safety, my social life, my freedom," the shaken prosecutor said, regaining his composure. "A perfect example is what happened right now. I always have to worry about what's going to happen next."[320]

As Pagones paused to consider his words, a reporter asked him if he had anything to say to Sharpton.

"Yes," Pagones replied. "Go away and leave me alone."[321]

As the press conference broke up, the media immediately hustled to the lobby hoping to find Sharpton and get a quote. He was still there and happily obliged.

"I am here to confront Pagones," Sharpton proclaimed, "and to deal with this bogus attempt to cover this up."[322]

The event was supposed to be about Pagones and his plight. Once again, however, Sharpton had interjected himself and made himself the feature act.

Having no desire whatsoever to deal with Sharpton's antics, Pagones and his family quietly exited the conference room through a side door. They were able to leave the hotel without further confrontation.

CHAPTER 16 - THE MURDER TRIAL BEGINS

THE TRIAL OF JEFFREY Dawson began late in the morning on Tuesday, January 10, 1989, before Judge Frank Vogt in Ulster County Court. Unlike the justice system structure in some other states, felony trials in New York are usually conducted in county court.

The twelfth juror and two alternates were chosen earlier that morning, while the first eleven members of the jury had been chosen the previous day. The jurors came from a variety of backgrounds and experiences, but all of them were white. This fact did not go unnoticed by Dawson, who lamented to the media that even a token black juror would have been better than none at all.

"It would be nice if you could get a tan face in there," he added sarcastically.[323]

Despite frequent requests from his attorney not to do so, Dawson repeatedly spoke with the media. Just a week earlier, Dawson gave an interview from the county jail. In that interview, he not only complained about his attorney, but also made damaging admissions.

Lippman, realizing that his client faced a strong likelihood of conviction, had been trying to convince Dawson to consider a plea bargain. This only resulted in further animosity with his client, who was convinced that his advocate was being controlled by the prosecutor.

"I feel as if Lippman is trying to jerk me, and all I want is a fair trial," Dawson said during his interview. "I want a lawyer who is going to do the job and not just listen to the district attorney."[324]

When he finished trashing his lawyer, Dawson recounted his entire statement to the police to the assembled reporters. He admitted to accidentally injuring Kithcart and leaving her alone on the ground, but insisted he did not kill her. He went away for two hours, he said, but when he returned, she had been moved about twenty-five or thirty feet from where he had left her.

"I checked for a heartbeat and a pulse," he added, "but I couldn't get anything, so I fled again."[325]

These statements were not helping Dawson. Once again, he was placing himself at the scene of the murder. The only possible benefit was to set up a defense that Kithcart had died accidentally by his actions, which would be manslaughter or criminally negligent homicide. Yet, Dawson repeatedly insisted that he would not enter a plea of any kind.

Seeing a chance to get the talkative defendant to give more statements for their stories the next day, reporters asked him about Todd Schleede, his former friend and witness for the prosecution.

"That's a lie," Dawson said, referring to Schleede's prior testimony. "I felt Todd Schleede made up the story because, like myself, he is on parole and got busted for robbery. In other words, he made a deal."[326]

To bolster his attack against Schleede, he told the reporters that, on the night Kithcart was killed, he was planning to rob a Stewart's Shop in Port Ewen and Todd Schleede was going to commit the crime with him.[327]

This statement might be helpful as an attack on Schleede's credibility, but it came at a price. Any potential jurors who read the next day's paper would conclude that the man on trial for murder pushed a woman down and left her lying in an abandoned railway bed in the middle of the night. Worse, he was only at the railway bed because his accomplice for a planned robbery had not shown up. If the accomplice had shown up, the two would have been busy committing armed robbery. It was not the best image to present at a trial.

Nevertheless, despite the continuing conflict, Lippman was still Dawson's appointed attorney a week later when the trial began. He stood, along with everyone else in the courtroom, as the members of the jury were brought in and took their seats.

Judge Vogt offered some preliminary instructions to the jury before announcing that the trial would begin with opening statements. He recognized District Attorney Mike Kavanagh, who strode confidently to the podium.

"On the morning of July the 12th, 1988, at around seven o'clock," he began, "the mangled and mutilated body of a nineteen-year-old Kingston girl named Anna Kithcart was found in a wooded area behind the Kingston Hospital. She was naked except for a bra that was pulled up above her breasts. A white moccasin was on her left foot."[328]

He paused for just a moment to let this image sink in before moving on to the injuries suffered by the victim, which he characterized as "atrocious, severe, and fatal."[329]

"Her skull was crushed," Kavanagh said ominously, "her larynx was fractured, her eyes were black, and her mouth beaten and battered…there were lacerations, contusions, and bruises all over the pour soul's body. And, on her abdomen and on her thighs, were scratched the letters 'KKK.'"[330]

Kavanagh told the jury that the injuries suffered by Kithcart looked like the work of a psychopath.[331] He used that word deliberately, knowing full well that he would later play the recorded conversation with Todd Schleede during which

Dawson used the same word.

Kavanagh informed the jury that police had spoken with the defendant before he was considered a serious suspect. During that interview, Dawson told them he had not seen Annie Kithcart that night. He had only been in the Royal Grill earlier that day for a quick game of Pac-Man before going home. He then stayed home the rest of the night with his wife. He had no idea what had happened to the poor girl.

"Ladies and gentlemen of the jury," Kavanagh said, raising his voice slightly, we will prove to you that every one of those statements was a bald-face lie."[332]

Right from the beginning, the district attorney was not only labeling Dawson a psychopath, but also calling him a liar.

"We will prove to you beyond any doubt that this defendant was with Anna Kithcart on the night of July the 11th," Kavanagh continued. "We will prove to you that this defendant had contact with Anna Kithcart on the morning of July the 12th. We will prove to you that this defendant was the psychopath who beat and battered this nineteen-year-old girl senseless. Then, he strangled her with his bare hands, killing her."[333]

Kavanagh's choice concerning the order of events during the crime was interesting. Even though the medical evidence was not definitive, he accused Dawson of beating his victim unconscious first and then strangling her. This told a story of a vicious and almost animalistic murder.

The prosecutor's trial strategy was clear. He planned to argue only intentional murder and intended to portray Jeff Dawson as a psychopathic killer. It was a direct assault against any attempt to label the young woman's death as accidental. It suggested that the prosecutor expected the defense's primary goal was to obtain some conviction less than murder as opposed to seeking a complete acquittal.

Kavanagh turned to the evidence found in the alley between the Royal Grill and Cheap Charlies on the day after the murder. He told the jury that Annie's bloodstained clothing was found along with two sticks and a man's white T-shirt that was also covered in blood. He promised to prove that the bloody T-shirt belonged to the defendant sitting before them.[334]

The prosecutor then pivoted to the involvement of his main witness: Todd Schleede. He started by telling the jury that Jeff Dawson had some level of conscience. The secret he was carrying was so awful and despicable that he could not keep it to himself.

"He had to tell somebody. He wasn't going to tell a stranger. He wasn't going to tell someone like you or people in this courtroom," Kavanagh said accusingly. "He was going to tell somebody he could trust…and he told a friend, an acquaintance, an individual named Todd Schleede, a convicted felon, a drug dealer, a burglar, a liar, a thief." He paused for a moment before sarcastically adding, "Someone he could trust."[335]

He repeated for the jury the details of the two conversations between Schleede and Dawson. As he finished describing the one recorded on a wire by police, he asked the jury to remember carefully Dawson's words that he took a knife to Kithcart's body because he wanted to make it look like a psychopath did it.

Kavanagh turned dramatically toward the defense table and pointed an accusing finger at Jeff Dawson. "This is the man who murdered that nineteen-year-old girl."[336]

Then, for reasons not entirely clear, the prosecutor broke from his dramatic tone and spoke in a less than flattering way about the victim.

"The picture we portray of Anna Kithcart in this trial, we hold no secret from you," he said. "Anna Kithcart was nineteen years old, and she was headed for trouble, there is no mistake about that. She hung around with the wrong people. She associated in the wrong type of places. But she didn't deserve this. No one deserves what happened to this poor soul that morning."[337]

Members of Kithcart's family were in attendance. Some shifted uncomfortably in their chairs while others stiffened with indignation. The words used by the district attorney were heartbreaking. Annie may have been experimenting with cocaine and alcohol in the last few months of her life, like many young adults. However, she was neither a criminal nor a drug addict.

It was bad enough that Annie had her young life snuffed out in a brutal murder. It was worse that the resulting media frenzy made it difficult to properly mourn her. Now, the district attorney, the man charged with getting justice for her, was publicly belittling her memory. For the people who loved her, it was almost too much to bear.

"Ladies and gentlemen," Kavanagh continued, "any fair view of the evidence in this case indicates beyond any question that this is the psychopath." Again pointing at Dawson, Kavanagh said, "This is the man who, in his own hands, took the life of this girl. This man, Jeffrey Dawson, is guilty of murder in the second degree."[338]

Thanking the jury, Kavanagh returned to his table and sat down. All eyes turned to the defense table as Lippman stood for his remarks.

"I'm going to be very, very brief with you at this point," Lippman began before adding, "There's no obligation for us to tell you at this point what the evidence will prove."[339]

He reminded the jury of Judge Vogt's admonition that anything said by either attorney was not evidence. He referred to Kavanagh's opening remarks as emotional and dramatic, but cautioned the jury not to consider the remarks as they were neither proof nor evidence. He asked the jury not to form any opinions about the guilt or innocence of his client.

"I am certain that if you keep an open mind and you listen and evaluate the evidence and evaluate the testimony fairly and honestly, at the conclusion of this case, you will have a reasonable doubt and you will return a verdict of not guilty."[340]

With that, Lippman thanked the jury and sat down. Dawson and his family members in the courtroom could not have been pleased with Lippman's remarks. He had offered no explanation or counter to the strong and forceful remarks of Kavanagh.

His opening statement effectively told the jury nothing. He gave no indication of a defense. He did not challenge any of the accusations leveled against his client. Jeff Dawson was on trial for murder, and Mike Kavanagh had just called him a vicious and brutal psychopath. Lippman responded by saying that his client did not have to prove anything.

Perhaps worst of all, he never once stated that his client was innocent. He never even put forth a denial of the charges. All he told the jury was that they should find a reasonable doubt. This suggested that the jury should return a verdict of not guilty because there was a problem with the evidence being presented, but not because his client was innocent. It was an extremely poor opening statement.

Judge Vogt broke the tense silence. "Ladies and gentlemen, we are going to recess for lunch at this time."[341]

As the jury filed out and the defendant was taken back to his cell, courtroom observers on both sides of the trial were less than pleased. The Kithcart family was stunned and angered at how Annie had been portrayed by the prosecutor, while the Dawson family was worried after hearing such a weak and ineffective opening statement from the defendant's advocate.

CHAPTER 17 - A BLUNDER

USUALLY, A PROSECUTOR'S FIRST witness or two are introductory or background witnesses. They are used to set the stage for the coming main event. District Attorney Mike Kavanagh opted against this method, choosing instead to call Todd Schleede, his single most important witness. Knowing his case would rise and fall with Schleede, the prosecutor decided to lead with him.

When Schleede sat in the witness chair, he looked straight at the prosecutor. He avoided making eye contact with his former friend at the defense table.

Kavanagh had Schleede tell the jury that he had lived in and around Kingston his entire life, and that he was currently working as a busboy in a local restaurant.[342] This was done both to humanize the witness and to give him a chance to get comfortable before the big questions.

Next, he had the witness identify the defendant and tell the jury that he had known Jeff Dawson for most of his life.[343]

Now, it was time to bring out Schleede's criminal record. When a prosecutor knows that his witness has a criminal past or some other potentially damaging history, he will usually bring it out during his questioning. The idea is to limit the damage during cross-examination. It is less dramatic when a defense attorney asks about something the jury has already heard.

Oddly, Kavanagh did not go into great detail about

Schleede's record. The witness admitted that he had been convicted of a prior burglary and a drug sale. He was not asked, however, to inform the jury that he was on parole.[344]

With his preliminary questions out of the way, Kavanagh started focusing on the issues of importance.

"I would like you to think back to the evening of July the 11th, 1988," he asked, "Do you recall at any time being at the Royal Grill bar located on Broadway in the city of Kingston?"

"Yes, I do."

"What time, Mr. Schleede, did you arrive at that bar?"

"About ten o'clock."

After confirming that the witness meant ten o'clock in the evening, the prosecutor asked, "Were you alone?"

"No, I was with my girlfriend."

"Her name?"

"Penelope DeGroat."

"Did you at any time that evening, while you were at the Royal Grill bar on Broadway, see the defendant, Jeffrey Dawson?"

"He was in the bar when I first walked in," Schleede answered.[345]

Schleede told the jury how he and Dawson had gone with DeGroat and another man named Mark Washington to DeGroat's home in Ulster Park. They drank beer and vodka for over an hour before heading back to Kingston. Dawson and Washington were dropped off around 11:30 p.m. on Jansen Avenue right behind the Royal Grill.[346]

"And after you dropped Mr. Dawson and Mr. Washington off...what did you do? Kavanagh asked.

"I went on home to my girlfriend's house in North Ulster

Park," he replied.

"What time was it that you got back there that evening, sir?"

"I would say approximately a quarter to twelve."[347]

Under careful questioning from Kavanagh, Todd Schleede testified that he stayed with his girlfriend for the rest of the evening. They never left the house until the following day. He also testified that he never saw Anna Kithcart that evening.[348]

This was important testimony. Kavanagh knew that the defense would likely point to Schleede as a possible suspect. He was therefore setting up an alibi for his witness on the night of the murder.

Having established this alibi, Kavanagh turned toward the afternoon after the murder when the witness picked up Dawson not far from the murder scene.

Schleede recounted to the jury how, as he drove with his girlfriend and the defendant down Foxhall Avenue, they passed police guarding the entrance to the area of the old railway bed. He described how Dawson had slid down in the back seat and announced that the police might be looking for him.[349]

The jury listened intently as Schleede told them how he eventually drove Dawson to his home, got out of the car with Dawson, and had a conversation with him.

"I got out of the car," Schleede explained, "and we go over by the steps and he tells me the reason why all the cops are there is because he murdered someone last night."[350]

"What did you do when he said that to you, sir?" Kavanagh asked.

"I believe I asked him, I asked him who it was," Schleede replied. "He told me it was Annie Kithcart and I…"

"Now, at the time he said that to you," Kavanagh

interrupted, "did you know about anything happening to Annie Kithcart?"

"No."

"First you heard of it?"

"Yes."

"What happened then, Mr. Schleede?"

"He gave me, he described," Schleede answered, stammering a bit with the emotion of what he was remembering, "he just said he took her clothes and put them by the bar--put them in a bag or something--and he said he washed all the blood off in the neighbor's pool."[351]

Kavanagh was about to move on when he realized he had forgotten something. "Incidentally, when you were talking with Mr. Dawson outside Brewster Street where he lives with his wife, Rose," Kavanagh asked, "did you notice anything unusual about his appearance?"

Picking up on the clearly leading question, Schleede replied, "I noticed a bruise under his eye."

"Had you seen that bruise there the night before?"

"No."[352]

The implication from this testimony was that Dawson had received the bruise either during or just before he committed the murder. The prosecutor wanted the jury to believe that either Kithcart had struck the defendant causing him to go into a rage or that Kithcart struck the defendant during the murder itself as she fought for her life. Either interpretation was beneficial to his case.

Kavanagh did not mention, however, that no bruise was visible on the defendant's face when he was arrested four days later. He left that argument for defense counsel. The only real evidence of this bruise was the word of Todd Schleede. That, Kavanagh knew, was not the strongest foundation upon which to build a credible case.

Having gotten through the first conversation between Schleede and Dawson with few objections or problems, Kavanagh brought up their second conversation on the Saturday after the murder. In response to these questions, Schleede described to the jury how the police taped a miniature microphone to his chest. He then went to Dawson's home to see if he could get him to repeat his previous confession. He was home, and the men spoke in the street in front of Dawson's house.

When Kavanagh asked Schleede to discuss the contents of this conversation, Lippman rose to his feet. "Your Honor," he said in objection, "I believe the tape would be the best evidence."

This was a clever objection by the defense attorney. The actual recording of the conversation was of poor quality and difficult to hear. Through the process of discovery, Lippman knew that the prosecution intended to present testimony of a technician who forensically enhanced the recording. Even with this enhancement, however, it was still difficult to hear clearly. By objecting to testimony about the conversation, he hoped to force the prosecution to rely only upon a poor-quality cassette recording.

Unfortunately for the defense, the judge overruled the objection and allowed the witness to answer.[353]

"I asked him what happened the night I dropped him off," he began. "He said he just bugged out. He said she fell down, hit her head, and he cut her face to make it look like a psycho did it. And I asked him did anybody see him go back there with her. He said no, and I asked him did he put the KKK on her. He shook his head no. And I asked him, did he have sex with her. He said no."

Kavanagh paused for a moment to form his next question. Schleede took the opportunity to add to his answer. "But,

I didn't use the term 'sex' though," he explained. "I asked him did he fuck her. He said no."[354]

"The conversation ends," Kavanagh continued. "What happens?"

"They come and they arrest him. Then we go down to the station."

After confirming that "they" referred to the Kingston Police Department, Kavanagh asked, "Now he's taken into custody. Where did you go?"

"Down to the station," Schleede answered. "They asked me a few questions, and that was end of it."

Kavanagh informed the court that he was finished with his direct examination. Now, the only question was whether his witness could survive questioning by defense counsel.

Barry Lippman walked quietly toward the witness. Schleede fidgeted nervously in his chair as the attorney set his legal pad on the podium and made eye contact with him.

"How old are you, Mr. Schleede?" the attorney finally asked.

"Twenty-six years old."

"You say you have been working for one month?"

"Yes."

"Prior to the job you now have as a busboy, were you employed?"

"No."

"At any time?" Lippman asked.

"No."

Surprised by his answer, Lippman asked if the busboy job was the first job he ever had. Schleede explained that while he had held jobs, he never was able to keep them for any length of time.[355]

"How were you supporting yourself in July of 1988?"

Lippman inquired.

"I have a..." Schleede said as he was again nervously stammering. He paused to regain his composure before continuing, "My father supported me, and my mother and my girlfriend."

"For how long prior to July had your father and your mother and your girlfriend been supporting you?"

"Just about the whole summer because I...I just got out from being violated on parole."

"You got out of prison?" Lippman asked.

"Out of county jail," Schleede corrected.[356]

Lippman had accomplished two of his goals in just a few questions. First, he demonstrated to the jury that the witness before them was a legal adult, but living off his parents. He might have a job now, but despite being twenty-six years old, he had never before held a job or supported himself in any way.

Second, he was now transitioned into the main reason why Todd Schleede had not been supporting himself. For a substantial portion of his young life, Schleede had been housed and fed by the jails and prisons of the State of New York.

For the next ten minutes, Lippman slowly walked the witness though his criminal history. Before July 1988, Schleede served two months in county jail because he failed to report to his parole officer. He had been on parole after a burglary conviction in 1980 and a subsequent felony for selling illegal drugs. He had also been convicted of the misdemeanor of petit larceny and served an additional nine months.[357]

To further cement his point, Lippman asked the witness to tell the jury how many times in total he had been convicted of crimes. After considering the question for a while, Schleede admitted with embarrassment to the jury that he did not know.[358]

"In July of 1988," Lippman persisted, "were you on parole?"

"Yes."

Lippman tried to get the witness to tell the jury what personal restrictions were placed on him by his parole officer, but the judge sustained an objection from Kavanagh.[359] So, Lippman moved on.

"Mr. Schleede, you say you knew Anna Kithcart?"

"Yes."

"How did you know her?"

"I lived in the same project house of hers."

"For more than ten years?"

"I believe about around…," he answered slowly. "My mother lived there about that long."

"Was she a friend of yours?"

"Yes."

"Did you ever go out with her socially?"

"No."

"Just knew her?"

"Yes."[360]

Having established that Schleede knew the murder victim, Lippman turned his attention to his relationship with the defendant.

"You say that Jeffrey Dawson was a friend of yours?"

"Well," Schleede answered hesitantly, "more like an associate."

"An associate?" Lippman asked incredulously.

"Yes," Schleede answered defiantly.

Undaunted, Lippman kept pursuing this line of questioning.

"Did you see him on a regular basis?" he asked.

"No."

"In July of 1988?"

"No, not regular," Schleede maintained. "Might run into him here or there, on the street, or at parole."

"What?" Lippman said, his voice rising in surprise. Having lost control of the witness and asked this foolish question, he opened the door wide for Schleede's next answer.

"When he would go to parole and see his parole officer," he answered. "We come to the same building."[361]

In a criminal trial, the prosecution usually cannot present prior convictions or other prior bad acts as evidence against a defendant.[362] If a defendant testifies, then he may be asked some limited questions about his criminal record. Even then, a judge will conduct a pretrial hearing to make sure the use of prior convictions or bad acts will not be too prejudicial against the defendant.[363]

Lippman had made a serious blunder. By not keeping control of the witness, he allowed the jury to learn that his client was on parole. Since one cannot be on parole without committing a felony, the jury now knew that his client had previously been convicted of a felony. Without knowing the specific charge, the jury could only speculate whether this prior crime was robbery, rape, or murder.

Realizing the damage done, Lippman changed topics and asked the witness about seeing Dawson on the night of the murder.

"You picked him up at the Royal Grill?"

"Correct."

"Now, you weren't supposed to be at the Royal Grill or any bar in July of 1988," Lippman stated.

Confused, Schleede replied, "Why not?"

"Isn't it a violation of the conditions of your parole?"

"No."

"To be in a bar?" Lippman asked mockingly.

Schleede held his ground, replying simply, "No, it is not."[364]

Although Lippman was surprised by the answer, he moved to his next question without slowing.

"Isn't it a violation of the conditions of your parole to commit another crime?"

"Of course," the witness replied, almost amused.

"And, in July of 1988," the attorney charged, "isn't it a fact that you were planning a robbery at Stewart's?"

"No," Schleede responded flatly.[365]

"Isn't it a fact that, prior to July 16, 1988, you robbed the Stewart's store in Port Ewen?"

"No," he answered again.[366]

With no further follow-up, Lippman switched topics again. "You didn't go to the police, sir, did you?"

"No, they came to me."

"They came to you?"

"Yes."[367]

Lippman spent the next few minutes trying to discredit the witness by highlighting that he never went to the police himself. Instead, he chose to have his girlfriend make an anonymous call identifying Dawson as Anna Kithcart's killer.

Schleede had already told the jury he had been in and out of county jail and state prison for most of his life. When he answered Lippman's accusations by testifying, "I didn't really want to get involved," the answer made perfect sense.[368]

Lippman would not let go of his attack even though it was clear to those in the court that it was going nowhere.

"Did you ask her to call the police because you believed the police were looking for you?"

"No," Schleede answered dismissively.[369]

"Were you aware at the time had Penny call the police that the police were actually looking for you?" Lippman suggested.

"No, I don't believe they were looking for me."

"You don't believe they were looking for you, sir?"

"I don't know," Schleede said beginning to show annoyance. "For what reason?"

"In connection with this incident," Lippman shouted.

Seeing his witness showing the first signs of losing his temper, Kavanagh stood and objected.

"Yes, we are getting argumentative," Judge Vogt announced. "Objection sustained."

Lippman asked only a few more questions, getting the witness to admit that he had waited several days after his conversation with Jeff Dawson before having his girlfriend make the call. He then informed the judge that he had no further questions.[370]

Kavanagh, realizing that his witness had actually done quite well, declined to ask any further questions.

Kavanagh made a mistake not setting forth Schleede's criminal record in more detail. Lippman initially did a solid job exploiting this mistake. However, his subsequent blunder and his inability to set forth an effective presentation during cross-examination resulted in an overall win for the prosecution.

CHAPTER 18 - MISSED OPPORTUNITIES

TODD SCHLEEDE HAD ONLY taken a few steps away from the stand when Judge Vogt instructed the prosecution to call their next witness. Kavanagh called Wally Richter, a twenty-three-year-old man employed for more than two years as a security guard for Kingston Hospital.

Richter told the jury that he had worked the overnight shift (11:00 p.m. until 7:00 a.m.) on the night of the murder.[371]

As part of his regular security rounds, he would walk through the old railway bed behind the hospital. If he found people hanging around back there, he would chase them out. That particular night, Richter checked this area between the hours of 12:30 a.m. and 1:00 a.m.[372]

At this point, District Attorney Mike Kavanagh broke from his questioning to have the witness identify an aerial photograph of Kingston Hospital, the wooded area containing the railway bed, and the other buildings nearby such as the Old City Hall Building and the Kingston Laboratory.[373]

Pointing to the portion of the picture illustrating the wooded area behind the hospital, Kavanagh asked Richter to tell the jury how this area appeared on the night of the murder.

"All broken," the witness replied. "A railroad track, but garbage."

"Is there a pathway a person can walk?"

"Yes."

"Did you walk that area that night?"

"Yes, I did," Richter answered obediently.

"Any lights in that area, Wally?"

"No."

"How did you see your way?"

"Flashlight."

"On your trip through that area between twelve thirty and one," Kavanagh continued, "did you see anything unusual?"

"No."[374]

Kavanagh had the witness tell the jury that once he completed his search of the area, he went back inside the hospital and remained there until the end of his shift. After work, he went straight home.[375]

The district attorney effectively used the witness for two purposes. First, his testimony showed that Anna Kithcart was killed sometime after one o'clock that morning. Second, it showed that the area was deserted that evening. Given Dawson's likely contention that someone else lurking in the railway bed had committed the murder, Richter's testimony of a deserted area became damaging.

Barry Lippman picked up on this point and sought to change the narrative on cross-examination. The defense attorney asked the witness if he had ever encountered people in that area at night.

"Bums sleep back there," Richter answered.

"Now, when you say bums," Lippman asked, "have you ever seen people drinking back there?"

"Yes, sleeping too," Richter offered.

"Seen young people back there?"

"Yes."

"Old people?"

"Yup."

"Men?"

"Yes."

"Women?"

"Yes."

"Group of people?"

"Yes."[376]

This was excellent testimony for the defense. The witness conceded finding numerous people of various ages hanging out on the old railway bed either drinking or sleeping it off. Unfortunately, instead of leaving well enough alone, Lippman asked one question too many.

"Would it be fair to say, Mr. Richter, that you encounter people back there on a regular basis?"

"Not really," the witness answered, shaking his head.[377]

Richter's answer made it clear to the jury that, while he had seen various people behind the hospital, that was over the two-plus years that he had been working. It was not, however, an everyday thing.

Lippman should never have asked that question. Once he had solid testimony from Richter, the conclusion that people were back there on a regular basis should have been held for his closing argument. By presenting it to the witness, he allowed his entire argument to be deflated.

When law students are taught the art of cross-examination, they are always told to leave summations for their closing argument and not to ask too many questions. A famous example usually given to them is of a young attorney named Abraham Lincoln, who was defending a man charged with assault for biting off another man's nose.

Lincoln got the accusing witness to admit that he never actually saw Lincoln's client bite the victim. Instead of stopping right there, Lincoln asked the witness to explain how he then could possibly testify that his client had bitten off the victim's nose. The witness replied that he had later seen Lincoln's client spitting out the remains of the victim's nose.[378]

Lippman's mistake was certainly not of that caliber. It was, however, quite unfortunate. It significantly weakened what was otherwise a very strong cross-examination.

The prosecution's next witness was Deborah Stewart, one of the two nurses who saw Joseph Kiernan walk out of the woods and heard him say that he had found a corpse.

She told the jury that she and Dorothy Clarke walked down the tracks after seeing Kiernan and that they had seen Kithcart's remains. She described the condition of the body to the jury in some detail, highlighting the damage to the face and the letters cut into the thighs.[379]

When they walked out of the woods, Kiernan was still waiting. Kavanagh had the witness testify that she then called the police. He also made sure to have the witness inform the jury that Kiernan had remained there and spoken with the police when they arrived.[380]

Once again, Mike Kavanagh was anticipating future arguments and claims from the defense. Expecting that they might point an accusing finger at Joseph Kiernan, Kavanagh elicited testimony showing that Kiernan did not flee and instead cooperated fully with the police.

Very surprisingly, Lippman opted not to ask any questions of the witness. She was excused.

Not asking questions of this witness was a definite mistake and a missed opportunity. Stewart was not going to give any answers that would completely exonerate Jeff Dawson. Nevertheless, questions should have been asked about Joseph Kiernan.

By this point in the trial, the jury had heard Kiernan's name, but knew nothing about him other than that he came out of the woods and reported finding a body. Lippman should have asked Stewart to describe in detail how Kiernan was dressed and how he appeared.

In her statement to the police, Stewart had described Kiernan as being unshaven and carrying a bedroll. Clarke gave a similar description. Considering that the previous witness admitted to finding "bums" sleeping in those woods, a description of Kiernan's appearance would have supported a later allegation that Kiernan was one of the bums who slept in the old railway bed.

He also should have asked Stewart if she could remember exactly what Kiernan had said to her. Kiernan told the police he had walked from the woods behind the old City Poorhouse and eventually made his way to the railway bed behind the hospital. However, in her written statement, Dorothy Clarke reported that Kiernan told her that he had just come from Shop-Rite, which was in a different direction and four miles away. Clarke also reported that Stewart was close enough to hear this remark. [381]

By bringing this information to the jury's attention, Lippman would have been able to show that Kiernan had either lied to Clarke or lied to the police. He could have later argued that Kiernan was a bum, seen walking out of an area where bums were known to sleep, who then lied about where he had really been. This would have made Kiernan a tantalizing suspect for the jury.

The final witness for the day was Allen Saehloff, a member of the Kingston Police Department for the previous seven years. He told the jury that he and his partner, Officer Gary Longto, as well as Officer Maurice Vandemark, were the first officers to arrive at Kingston Hospital.[382]

He recounted walking down the path behind the hospital

and observing the body of Anna Kithcart. He and his partner secured the area with police tape in an effort to preserve the crime scene.[383]

Kavanagh picked up several photographs before asking, "Do you remember how the area appeared, how it looked to you when you saw this girl's body?"

"Yes."

The prosecutor handed six photographs to the witness and asked him to examine them. After a moment, he asked if the photographs accurately depicted the scene as he observed it that morning.

"Yes, sir," the officer responded.[384]

After a few more questions, Kavanagh had the pictures entered into evidence and presented to the jury for viewing. The photographs showed the taped-off entrance to the railway on Foxhall Avenue, Kithcart's remains as they were found, and the area immediately around her body. They were extremely gruesome pictures. Kavanagh wanted them seen by the jury so that they would understand the sheer brutality of the murder and generate sympathy for the victim.[385]

When the jury finished with the pictures, the district attorney had a few more questions. After having Saehloff repeat that he and his partner secured the crime scene, Kavanagh asked the witness if he knew who was in charge of collecting evidence from the scene. Saehloff replied that it was Detective Richard Krom.[386]

Again referring back to the pictures the jury had just seen, Kavanagh asked, "Was the area that is pictured in those photographs…in the same condition when Detective Krom arrived as it was when you got there that morning and you secured it?"

"Yes, sir," Saehloff answered.[387]

This testimony was necessary to show that the crime scene

found by the detective who collected evidence had not been altered or tampered with. Kavanagh was securing his chain of evidence. To prove the chain of custody, and ultimately show that the evidence has remained intact, a prosecutor generally needs witnesses who can testify that the evidence offered in court is the same evidence collected or received and that there was no tampering with the evidence while it was in custody.

By demonstrating that the crime scene was properly secured prior to Detective Krom arriving, the prosecutor was attempting to prevent an argument of evidence contamination or destruction.

Finally, Kavanagh had the witness testify that he saw Joseph Kiernan when he arrived at the scene. He told the jury that Kiernan remained with an officer on Foxhall Avenue. The prosecutor elicited this to show that Kiernan did not return to the railway path and that he continued to stay at the scene.[388]

The defense attorney started his cross-examination by revisiting some points he had made when he questioned the hospital's security guard. After getting the police officer to admit he was familiar with the area behind Kingston Hospital, Lippman asked, "Have you had occasion to go down that area in the past?"

"Yes."

"Do you ever receive complaints or calls, one sort or another, to go back there?"

"Yes, sir."

"And, in fact, would it be fair to say that was a known hangout?"

Kavanagh objected to the question. However, the judge denied the objection and instructed the witness to answer.

"There were noise complaints and types like that, yes."

"You ever have a complaint of people drinking back there?" Lippman continued.

"On occasions," he answered.

"Well, do you recall the last time you received a complaint of noise back there?"

Before the witness could answer, the district attorney was on his feet objecting again.

"Well, I think you made your point, Mr. Lippman," Judge Vogt ruled. "Go to something else. Objection sustained."[389]

Lippman brought the officer's attention back to the area where the body had been found and asked if he had noticed a blue shirt near the body. Saehloff said he had seen it.

"Was that one of items that was taken into police custody?"

"I believe it was, sir."

"Did you ever determine whose shirt that was?"

"Myself, no, sir," he replied.

"Do you know whether anyone at the Kingston Police Department ever determined who owned that shirt?"

"I do not know, sir."[390]

This was a smart move on Lippman's part. He knew that many of the items found at the scene were junk and trash that had been dumped in this area over the years. However, some of these things, like a shirt, could be used to allege that another person had indeed been present that night.

Lippman then turned to the orange washbasin found a few feet from the body. After confirming that Saehloff had seen this item, he asked, "Would you say there was blood in it?"

"No," the witness said, correcting the defense attorney. "It was inverted. It was upside down. There was some (blood) on top, on the ground around it."

"Do you know where that basin came from?"

"No."

"Did you ever determine who owned that basin or who put it there?"

"I have no idea, sir."

"Do you know if anyone in the Police Department ever determined where that basin came from, or who had owned it or possessed it?"

"I do not know."

Pressing his perceived advantage, Lippman asked, "Do you know if any fingerprints were taken from that basin?"

"I do not know that."[391]

Lippman then referred the officer to some other items present at the crime scene including three pearl-colored buttons, a brown paper bag, and various beer bottles.[392]

He finished his cross-examination with a few questions about Joseph Kiernan. However, he only asked if the witness had spoken with him. (He had not.) Lippman again failed to have any physical description of Kiernan entered into the record.

District Attorney Kavanagh had a few follow-up questions that focused entirely on the variety of debris found in and around the crime scene. In response, Saehloff said that whenever he went to the old railway bed, there were always bottles, clothing, and trash scattered about.[393]

With that, Officer Saehloff was excused and left the courtroom. Looking at the clock, Judge Vogt announced that the trial was finished for the day. Cautioning the jury to keep an open mind and not to make any conclusions about the case until all of the evidence was presented, he adjourned the case until eleven o'clock the next morning.

SIDETRACKED | 161

CHAPTER 19 - DR. MCNAMARA

THE NEXT MORNING, THE prosecution opened the scientific portion of its case by calling Dr. Harry McNamara to the stand. He carefully presented his qualifications to the jury and described for them the nature of his job as a medical examiner.[394]

"Now, in connection with your responsibilities as medical examiner of Ulster County," District Attorney Mike Kavanagh asked, "did you have occasion to respond to an area located behind the Kingston Hospital on the morning of July the 12th, 1988?"

"I did," the doctor answered.[395]

Through a series of questions and answers, McNamara recounted his arrival at the crime scene and provided a detailed description of both the railway bed and the location of Anna Kithcart's body.[396]

The prosecutor presented the witness with eight photographs of the body as it was found. They were taken from various angles and focused on different parts of her body.[397] The doctor testified that each picture fairly and accurately depicted the appearance of the body when he viewed it that morning.[398]

"Doctor, when you arrived at the scene and you saw this girl," Kavanagh continued, "did you notice any obvious injuries on her remains?"

"She appeared to have some injuries to the front of the

head," the witness replied. "She had a piece of glass in her neck, and she had scratch marks on the thighs and abdomen. That was just by superficial inspection."[399]

"The injury to the head, could you describe how it appeared to you," Kavanagh asked, "where was it located, what it looked like when you observed it that morning?"

"She appeared to have sustained some fairly severe cuts from some type of blunt force."

"Where was it located?" Kavanagh pressed.

"In the frontal portion of the head," McNamara answered.

"Forehead?" Kavanagh asked, trying to use more casual language for the jury.

"Yes."

Having presented to the jury that the victim had severe wounds on the front of the head, Kavanagh now asked about the back of the head. Knowing that the defendant had told the police and the media that Kithcart had struck the back of her head, the prosecutor intended to attack this position even before the defense could present it.

"Did you examine the back of the head?"

"In the morgue," the doctor replied.

"In the morgue," the prosecutor repeated. "Tell us about that."

"Well, once the crime scene work was finished," McNamara said, "we placed the body on a white shroud, put it in a body bag on a stretcher, wheeled it into the morgue where we do a closer inspection and also got X-rays of the skull."[400]

Kavanagh was becoming frustrated, though he did an excellent job of hiding this from the jury. Twice he had asked the doctor about his exam of the back of the head, and twice the doctor had not really answered the question.

"This closer inspection you did in the morgue of the back

of the head," Kavanagh asked in a very deliberate tone. "Would you be kind enough to tell us what it revealed?"

Finally getting the hint, the doctor responded more directly. "There were no lacerations on the back of the head," he said, "there was apparently a small contusion of some type, but not cuts."

"No bleeding from the back of the head?" Kavanagh persisted.

"No, sir."[401]

Having finally gotten his answer, the prosecutor moved on and asked about the X-ray results. McNamara informed the jury that Anna Kithcart suffered a skull fracture in the right front of her head.[402]

For the next few minutes, Kavanagh had the doctor describe the various other injuries on the victim's body. These included bruises on the knees, left arm, left upper chest, and neck, as well as the scratches on the thighs and abdomen.[403]

"Based upon what you saw," the prosecutor asked, "based upon your experience as a medical doctor, can you give some idea as to when these injuries that she sustained were inflicted?"

"Estimation of death is not completely accurate scientifically. It's a guess as to the time frame," McNamara answered. He hesitated for a moment and then added, "Between two a.m. and four a.m."

"What do you base that upon, doctor?"

McNamara explained that his estimate was based upon the amount of rigor mortis and the temperature of the corpse.[404]

Rigor mortis is the medical term for the stiffening of muscles, joints, and even internal organs that begins to set in approximately two hours after death. Coroners frequently use this as an indicator of time of death.

Kavanagh was not quite finished with the witness. McNamara had taken some samples for lab testing. In order to enter those lab results into evidence later in the trial, the prosecution needed to show how the evidence was initially collected.

McNamara testified that he took a blood sample from a small plastic basin found about five feet from the body. He also collected blood and hair from the murder victim. He further took samples of some of the dirt smeared on the victim's knee and foot, as well as swabs from her nose, mouth, and vagina.[405]

The doctor further testified that he had later been asked to take samples from Jeffrey Dawson and Joseph Kiernan for testing. In addition to blood, hair was collected from each man's head, chest, and pubic area.[406]

After having the witness confirm that all of the evidence he collected was given to Detective Krom for delivery to the State Police Laboratory, Kavanagh announced that he was finished.

Although it was necessary for McNamara to discuss his initial observations and examination of the body, the prosecutor did not intend to solicit testimony from him concerning the cause of death. Instead, he planned to save that for Dr. Eric Mitchell, the forensic pathologist who performed the autopsy. Lippman had other ideas.

"Prior to the time that the body was transported, did you make a determination as to the cause of death?" Lippman asked.

"Taking an X-ray, we knew there was a fracture of the skull. We knew she had a crushing, severe injury to the forehead. We didn't make a final determination at that time," the doctor replied. "We were sure that was part of the picture. Until the autopsy was completed, we did not have the full picture."

Lippman, not wanting to let the doctor avoid his question, asked, "Did you make a preliminary determination?"

"Just that there were severe head injuries, a fractured skull. It was an obvious homicide."

"And at that time," the defense attorney persisted, "was it your opinion that the fracture of the skull was the cause of death?"

"I probably assumed that at the time, but until the autopsy was completed, we didn't…"

"Did you note at the time of your examination of the body, doctor," Lippman interrupted, "a fracture of the larynx?"

"That would not be obvious from external examination," McNamara answered weakly, before explaining that the fractured larynx was noted during the later autopsy. He had been informed of that via a telephone report from the pathologist.[407]

Moving away from this subject, Lippman asked the doctor whether during his examination he noticed a fluorescent substance on the victim's thighs. McNamara said he had not, but was later told that such a substance was found during the autopsy. The nature of the substance had not been identified.[408]

"When we talk about a fluorescent substance," Lippman continued, "this is something that appears under ultraviolet light only?"

"Yes," the doctor agreed.

The attorney asked McNamara if he had ever come across a homicide in his career involving the use of a fluorescent substance. The doctor said he had not.

"Have you ever taken any courses dealing with ritualistic murders?" Lippman asked.

The district attorney was on his feet immediately announcing his objection. The judge overruled him and allowed the witness to answer. McNamara said that he previously attended a conference on ritual abuse.

"And did that include witchcraft?" Lippman continued.

"Not that I recall."[409]

Lippman then asked the doctor about the basin from which he had taken a blood sample. The doctor would not give an estimate concerning the amount of blood on the basin, though he admitted there was a significant amount.

"Have you ever had occasion," Lippman continued, "to investigate any homicides involving a satanic murder or some ritualistic murder?"

He answered, "No," mere moments before the district attorney shouted out his objection. The objection was overruled, and the doctor repeated his denial.[410]

The question about the unknown fluorescent substance was important. Anytime a defense attorney can bring out facts or circumstances that the prosecution cannot explain, it leaves the members of the jury with an unanswered question. Unanswered questions in a murder case almost always favor the defense because they can often lead to a reasonable doubt. A juror with a reasonable doubt is supposed to cast a vote for not guilty.

However, suggesting a satanic ritual or other ceremonial murder was a poor decision by the defense attorney. The members of the jury were all from Ulster County, a small and rather conservative county in Upstate New York. The idea of a group of Satan worshippers killing young women in their county was not something they were likely to believe or accept. Suggesting such a thing was a mistake that quite possibly weakened his otherwise decent cross-examination.

Perhaps realizing this, Lippman dropped his line of questioning and asked more questions about the victim's injuries and the doctor's observations.

"Do you know whether the body was moved from the time of death to the time you first observed it?"

"I would feel that the body had been moved," McNamara confirmed.

"Can you determine the distance that the body was moved?"

"No," he replied. "I would say not a long distance. Five, ten feet, maybe a little longer."

Despite repeated questions from the defense attorney, McNamara was unable to say when the body had been moved, other than to confirm that it was done sometime after death.[411]

After confirming that the victim had a bruise on the back of her head, the attorney asked, "In your opinion, would that injury have been the cause of death?"

"I would say in my opinion, no."[412]

This was an important piece of testimony. Jeff Dawson had told reporters and the police that he had pushed Kithcart, causing her to strike the back of her head. If this injury were the cause of death, then Dawson would at least be guilty of manslaughter. With this medical opinion, Lippman now had a counter to that charge.

"Do you have an opinion, doctor, as to the time of the injury to the back of the head?"

"No."

"Could that injury have occurred prior to the fracture of the skull?"

"Possible," McNamara replied.

"Is there a scientific way to determine that?" Lippman asked.

"I think maybe your autopsy will indicate that," the doctor

answered, successfully dodging the question.[413]

Lippman announced to the court that he was finished with the witness. He had obtained a few concessions, but his questions about satanic murders did not help his cause.

District Attorney Kavanagh decided to ask more questions of his witness. Interestingly, he did not ask a single question about the mysterious fluorescent substance, choosing instead to focus on Kithcart's body being moved.

"You say that you think the body was moved?"

"That's right," McNamara answered, "My opinion."

"I understand," Kavanagh countered. "What do you base that upon?"

"Based it upon the brush marks on the back of the legs and the fact that one shoe is on and one shoe is missing," he replied.

This was the first explanation offered as to why one shoe was left at the scene. The doctor quite logically concluded that one of the girl's shoes fell off when her body was dragged. In the near pitch darkness, the killer simply could not find the other shoe to remove it. It was definitely speculation, but extremely good speculation.

"So, these brush marks on the back of the legs, you base that upon the fact, am I correct, that apparently the legs were in contact with the ground?"

"That's correct," the doctor answered.

"They were scratched?"

"That's correct."

"And you assume that the contact that made those scratches was as a result of the body being pulled?"

"That's correct," McNamara repeated.

"Now, as far as the body being moved," Kavanagh

continued, "you indicated to Mr. Lippman that you thought it was after death?"

"That's correct," the witness repeated for the fourth time.

"Why?"

"The scratch marks seemed to be not showing any hemorrhage."

"So, in other words," Kavanagh said, once again having to explain his witness's answer in plainer language to the jury, "if there is no hemorrhage, the heart is not beating, so the blood is not pumping to that part of the body. Is that so?"

"That's correct," the doctor responded. "Yes."[414]

Having confirmed that the body had indeed been moved postmortem, the district attorney now needed to establish when all of the wounds had been inflicted in relation to one another. He knew, based upon Dawson's statement to the police, that the defense would likely allege that another person came by after Kithcart fell and committed the murder. Kavanagh wanted to limit the timeline as much as possible.

"Now, these injuries to this girl that you saw at seven thirty that morning," the district attorney asked, "do you have an opinion that you can give these jurors with a reasonable degree of medical certainty as to whether or not these injuries were all inflicted at about the same time?"

"My opinion was that they were all inflicted at about the same time."

"Upon what do you base that opinion?"

"You have got the blood pattern, the bruises, everything to fit right into the pattern," he answered.[415]

This was very effective testimony. Obviously, the closer in time that all of the wounds were inflicted, the more likely it was that one person inflicted them. Knowing this, Lippman asked permission to question the doctor further.

"The body had a number of different injuries, so to speak. Isn't that true, doctor?"

"That's correct."

"The fracture of the face?"

"Fracture of the skull," the doctor corrected.

"Bruises and contusions about the body?"

"Yes."

"Some of the bruises on the body could have occurred days before. Isn't that so?"

"I think that would be indicated in your pathology report," McNamara answered, trying to again avoid a question.

"Well, from the observations that you made of the body," Lippman pressed, "did you observe any bruises whatsoever that could have existed or been caused days before this incident?"

"Not that I can recall."

"What about a day before the incident?"

"I just don't recall," the doctor insisted.

As soon as Lippman started walking back to his table, the district attorney was up and posing more questions to the doctor.

"Mr. Lippman asked you about those injuries being caused days before the injuries," Kavanagh began, "the KKKs, do you have an opinion as to when those injuries were inflicted upon this girl's torso?"

"I would say they were fresh, relatively fresh."

"The bruise to the back of the head," Kavanagh pressed. "Do you have an opinion as to when that was inflicted upon this girl?"

"Well," McNamara said, pausing for just a second, "relatively fresh."

"And the laceration to the forehead, that resulted in a frontal skull fracture that you saw, when would that have been caused?"

"Roughly around the time of death."

"The crushed larynx, you didn't see it, but based upon your experience as a medical examiner of Ulster County," Kavanagh continued, now on a bit of a roll, "when in terms of death would that have been caused?"

"About the same time," he replied.[416]

This was extremely problematic testimony for the defense. Given Dawson's version of events, the defense had to show that there was enough time after Kithcart struck the back of her head for Dawson to have left the area and another person to have arrived at the scene and inflicted the balance of the wounds, all without being seen or heard by Dawson.

Because the district attorney had been permitted to question his witness for a third time, the defense was entitled to another opportunity. Lippman went right after the witness.

"Well, when you use the term, doctor, 'in and about the time of death,' what sort of a time span are we talking about?"

"I give you my best estimate," McNamara answered, "two to four a.m."[417]

The doctor had misunderstood the question. Lippman asked about the time frame for all of the injuries, but McNamara had responded with the estimate time of death. It was a mistake by the witness that could be exploited by the defense. At this point, Lippman should have sat down. Instead, he continued his questions.

"Even within that framework, doctor, isn't it conceivable that the bruise to the back of the head occurred at two a.m.?"

"I can't sort and say one thing happened at two or at four," McNamara retorted. "Chances are that all of these things happened within a very short time span."

"Perhaps over a couple of hours?" Lippman asked, once again offering that one question too many.

"Over ten minutes," the doctor offered. "Fifteen minutes max."[418]

This answer was devastating. With all of the extensive injuries occurring within a fifteen-minute window, the chances of convincing the jury that someone else had done everything after Kithcart struck her head were extremely poor.

Trying to recover, Lippman shifted his inquiry slightly. "Assuming the deceased died as a result of the fractured skull, how long after sustaining that fracture, in your opinion, would she likely have survived?"[419]

"It would almost have been instantaneous," McNamara answered. "It would be a fairly short period of time."

"If strangulation was the cause of death, can you estimate how long one would live after that injury was inflicted?"

"Not really," the doctor replied. "But all I can say is that the strangulation occurred first. She was still alive when the head injuries occurred because there was very active bleeding there."

Now, Lippman tried to subtly return to the ten- to fifteen-minute answer, by asking, "And those injuries occurred in your best opinion between two a.m. and four a.m., is that correct?"

The court was more than a little surprised when Judge Vogt spoke in response. "No, I don't believe that was his testimony," the judge admonished, "He said injuries occurred. That was the time of death."[420]

Now, it was even worse. Juries may believe or disbelieve witnesses or attorneys, but they always believe the judge.

Any chance of getting the jury off the ten- to fifteen-minute time frame was gone.

Lippman took a moment to phrase his next question. "The various bruises and contusions, doctor, couldn't the bruises have occurred prior to two a.m.?"

"We have covered that, Mr. Lippman," Judge Vogt interjected, before turning toward the witness. "Go ahead, answer if you can."

"The bruises could have occurred prior to two a.m." McNamara said, "I am just making an assumption that everything went pretty simultaneously."

"That is just an assumption on your part?" Lippman asked, a look of surprised optimism on his face.

"An assumption," the doctor repeated.[421]

This time, Lippman took that gift of an answer and sat down. His mistake of asking too many questions on the time frame was severe, but at least he could label the fifteen-minute time window as a mere assumption. It was not great, but it would have to do.

CHAPTER 20 - PHYSICAL EVIDENCE

THE NEXT WITNESS WAS Detective Richard Krom, the primary evidence technician of the case. He told the jury that he had been working for the Kingston Police Department for fourteen years, the last two as a detective.[422]

Knowing he had a rather long direct examination planned, the district attorney immediately brought the witness's attention to the morning of July 12, 1988, and asked him if he had been ordered to respond to the area behind Kingston Hospital.

Krom answered that he had been ordered there and arrived at approximately 7:25 a.m.

"What was your purpose in going to that location on that date?" Kavanagh asked.

"I was assigned to go to that location as a crime scene investigator," the witness replied.

"When you got to the area, could you briefly describe how it appeared to you on arrival?"

"Yes, sir," Krom said. "The area was located on the old railroad bed tracks in the rear of Kingston Hospital. The railroad bed connects Foxhall Avenue with East O'Reilly Street. It was a pathway and heavily wooded. There was a considerable amount of debris, garbage, papers, bottles, things of that nature in the pathway."[423]

Krom stopped talking, but Kavanagh asked him to continue

his description.

"As I walked down the walkway, I observed a female, a nude female lying on the side of the pathway. She appeared to be, at my first observation of her, a white female. As I got closer to her, I saw that she was a light-skinned black female. She was nude at the time except for a bra, which had been pushed above her breasts, and a moccasin. The victim's face was covered with a substantial amount of blood. There appeared that the forehead or facial area was crushed, crushed inward. There was a piece of glass that was embedded in her neck, and there were numerous lacerations and cuts on her body. There were the letters 'KKK' carved on the inside of her thighs, also on her abdomen."[424]

Having once again had the gory description of Anna Kithcart's remains brought to the jury's attention, Kavanagh asked Krom what he had done upon seeing the remains. Krom told the jury that he made sure that the area was secure. He observed that both entrances to the railway bed were secured.

"Did you focus in on any particular area of this scene in terms of executing your responsibilities?" Kavanagh asked.

"The area in and around the body," Krom explained. "There was an area right directly on that pathway of the old railroad bed. The area, as I stated before, was strewn with debris of all sorts. That particular area I focused in on because articles appeared to be moved in that area. There appeared to be a struggle in that area."[425]

"When you say 'struggle,'" Kavanagh inquired, "what did you see that prompted you to arrive at the opinion that there appeared to be a struggle?"

"Certain areas near the body were matted down, things--items that were lying on the ground--appeared to be turned over or moved."

"You indicated to the jury at the outset that when you first saw the deceased's body, you noticed a large quantity of blood on her face or forehead," Kavanagh reminded Krom. "Did you notice any similar bloodstains in or around the body?"

"Yes, I did."

"Tell us about that," Kavanagh instructed.

"Below the body was a broken washbasin," Krom replied. "The washbasin was plastic in nature. It was broken. It was upside down. The bottom was caved in. In that washbasin was what I believed to be blood, a pool of blood. There were also spots of blood that were in the area of the washbasin, in the area that appeared to be the struggle, and were between that washbasin and the body."[426]

"How far was this washbasin located from the remains of deceased?"

"Approximately eight feet," Krom replied.

Kavanagh produced a large plastic evidence bag containing a bloodstained, plastic washbasin. Krom quickly identified it as the one he found behind the hospital. Kavanagh then produced a photograph that Krom confirmed was of the same basin as it appeared when found. Both the picture and the washbasin were entered into evidence.[427]

Kavanagh produced two more exhibits and presented them to his witness. Krom identified the exhibits as two fireplace-type bricks.

Pointing at the bricks, Kavanagh asked, "What would those have to do with this case, officer?"

"The bricks were found in the area below the body that I refer to as the struggle area," Krom advised. "The bricks were located by me, and I found them to have a small drop of blood or bloodstain on them."

"How far from the remains were these two bricks located,

officer?"

"Approximately three to four feet."

The bricks were then formally entered into evidence.[428]

"Officer," Kavanagh continued, "taking these two exhibits out of the bag that they are contained in, you indicated that they seemed to be part of the same brick, am I correct?"

Krom had not said anything of the sort in his testimony. However, since no objection was made, Krom simply answered, "That is correct, sir."

"What is it about those two bricks that caused you to arrive at that opinion?"

"The bricks appear to have been moved," the detective replied. "They do not appear to have been sitting there for any period of time."

"I object," Lippman said finally, "unless the officer can state the basis for that."

It was not the correct objection. The proper objection was that Detective Krom had not been shown qualified to make such an opinion.

"Well, I assume that is going to be the next question," Judge Vogt announced. "Then you can make your motion to strike."[429]

Detective Krom did not wait for another question. He said, "Bricks looked to have been moved. Also, each brick has a bloodstain on it. Also, the bricks appear to have been broken. They were of the same brick."

After the answer, Lippman simply sat down and said nothing, apparently deciding not to make his motion to strike. This was yet another major blunder. The prosecution had not yet made the allegation, but it was clear to everyone in the courtroom that these bricks were being presented as the possible murder weapon. The unspoken contention was that the brick had broken when it was used to strike Anna Kithcart on the head.

There was nothing presented that in any way qualified Richard Krom as a mason or forensic expert capable of rendering an opinion as to whether the two bricks were once part of the same brick. Yet, without any objection, both pieces of brick were formally accepted into evidence.

The bricks almost certainly would have been taken into evidence simply because of the bloodstains. The blood gave them relevance. However, to allow the prosecution to submit a conclusion that the two pieces were part of the same brick without a qualified witness was a substantial error.

Taking full advantage of his colleague's mistake, Kavanagh had his witness tell the jury that there were bloodstains on the bricks and that they had been sent to the New York State Police lab for analysis. He had Krom set forth all of the necessary evidentiary foundations so he could call the lab technician later in the trial.

Maintaining his momentum, Kavanagh produced another evidence bag. This one contained a bloodstained piece of Styrofoam. Krom told the jury that he had discovered this item in the area of the struggle. It was about four feet from Kithcart's feet. He had collected it as evidence and sent it to the lab along with the washbasin. It was entered into evidence.[430]

"How much evidence did you gather in the scene of this young girl, in the area of this young girl's body, detective?"

"Approximately twenty-six items," the witness answered.

The prosecutor asked Krom to describe generally the types of items he collected. Kavanagh knew that because the area was full of refuse and debris, the police had collected a great many items, some of which had nothing to do with the case.

Krom mentioned a variety of objects including a blue,

long-sleeved shirt, a duffel bag containing women's undergarments, soil samples, and several other articles of clothing and trash.[431]

To give the jury a further understanding of the sheer amount of junk and trash scattered about the scene, Kavanagh asked the detective to estimate for the jury the number of items found around the body. Krom smiled and replied, "It was astronomical, mind-blowing."[432]

"You mentioned also in your testimony," Kavanagh asked, "that you observed a piece of glass in the deceased's neck?"

"Yes, sir."

"What was done in regard to that piece of glass?"

"The piece of glass that was found in the victim's neck was left exactly as we found it," Krom said. "It was photographed. Notes were taken when the body was turned over to Dr. McNamara. The piece of glass was untouched, went with the body."

"Went with the body to the autopsy?" Kavanagh asked.

"Yes, sir."

He showed the witness a photograph, and Krom quickly noted that the piece of glass could be seen in the victim's neck in that picture. It was just as he had seen that morning.[433]

Kavanagh fully intended to offer that piece of glass into evidence. He could not do so until the forensic pathologist testified. He just needed Krom to complete the chain of custody narrative.

Having finished with Krom's activities at the first crime scene, the prosecutor turned to the second. "I would like to direct your attention to the next day, July the 13th, 1988," Kavanagh said. "Did you have occasion on that date to go to an area on Broadway in the city of Kingston near an establishment that was popularly known as Cheap Charlies?"

"Yes, I did."

"For what purpose?"

"I was notified by Sergeant Dunn and Officer Spetalieri that articles of clothing had been found which were believed to be pertinent to this particular case, and I was notified to respond to that."[434]

Kavanagh asked the detective to tell the jury what he did when he arrived. Krom said the area was an alley between the Royal Grill and Cheap Charlies. He made sure that the alley was secured and had photographs taken of the alley, both entrances, and every item that was eventually collected as evidence.[435]

"All right, you say you collected evidence," Kavanagh said. "What did you find?"

"In the alleyway was a white towel. The towel was lying on the sidewalk. On top of the towel were numerous articles of clothing. The towel and the articles of clothing were soaked and wet. The articles of clothing were bunched up on the towel, and protruding from the top of the clothing was a stick, a common stick you would find in the woods, approximately sixteen inches in length. Each item was removed and placed in evidence bags and marked by me."

"What did you remove from the towel?" the prosecutor inquired.

Krom reported that in addition to the stick that he had just mentioned, he found a green and brown terry-cloth shirt and pants, two T-shirts, a pair of women's underwear, and a second stick measuring about fourteen inches in length.[436]

Krom told the jury that all of the items were sent to the State Police lab for analysis, as well as numerous pieces of glass found in the alley near the pile of clothing.

In painstaking detail, Kavanagh produced each item of clothing described by Krom, as well as the two sticks and the white towel. Krom identified each one as having come from the alley. He also identified photographs that showed the pile of clothing exactly as it had been found that morning. When this was completed, the district attorney asked to enter all of the exhibits into evidence.

Lippman objected and requested to *voir dire* the witness. The legal term *voir dire* refers to a mini-hearing or brief examination used to either select jurors, contest qualifications of an expert, or contest entry of evidence. In this case, Lippman was asking to question Krom specifically on the offered evidence. The judge granted the request.

"These items, detective, that you say you found in the alley," Lippman began. "Do you know how long they were there?"

"No, sir," Krom answered. "I do not."

Lippman asked Krom if he personally had received the call from the person who found these items. Krom said it was Sergeant Dunn who had received the call.

"Did Sergeant Dunn first come across these items?" Lippman asked.

"No, sir," Krom admitted. "I believe he was notified by someone else."

"Do you know who put them at that location?"

"No, sir, I do not."

This was actually a dangerous question. Krom could have answered that it was his understanding that Jeff Dawson placed the clothes there. Given his knowledge of Dawson's recorded statement to the police, he would have been justified in this reply.

Lippman asked a similarly dangerous question when he asked Krom if he knew who had contact with the items before he arrived. The detective did not take advantage of this gaffe.

His *voir dire* completed, Lippman turned to the judge and objected to the acceptance of the clothing, sticks, and towel. The basis for his objection was likely going to be insufficient foundation, though he never got the chance.

Judge Vogt interrupted before the attorney could get out another syllable. "Objection overruled. Mark them entered."[437]

With the major pieces of evidence successfully entered, the district attorney had only a few more points to make with this witness. With McNamara having testified earlier that day about taking various samples from Kithcart's body, Dawson, and Joseph Kiernan, the prosecutor had Krom inform the jury that, after receiving all of these samples from the doctor, he brought them to the State Police lab for testing. The chain of custody of this evidence was now established from their initial collection until their receipt by the lab. The foundation was set for later forensic testimony.[438]

The final thing Kavanagh asked his witness concerned evidence he received from Dr. Eric Mitchell, the forensic pathologist who conducted the official autopsy. The jury had already been told that the body of Anna Kithcart was sent to Mitchell in Syracuse. The bra and moccasin found on the body, as well as the glass imbedded in her neck, had also gone to Syracuse.

Kavanagh planned to call Mitchell as a witness very soon to discuss his findings. However, even with that testimony, the evidence could not be admitted without one further link in the chain of custody. That link extended from Mitchell back to the Kingston Police Department.

Detective Krom testified that he received evidence from Mitchell's office. Kavanagh had him identify a list of all of the items he received, which was entered into evidence over Lippman's objection.[439]

The prosecutor produced another exhibit, handed it to his

witness, and asked him to identify it.

"This is a lady's bra," Krom replied. "This was the bra that was on the victim at the crime scene upon my arrival."

Kavanagh turned to the bench and asked that the bra be accepted into evidence. Judge Vogt turned to the defense table fully expecting an objection. The prosecution had not established what, if anything, had happened to the bra while it was with Dr. Mitchell. This was an obvious gap in the chain of custody. Lippman offered no objection, however, and the judge marked it received in evidence.[440]

Finally, Kavanagh presented one last exhibit to Krom. The detective identified it as the glass that had been in the victim's neck. He told the jury that, after receiving this evidence back from the pathologist after the autopsy, he had brought it to Investigator Vincent Rossetti of the New York State Police. Krom explained that Rossetti was to examine the glass for possible fingerprints.[441]

After taking the exhibit from the witness, Kavanagh advised the court that he had no further questions.[442] Kavanagh did not offer the glass into evidence. He was well aware that he needed testimony from Rossetti to complete the chain of custody. It was not likely that Lippman would repeat the mistake he made in not objecting to the chain of custody of the bra.

Seeing the lateness of the hour, Judge Vogt announced that he was adjourning for the day. Barry Lippman would get his chance at cross-examination in the morning.

CHAPTER 21 - LIPPMAN FIGHTS BACK

A FEW REPORTERS STOOD watching as Jeff Dawson was marched from the police van into the courthouse the next morning. He was wearing the same brown suit with light brown pinstripes and white, knit skullcap from the day before. As he passed by, one of the reporters asked him how he thought the trial was going.

"No black man could get a fair trial in Ulster County," he mumbled without looking up.[443]

At the beginning and end of each trial day, the press kept as close as they could to the defendant. He often made comments, usually against his own lawyer. This was always good for headlines.

Just the evening before, Dawson was asked why he was constantly perusing through his attorney's file while Lippman was questioning witnesses. Dawson responded by complaining that Lippman would not give him copies of motions and documentary evidence.

"All these things that I've been reading are things I don't have and I got to have," the defendant protested.[444]

When Lippman walked out of the courthouse almost immediately after these comments, the press told him about Dawson's complaints and asked for a response. To his credit, Lippman did not take the bait.

"I don't have any comment. He can say whatever he wants. He's doing all the talking," he said.[445]

Despite the pressure of a difficult murder trial and an even more difficult client who neither liked nor trusted him, Lippman was ready when Detective Krom resumed the stand that Thursday morning. He knew that he would not be able to counter the various pieces of evidence entered the day before. However, he might be able to convince the jury to focus on something else.

After asking a few questions about the items Krom had taken into evidence, Lippman asked, "Now, you did collect quite a number of items from the area of the body. Is that right?"

"Yes, sir."

"Those weren't all of the items you observed in the vicinity of the body, were they?"

"No, sir," Krom replied.

"Were there many items that were not collected by you?"

"Yes, sir."

"What, if anything, was done with those items?"

"The items that were not collected?" Krom asked, seemingly confused.

"Yes."

"The items are still at the scene," Krom answered.

"Do you know whether all of the items that you did not mark and take into custody are still there?"

"No, sir, I do not."[446]

This was a rather shrewd series of questions by Lippman. He had set up a scenario whereby he could argue later to the jury that important evidence might have been left behind. In reality, the items left behind were just trash and rubbish. However, a defendant has no obligation to prove his innocence. He needs merely to present reasonable doubt. Unanswered questions almost always favor the defense. If

Lippman could convince even one juror that the police had left behind important evidence, his client might just go free.

The attorney next turned to items that were collected by the detective, but had not been shown to the jury or brought into court.

"You mentioned a blue shirt that you did pick up from the scene. Is that correct?"

"Yes, sir."

"Did you ever determine whose shirt that was?"

"No, sir, I did not."

"Or who left it at the scene?" Lippman asked, his voice rising slightly for effect.

"No, sir," Krom repeated. "I did not."[447]

Lippman next asked about three buttons that had been found at the scene. Krom confirmed that he had found them, but conceded that he had never compared them with the clothing found later in the alley or whether that clothing was even missing any buttons.[448]

"One of the items you picked up was a duffel bag?" Lippman inquired.

"Yes, sir," the witness replied continuing to keep his answers short and to the point.

"Could you describe this duffel bag?"

"Yes, sir," Krom replied. "It was a small, dark-blue duffel bag with two cloth-type carrying handles."

"What was in that duffel bag?"

"A lady's bra and also a lady's pair of panties, underwear."

"Did you ever determine to whom the duffel bag or the contents of the duffel bag belonged?"

"No, sir, I did not," Krom answered, returning to his staccato responses.[449]

This was again very clever strategy by Lippman. A mysterious blue shirt and a bag of women's underwear that the police took the time to collect, but the prosecution never presented to the jury, could potentially for the basis of a reasonable doubt.

Finally, Lippman turned his inquiry to the subject of Joseph Kiernan. To the jury, Kiernan remained a shadowy figure who had found the body and been at the scene. Little else had been presented to them about him. Lippman planned to change that.

"Did you have any contact with Joseph Kiernan in connection with your investigation?"

"Yes, sir."

"Did you question him?"

"Yes, sir."

"And were you present when a statement was taken from him?"

"A written statement," the detective replied. "Yes, sir."

The district attorney, knowing full well where Lippman was going with this, stood and objected. To his surprise, the judge allowed Lippman to continue.

"Did Joseph Kiernan eventually admit to having sexual contact with that body?"

"Yes sir, he did," answered Krom, causing some of the jurors to visibly stiffen in their seats. This was the first time Kiernan's alleged actions involving the body had been presented to the jury. It certainly caught their attention.

"Did he admit to cutting up the body?" Lippman asked.

"No, sir," Krom countered. "He did not."[450]

This answer was a little surprising considering that the police chief had told the media at the press conference right after Dawson's arrest that Kiernan had admitted to carving up the body. However, Lippman wisely did not inquire further. He knew Krom would certainly have an explanation, and he did not want that explanation offered to the jury.

Lippman turned toward the defense table, seemingly done with the witness. Then, he stopped and turned back to ask about just one more thing.

"When for the first time did you see Jeffrey Dawson following this incident?"

When Krom replied that it was on the day of the arrest, Lippman asked, "And at that time, did you observe any type of bruise on Jeffrey Dawson's face?"

"No, sir," Krom confirmed. "I did not."[451]

Lippman looked to the bench and announced that he had no further questions for the detective. He walked back to his seat quite pleased. This was by far Lippman's best moment in the trial thus far. He placed possible questions in the minds of the jury about the mystery shirt and duffel bag. He introduced Kiernan's repulsive behavior and made him a possible suspect. Lastly, he used a police detective to challenge the credibility of Todd Schleede, who just days before had testified that he saw a bruise on Dawson's face. Yet, the detective in charge of collecting evidence saw Dawson at his arrest and observed no bruise.

Mike Kavanagh knew that Lippman had damaged the case. The prosecutor approached his witness hoping to repair it.

He started by asking Krom to tell the jury exactly where he found the blue shirt in relation to the body. Krom said it was ten to twelve feet from Kithcart's feet and just beyond the area of the apparent struggle.

When asked to describe how the shirt appeared when found, Krom responded that it was rain-soaked and appeared to have been there for a period of time.

"When you say a period of time, are you talking about five

minutes?" Kavanagh inquired.

"No, sir," Krom answered. "I would say longer than four or five days."[452]

Kavanagh next asked about the duffel bag. Krom told the prosecutor that the bag had been found over seventy yards away from the body. It was actually up the embankment and nearly out of the railway bed completely.

Kavanagh also took great pains to have the detective repeat for the jury that the victim's bra was found on her body and her panties were found in the alley a few blocks away.[453]

The clear implication of this was that the bra and panties found in the duffel belonged to someone else and had nothing to do with the murder.

Kavanagh's re-direct examination had been brief, but effective. He presented alternate explanations for the shirt and duffel bag. He had not been able to deal with Kiernan or the report of Krom not seeing a bruise on Dawson's face. It was about as much as he could have expected.

Lippman was not content to concede anything. He rose to again question the detective.

"Detective Krom," he began, "in addition to your duties as a detective, you are specifically assigned to secure the crime scene and inventory evidence. Isn't that true?"

"Yes, sir," Krom agreed.

"Do you have specific training or have you taken particular courses which indicate what evidence to look for as perhaps being important in the course of your arrival at a crime scene?"

"Yes, sir, I have," the detective agreed again.

"And in fact, you told us many things that you didn't pick up, isn't that correct?"

"Yes, sir."

"And those that you considered important, you did pick up?"

"Yes, sir."

"And when you picked up the blue shirt and secured that as part of the evidence in this case," Lippman asked finally getting to his intended point, "you considered that blue shirt as possibly being important in this case?"

"At that time," Krom admitted, "yes, sir."[454]

With that, Lippman quietly returned to his seat. He had done a rather efficient job of keeping the cryptic blue shirt relevant for the jury. The prosecution would maintain that the blue shirt had nothing to do with the case, but the defense could continue to ask why had it been taken into evidence by a trained investigator if it meant nothing.

In all, while Krom had been effective for the prosecution and had set the stage for later forensic testimony, Lippman had scored his first real points of the trial and had won the round.

CHAPTER 22 - TESTIMONY FROM FAMILY

THE COURT BECAME COMPLETELY silent as the next witness walked slowly to the witness chair. She was Margaret Kithcart, Annie's mother. Until now, she had not spoken publicly about her daughter's death.

Mike Kavanagh started very slowly with the witness, allowing her to become more comfortable with each question. She told the jury that her daughter had lived with her in downtown Kingston for the last nine years.[455]

The prosecutor handed the witness a photograph and quietly asked, "Ma'am, do you recognize the person pictured in that photograph?"

Mrs. Kithcart looked down at the photograph and flashed a brief smile showing a mixture of love and sadness. She took a breath and replied, "That's my daughter."

"Anna Kithcart?" Kavanagh asked, to clarify.

"Yes," she answered, her voice barely a whisper.[456]

With the preliminary matters complete, Kavanagh asked the grieving mother to recall the day of July 11, 1988. "Do you recall on that date," he asked, "when you last saw your daughter?"

"It was between nine and nine thirty that night."

Kavanagh asked her to explain the circumstances of her last encounter with her daughter. Mrs. Kithcart told the jury that Annie had gone out at around nine thirty after borrowing some money. She told her mother that she was meeting some friends that night.

"Now, at the time she left the house," Kavanagh continued, "do you recall what she was wearing?"

"Yes," she replied, "it was a gray striped outfit, like sweatshirt material."

Kavanagh approached the witness and handed her two evidence bags containing familiar garments. Tears came to Mrs. Kithcart's eyes as she carefully held and looked at them. Kavanagh then asked her if she could identify the clothing. She closed her eyes, bracing herself against more tears that she was fighting to hold back. A moment later, she opened her eyes and informed the jury that the bags contained the pants and top her daughter had been wearing the last time she saw her.[457]

Kavanagh took the garments from her and started to offer them into evidence, before remembering that the court had already done so the day before.

Kavanagh finished his direct examination by having Mrs. Kithcart discuss how she learned of her daughter's death, first from a neighbor, and later from Detective Harris of the Kingston Police Department.[458]

As Barry Lippman rose to question Mrs. Kithcart, he knew full well that he had a difficult task ahead of him. There were some points that he needed to make, but he had to be exceedingly careful not to upset the victim's mother. If he did, the jury would absolutely hate him. That would not help his client in any way.

"Do you recall whether your daughter was wearing any jewelry that night when you saw her?" he asked cautiously.

"I believe she had a necklace and a pin on," she responded. "I thought she had a ring on, but we found the ring. We never found the necklace."

"Did you ever get those items or see them back again?"

"No."[459]

If Annie was wearing any jewelry when she was killed, it had not been recovered. This would be something to discuss later. For now, Lippman felt it best to stop his questioning. Kavanagh had no re-direct, and Mrs. Kithcart was excused.

The district attorney then announced to the court, "The People call Rose Dawson."

Lippman objected immediately and asked to approach the bench. During the bench conference, Lippman asked the court to disallow Rose Dawson as a witness, citing the marital or spousal privilege. Rose Dawson was the defendant's wife, and Lippman did not believe she should be allowed to testify.

The spousal privilege is a legal doctrine protecting confidential communications between a husband and a wife. Under New York law, a husband or wife shall not be required or, without consent of the other if living, allowed to disclose a confidential communication made by one to the other during marriage.[460]

Judge Vogt was prepared for this objection. Having noticed that Rose Dawson was on the prosecutor's witness list, he had already reviewed his law books on the issue.

"The court takes note of the fact that the prosecution intends to call the defendant's wife to the stand and proposes to ask her certain questions with respect to observations she made of the defendant on the morning following the slaying of the victim."[461]

The prosecutor jumped in at this point and noted that they intended to have the wife testify that she saw her husband come home completely wet, and that he had told her he had been swimming in a neighbor's pool.

Over Lippman's strongly worded, but respectful protests,

Judge Vogt ruled that the defendant had told the police that he had been swimming in the neighbor's pool and thus had waived the privilege on that point.[462]

As the attorneys returned to their respective tables, Rose Dawson took the stand. Her body language practically screamed that she wanted to be anywhere else in the world than on the witness stand testifying against her husband.

Kavanagh had her tell the jury that she was the defendant's wife. Although she had since moved to the town of Catskill, she and her husband lived in an upstairs apartment on Brewster Street in Kingston in July of 1988. The landlord, who lived on-site, was named Mary Paschell.[463]

"On July the 11th, the night before Anna Kithcart's death, do you recall being at home at 42 Brewster Street?" Kavanagh asked.

"Yes, I do," she answered.

"Was your husband at home with you?"

"No, he wasn't," she replied uncomfortably.

"What time was it that you last saw your husband on the night of July the 11th?"

"I believe it was like eight, eight thirty in the evening."

"And when was it that you next saw your husband?"

"The following morning," she answered vaguely.

"What time," Kavanagh persisted.

"Around four, four thirty, somewhere around there."

"And where were you at the time you saw your husband at around four or four thirty in the morning?" Kavanagh asked, placing emphasis on the time for the jury.

"I was home," Rose Dawson responded.[464]

Then, for reasons not entirely clear, Kavanagh moved away from the encounter that morning and asked Rose whether she and her husband had been to the police station on July 13. She said they had.

The district attorney slowly walked the witness through the couple's entire experience at the police station that day. They were told by Mary Paschell that the police were looking for Jeff, so they walked downtown to the police station where they were interviewed, together and separately. She admitted giving the police a false alibi for her husband.[465]

Lippman made two half-hearted objections during this testimony that were denied. He was glad these objections were denied as they were actually just show for the jury. He knew that Kavanagh had just made a mistake, and he was planning how to exploit it.

After finishing with the events of July 13, Kavanagh returned the witness to the early morning hours of July 12, when her husband had just returned home.

"Describe to the jury your husband's appearance when you saw him at four or four thirty in the morning," Kavanagh instructed, again emphasizing the time.

"He came in wet."

"How was he dressed?"

"He had a pair of blue jogging pants on and no shirt and something white in his hand," she replied. She did not know exactly what was in his hand other than it was some article of clothing.[466]

"When you last saw your husband on the night of July the 11th at eight or eight thirty," Kavanagh asked, still highlighting the time, "can you tell us what he was wearing?"

Rose said her husband had been wearing blue jogging pants, white sneakers, a white T-shirt, and a white cap.

"Now you said he had a pair of blue jogging pants?" Kavanagh asked with surprise in his voice.

"Yes," she insisted.

Kavanagh handed the witness her prior statement to the police and asked whether she had reported blue jeans instead of blue jogging pants. Lippman objected, but the judge permitted him to proceed. Nonetheless, Rose maintained that her recollection was that her husband had been wearing blue jogging pants and not jeans.[467]

Kavanagh knew that the police had seized a pair of blue jeans from the defendant's home, and he was hoping Rose would confirm that the defendant had been wearing them the night of the murder. She would not.

So, Kavanagh decided to finish with this witness, but not before asking her about the night her husband was arrested. Rose testified that she had been home and was watching out the window while her husband spoke with Todd Schleede.[468]

Kavanagh made sure that Rose told the jury that she did not see anyone else around when her husband spoke with Schleede. Kavanagh planned to soon present the audio recording of the conversation between Todd Schleede and Jeff Dawson. By having Dawson's wife testify that she did not see anyone else around during the conversation, he hoped to avoid any contention that someone other than Jeff Dawson had spoken those fateful words.

Barry Lippman did not ask a single question about his client's appearance on the morning after the murder. Instead, he focused exclusively on the trip Rose and Jeff Dawson had taken to the police station on July 13.

Just before the trial, the court had held a suppression hearing to determine whether the prosecution would be able to use Jeff Dawson's statements to the police. Lippman had argued that since the defendant had requested a lawyer on his first trip to the station, the police were not permitted to question him thereafter without his lawyer being present.

In New York, once a suspect in custody requests an attorney, the police may not question him unless his attorney is present.[469]

Additionally, Lippman argued that his client was in legal custody when he was questioned on July 13, but was never read his Miranda rights. As such, all statements made after that point were poisoned by this failure and should have been suppressed.

Under the now famous Miranda decision from the U.S. Supreme Court, once a suspect is in custody, he must be advised of his or her rights against self-incrimination before he is questioned. Whether or not a suspect is considered to be in custody comes down to a question of whether the suspect reasonably felt he was not free to leave.[470]

After taking testimony from the officers, Judge Vogt issued a written ruling which he read into the record finding the defendant was not in custody on July 13 because he was free to leave at any time. He also found that the defendant did not specifically invoke his right to counsel. As such, he declined to suppress either the statement made by Jeff Dawson to the police or the recorded conversation between Dawson and Schleede.[471]

When Kavanagh asked Rose Dawson about the day she and her husband visited the police and gave a statement, he opened the door for Lippman to ask more questions on this issue. Lippman's hope was either to get enough information to support a motion for Judge Vogt to reconsider his ruling or to establish a solid record for appeal in case his client was convicted.

Lippman was only a few questions into his cross-examination when Kavanagh objected and asked for a bench conference. The judge simply waved him off. The prosecutor had made the mistake of opening the door and now he would have to sit idly by while Lippman walked through it.

For the next fifteen to twenty minutes, Rose Dawson told the court that she and her husband were kept at the police station from 11:30 a.m. until 9:00 p.m., a total of nine and a half hours.[472]

At one point, she was left alone in a room for three hours while her husband was questioned in another room. She repeatedly asked to leave but was told she could not. She said her husband asked repeatedly if they could leave but was told they both had to stay until the District Attorney's Office called and gave permission.[473]

After Lippman sat down, the district attorney asked a few more questions, but the most he could get the witness to admit was that she and her husband had voluntarily gone to the police station. She maintained, however, that Jeff was later not permitted to leave.[474]

The next witness was the defendant's former landlord, Mary Paschell. Her testimony went rather quickly. She had been working the night shift at a local diner (9:00 p.m. to 6:00 a.m.) on the day the murder was discovered. She arrived home at about 6:20 a.m.[475]

A few hours later that day, July 13, at about 11:20 a.m., the police came to the door, waking her from her sleep. She answered the door and was told they were looking for Jeff Dawson. She told them he was not there and started to leave a note for Jeff and Rose. She then discovered that they were there so she told them personally.[476]

Her testimony did not offer very much. She did contradict Rose Dawson slightly when she reported that the Dawsons went to the police station and were back in the house by eight that evening. [477]

Detective Wayne Freer, a thirteen-year veteran of the Kingston Police Department was Kavanagh's next witness. The prosecutor had no real surprise or drama in store for this witness. He was intended only to set the foundation for two much stronger witnesses. Lippman had other plans.

The detective testified that he picked up Todd Schleede from his home on Saturday, bought him to the station, and took his written statement. He also helped place the recording device on Schleede for his conversation with Jeff Dawson.[478]

After Dawson was arrested, Freer was part of a police team that executed a search warrant on the defendant's apartment. He seized a pair of blue jeans off the bedroom floor and a white hat. He gave them to Detective Krom to be logged as evidence. Kavanagh produced both the jeans and hat, and the witness promptly identified both. They were accepted into evidence without objection.[479]

Finally, Kavanagh had the witness tell the jury how he had gone to the Ulster County Jail to obtain evidence from Joseph Kiernan. From his effects, Freer seized the pants and coat Kiernan had been wearing on the morning he discovered Kithcart's body. Again, Kavanagh produced the items, and Freer identified them.[480]

As Kavanagh sat down, Lippman went after the witness, but in an unexpected way.

"On July 16th, when you went to Mr. Schleede's trailer, were you aware that the manager of the Stewart's store in Port Ewen had been robbed on or about the 13th of July?"

"Yes," Freer answered.

"Is it fair to say that the robbery was purportedly committed by two men wearing ski masks?" Lippman asked.

Freer never got a chance to answer because Judge Vogt sustained the district attorney's objection. Lippman seemingly did not care about the ruling and quickly plunged forward.

"At the time you went to Mr. Schleede's trailer, you knew that Todd Schleede had a history of robberies at Stewart's stores. Is that correct?"

Freer again did not answer as Vogt sustained another

objection from Kavanagh. Lippman kept going with his inquiry, barely taking a breath.

"On July 16th, was the Kingston Police Department involved in the investigation of the Stewart's robbery?"

This time, Freer blurted out, "Not that I know of," before a third objection was sustained.

Undaunted, Lippman asked, "To your knowledge, wasn't Todd Schleede a suspect in that robbery?"

When that question was squashed by a fourth sustained objection, Lippman repeated, "Do you know that Todd Schleede was suspected in that case?"

Before Kavanagh could object a fifth time, Judge Vogt ordered both attorneys to the bench.[481]

The judge and the attorneys spoke briefly in a sidebar while the jury waited. When Lippman was permitted to resume his questioning, he again asked about Todd Schleede but not in the same accusatory manner.[482]

He asked the detective whether he had made any deals with Schleede to not prosecute him concerning possible robberies, whether he had given Schleede suggestions on how to entrap Jeff Dawson, or whether he had been the one to convince Schleede to wear the wire. Freer denied it all.[483]

Lippman then went off in a completely different direction asking, "In the course of your investigation, did it come to your attention that an individual by the name of Tommy Phillips was wanted by the police in Florida for raping, tying up, and cutting a girl?"[484]

"I object, Your Honor," Kavanagh shouted, rising from his chair.

"Sustained," Judge Vogt answered immediately. "The jury is instructed to disregard counsel's question."[485]

Lippman had no intention of backing down on this point. He

took some documents from his table and handed them to the witness.

"Did you make any record or notes with respect to your investigation in this case?"

"Yes, sir," the detective replied.

"On July 16, 1988, did you note in your records…"

"I object, Your Honor," Kavanagh interrupted. "Mr. Lippman is reading from the record now."

"I am not reading from anything," Lippman retorted, his volume increasing with anger.

Judge Vogt called an end to the argument and instructed counsel to approach the bench again. After a brief conference, it was decided that Lippman would not ask any more questions about Tommy Phillips in front of the jury. However, Vogt said he would hear oral arguments at the end of the day outside the presence of the jury. If Lippman could convince him, he would allow Detective Freer to be called to the stand again to address the matter.[486]

After the conference, Lippman had only a few more questions. He asked whether Freer had been involved in the interrogation of Joseph Kiernan. Freer said his involvement in that was limited.

As he returned to the defense table, Lippman was generally satisfied with his cross-examination. He had not expected Judge Vogt to give him much leeway, but he had used the little he had been given to continue to accuse Todd Schleede of being a serial robber. He had also tried to plant the idea that a man wanted in Florida for a similar crime might be a possible suspect.

The next two witnesses were on the stand only briefly, and Lippman did not bother to question them. Detective Dennis Day testified that he had been assigned to drive the body of Anna Kithcart to Syracuse for the autopsy and then back again. He also said that Dr. Eric Mitchell, the pathologist, provided him with samples and other evidence that he brought back to Kingston and gave to Detective Krom.[487]

Detective John Wallace told the jury that on July 20, 1988, he picked up a set of dental impressions from Dr. Randolph Myerson, a local dentist, and logged them into evidence at the Kingston Police Station.[488] The jury and courtroom observers were left wondering what the dental impressions were all about.

After Wallace walked out of the courtroom, Kavanagh announced to the judge that he had no more witnesses for the day. His next witnesses would be dental experts that would require a substantial amount of time. Judge Vogt agreed and sent the jury home for the day.

Once the jury had filed out, Vogt invited Mr. Lippman to present his oral argument concerning Tommy Phillips. The members of the media in attendance, who up until now had heard nothing about this mysterious man wanted in Florida, got their pencils and recorders ready hoping for a headline.

"Detective Freer's notes indicate," Lippman began, "that he had received information on July 16th that an individual, who apparently was in Kingston and whose name was mentioned in connection with this investigation, was wanted by the police in Florida for taking a girl into the woods, tying her up, and raping and cutting her."

Lippman paused, seemingly for effect, before continuing. "I attempted to question Detective Freer about the fact that this information came to his attention. I believe, Your Honor, that I have a right to do that and inquire as to what steps, if any, Detective Freer, or anyone else in the Police Department for that matter, took to inquire into that situation."[489]

The district attorney was ready with a response. He informed the court that the note in question involved a meeting Detective Freer had with an informant in a city park. The informant did mention his understanding of Tommy Phillips being wanted in Florida. However, the informant did not give information that Phillips had been in Kingston or was ever in contact with Anna Kithcart on the night of the murder or any other time."[490]

Judge Vogt was not impressed with Lippman's plea. "I distinguish this sort of thing from Kiernan. That is different because there is a connection there," the judge ruled. "We are certainly not going to inquire into every unsubstantiated attempt or statement made by people as to what was done by the Kingston Police Department. It is all irrelevant. It is collateral and has no place in this trial."[491]

Lippman knew that the judge was correct. If he allowed questions on every single thing said by people during the entire investigation without something clearly tying it in, a trial would take months. He still had another card to play though.

"I think, if I may make one further point," Lippman argued. "In this particular case, we are dealing unquestionably with someone who was in contact with the body."

"All right," the judge conceded. "There is evidence that Kiernan had contact with the body."

"But," Lippman continued, "there is a serious question as to what contact he had with her."

"That may be," Vogt retorted. "That's a matter of proof."

"That's why I thought it was so very, very important that I be privy to all of the questioning and all of the statements that were taken from Mr. Kiernan," Lippman said, getting to his ultimate point. "I have not received them and I am asking, demanding at this time, the written statement that was taken from Kiernan."[492]

With no hesitation, Judge Vogt replied, "I am directing the district attorney to turn that over to you."

Lippman was not satisfied. He pointed out to the judge that he also wanted the questions and answers asked of Kiernan during his lie detector test.

Kavanagh immediately objected. He argued that since lie detector tests are not admissible in court, he should not have to turn over any portion of it.

The judge ordered the prosecutor to provide the court with that information. Vogt said he would review it and decide whether or not it would be disclosed to the defense.[493]

The third day of trial had not gone well for Kavanagh. Lippman had performed very well in challenging the prosecution's witnesses. Kavanagh was not overly concerned though. He knew that his strongest witnesses and evidence were coming up.

CHAPTER 23 – THE DENTISTS

THE NEXT MORNING, THE first witness was Randolph Myerson, a local dentist. He started his testimony by discussing his credentials in dentistry.[494] When he finished with his *curriculum vitae*, District Attorney Mike Kavanagh turned to the real purpose of his testimony.

"Doctor, on or about July 20, 1988, did you have occasion to come into contact with the defendant, Jeffrey Dawson?"

"Yes, I did."

"For what purpose?"

"For the purpose of obtaining impressions and making impressions of the individual's teeth," Myerson replied.[495]

Myerson explained to the jury that dental impressions are a negative imprint of the teeth and soft tissues in the mouth from which a positive cast can be formed. They are made with a set of trays filled with a doughy material that are then placed into the mouth. Once the material sets, it is removed from the mouth, cleaned, and dried. It is then filled with plaster. Once the plaster dries, it is removed from the impression itself. The ultimate result is a custom dental mold of the subject's teeth.[496]

Kavanagh produced a dental impression and mold and handed them to the witness. Myerson identified them as the ones he prepared from the defendant's teeth and gave to the police. They were entered into evidence.[497]

The prosecutor asked if there was anything unique or unusual about Jeff Dawson's teeth. Myerson answered that Dawson's upper, front teeth were wider than average and that his teeth's biting surfaces were worn down. Additionally, his upper and lower right canine teeth each had a notch, though the one on the upper tooth was much more noticeable.[498]

Myerson said he also took impressions of Joseph Kiernan's teeth and made a mold from them. Kiernan's teeth were quite different. He had no upper teeth and only a few lower teeth in the front.[499]

Kavanagh did not go any further with his witness. Myerson created the dental molds, but a different dentist would testify to their importance in this case.

Lippman's cross-examination was very limited. He got the doctor to admit that the wearing down he observed on Dawson's teeth was not that unusual. In addition, Myerson agreed that he never took dental impressions from Todd Schleede.[500] Once again, Lippman was using his cross-examination of a witness to point an accusing finger at Schleede.

When Lippman sat down, Kavanagh stood up and asked Myerson, "Any two sets of teeth alike?"

"Highly unlikely," the dentist answered. "In the field of forensic dentistry, teeth are considered like fingerprints in terms of their ability to present unique sets of characteristics that can almost perfectly be distinguished from different people, if one has a good enough bite mark or impression."[501]

Lippman aggressively questioned Myerson on this point, but the dentist refused to budge on his contention that bite marks were as distinct as fingerprints.

This was very much an overstatement. While there have been many convictions based upon bite mark evidence, its reliability and credibility has been strongly criticized by several scientific bodies, including the National Academy of Sciences (NAS) and the President's Council of Advisors on Science and Technology (PCAST). The Texas Forensic Science Commission has recommended a moratorium on its use in court.

More than two dozen convictions based on bite mark evidence have been overturned. Two men sentenced to death on bite mark evidence were later proven innocent by DNA testing.[502] A man named Keith Harward spent more than thirty-three years in prison after being convicted of rape and murder. Bite marks on the victim had been the primary pieces of evidence against him. At trial, six experts testified that bites matched Harward's teeth. However, subsequent DNA testing proved his innocence.[503]

In modern criminal investigations, DNA analysis has become the preferred forensic evidence and is certainly more credible and reliable. In 1989, DNA analysis was in its infancy, and bite mark evidence was considered solid science, having come to prominence in the 1979 trial of serial killer Ted Bundy. There was really little that Lippman could do to challenge the bite mark analysis, despite the true limitations of the science, unknown at the time.

Mike Kavanagh's next witness was Dr. Edward Mofson, a forensic dentist certified by the American Board of Forensic Odontology.[504]

Although the jury had already been told about forensic dentistry from the previous witness, Kavanagh had Mofson give his own version.

"Forensic dentistry," Mofson explained, "is the application of knowledge of dental science in areas of the law such as incidental identifications of unknown deceased persons, analysis of bite marks, evidence management of mass disasters, and situations where there are large numbers of people who need to be identified by dental means."[505]

Kavanagh was not interested in the identification of an

unknown deceased. He focused instead on bite mark analysis.

"Now, is it possible," the district attorney asked, "to examine a substance such as human tissue after the subject has expired and identify marks on that body positively and conclusively as being human bite marks?"

"Yes," Mofson replied, "it is."

"Can you tell us generally," Kavanagh continued, "what goes into the process of uncovering those types of marks and making that type of conclusion?"

"There are certain general characteristics that characterize a human bite mark such as the size of the mark, shape of the mark, interrupted linear abrasions in an arch, and shape or curb shape pattern within the limits of the size of the human dental arch."[506]

Kavanagh next asked his witness whether a forensic dentist could examine bites on human tissue and identify the person who made the bites through comparison with the subject's known dental mold. Mofson answered yes.

"Doctor, were you called upon by the Onondaga County Medical Examiner's Office in the examination of the remains of a young girl, identified to you by the name of Anna Kithcart?"

"Yes, I was," Mofson responded. He further explained that he was contacted specifically to examine a bruise on the right side of the victim's neck that was suspected to be a human bite. After his initial viewing of the wound, he felt that the size, shape, and pattern of the mark were consistent with a human bite.[507]

Kavanagh produced a photograph taken at the autopsy, and Mofson testified that this picture depicted the bruise on the throat believed to be a bite. The photo was entered into evidence.[508]

Under further questioning, Mofson advised that while viewing the bruise with the naked eye was enough to conclude that it was a human bite, additional amplification was needed to make a proper forensic review. So, he used a laser light to highlight certain details. Then, photographs were taken of the laser enhancements to preserve them for later analysis. Two such photographs were presented, identified, and entered into evidence.[509]

Mofson advised the jury that, by carefully studying these laser-enhanced pictures, he was able to confirm his initial suspicion that the bruise on Kithcart's neck was in fact a human bite mark.[510]

Kavanagh asked the dentist to step down from the stand. When he had done so, the prosecutor asked him to show the jury where the bite was located and the position of the person doing the biting.

Mofson said the person inflicting the bite had his or her forehead in the center of the neck facing the left shoulder. His chin was over the right shoulder with his head at a right angle to the victim's neck.[511]

After the brief demonstration, Mofson returned to the witness chair.

"Could you tell," Kavanagh asked, "whether or not the person who made this bite on this girl's neck had both upper and lower teeth?"

The dentist agreed that the biter had upper and lower teeth, but admitted that the marks from the lower teeth were blurred and less distinct. He was unwilling to make any identification based on the lower teeth.

"You are hesitant about being able to identify the specific lower teeth that made those marks?" the district attorney asked.

"That's correct."

"But, there is no question," Kavanagh persisted, "that the person who made the bite had lower teeth, is that correct?"

"I believe so," Mofson answered, "yes."[512]

Kavanagh was insistent on this point because he wanted to exclude Joseph Kiernan as the biter. There was no question that Kiernan had been at the scene and made admissions involving physical contact with the body. It was necessary for the prosecutor to limit Kiernan's involvement as much as possible. He knew that the defense would point to the transient as a possible murderer. Kavanagh could not call Kiernan to testify because he would likely take the Fifth Amendment and refuse to testify. If the jury heard Kiernan refuse to testify, they might become more open to various conspiracy theories from the defense.

The next point to address was whether the bite was made before or after Kithcart's death. Mofson replied that he tended to believe that the bite was made before death since there was bruising around the bite. However, he deferred to Mitchell, the pathologist, as this was beyond the dentist's area of expertise.[513]

"Fair enough," Kavanagh said, moving to his next point. "Given what you found on the girl's neck, would you be able to make a comparison with that mark for identification purposes?"

"I believe there is enough evidence," Mofson replied, "enough information in this mark to compare to a dentition, yes."

The prosecutor retrieved the dental molds made of the defendant's teeth by Myerson and handed them to Mofson. The dentist told the jury that the dentitions were of high quality and professionally done.

After confirming that the witness had already made a comparison between the bite mark and the defendant's dental mold, Kavanagh asked the big question.

"Based upon that comparison, do you have an opinion that you can give with a reasonable degree of scientific and medical certainty as to whether or not Jeffrey Dawson's teeth made the mark on Anna Kithcart's neck?"

"Yes, sir," Mofson responded. "It is my opinion within a reasonable degree of dental certainty that the marks on Anna Kithcart's neck are human bite marks and that they were made by that dentition."[514]

The murmuring in a courtroom that always follows a big evidentiary pronouncement had barely ended when Kavanagh asked the judge to allow the witness to step down from the stand and use a blackboard to demonstrate to the jury the basis for his conclusions. Judge Vogt granted the request on the condition that, at the end of the demonstration, a picture be taken of the blackboard and the photo entered into the evidentiary record.

For the next ten minutes, Mofson drew on the board and described his conclusions. He first drew a diagram of the victim's head and neck and sketched the bite. Next, he drew a larger representation of the defendant's mouth and numbered the teeth using the universal dental notation system. The right third maxillary molar or wisdom tooth is designated as "1" and each tooth across the top is numbered in order through "16." The numbering continues on the bottom starting with the left third molar and across to the other side of the lower jaw, ending at "32."[515]

He told the jury that the bite mark on the victim's body showed a groove in the biting surface of tooth No. 6, the upper right canine tooth. He felt this was consistent with the notch in the defendant's upper right canine.[516]

He further explained that the worn-down biting surface and distance between the teeth marks were consistent with the defendant's right lateral and central incisors (teeth Nos. 7

and 8).[517]

Mofson then identified two of the marks as being teeth Nos. 10 and 11, the left lateral incisor and left upper canine teeth respectively. However, the dentist told the jury that he did not have an explanation for these two marks in his initial examination.

"Then, I went back and looked at it again. I looked at it about three times to be sure," he continued. "It occurred to me that if some motion took place during the course of the bite, that if either the person doing the biting, the person being bitten, or both moved while the bite was being inflicted, then it would cause the teeth to slide, grab, or at least take another position on the tissue. Then, if the bite were inflicted again, it would leave almost a second bite superimposed on top of the first bite."[518]

Mofson testified that if one assumed this chain of events, then the bite would be entirely consistent with the dental mold of the defendant.

The district attorney announced he was finished with his direct examination. Barry Lippman walked towards Mofson knowing that he had a very difficult job ahead of him.

Lippman asked the dentist whether he had observed any punctures of the skin in the area of the neck.

"Yes, there were punctures of the skin, although it was not part of the bite mark," the witness replied. Mofson knew that the attorney was asking about the bite mark, but his answer made it clear he intended to fight Lippman on every single point.

To his credit, Lippman did not let this bother him. Instead, he decided to clarify the definition of the word bite.

"When you use the term bite, you don't necessarily mean a puncturing of the skin. Is that correct?"

"That's correct."

"By bite, you mean the formation of the shape of the teeth?" Lippman asked.

"By bite mark," the dentist replied in a rather arrogant tone, "I mean any kind of a mark left by a bite. It could be a bruise, or could be abrasions, or could be a tear. A combination."

"A bruise left by the mouth would be considered a bite mark?"

"A bruise left by the teeth would be a bite mark."[519]

Now Lippman turned to the heart of Mofson's testimony, his conclusion of a forensic match between the bite mark and the plaster mold of his client's teeth.

Pointing to the area on the blackboard depicting teeth Nos. 10 and 11, Lippman asked, "Doctor, you indicated that that area didn't seem to match precisely with the dentition that was provided to you. Is that correct?"

"What I indicated," Mofson countered, "was that under the first analysis, although I had matched most of the little bruises to areas on the teeth that I felt matched, the bruises there were two areas in particular that I had not accounted for at that point in time."

"When you say that you had not accounted for them," Lippman pressed, "those bruises didn't seem to correspond with the appropriate portion of the dentition that you had been provided with. Is that correct?"

"At that point in my analysis, that is correct."

"And is it fair to say that you attempted to speculate as to why it didn't match up correctly?"

"Well," the dentist said defensively, "what I wanted to see was if I accounted for the marks. The marks were an inconsistency. By inconsistency, I mean marks that are not explainable by the bite, by the teeth that made the bite."[520]

Lippman titled his head slightly and smiled, trying to show

the jury his incredulity at the doctor's answer.

"Isn't it fair to say," Lippman continued, "that you assumed at that point that the mark which you observed was caused by the dentition sample which was provided to you?"

"No, that is not correct," the witness retorted. "I came to that conclusion after comparing that dentition with the bruises on the tissue. I had a lot of evidence that agreed with the high degree of consistency between the bruises and the dentition."

"One possible explanation for the fact that the marks that you observed," Lippman said accusingly, in a tone showing both disgust and disbelief, "is that the mark, if it was caused by a bite, was not caused by the individual whose dentition sample had been provided to you. Isn't that true?"

"Well, that would be possible," Mofson answered, "but then you would have to throw out all of the other evidence that indicates it was made by that dentition. There was far more evidence indicating a match, than there was evidence that it was not explainable by a match."[521]

Lippman did not back down. "In order to make that explanation, you *assumed*," Lippman accused, stressing that word, "that there must have been a movement of either the victim or the person who caused that mark to be placed there, or both?"

"I felt that is a reasonable explanation of the additional marks."

"But, if in fact there was no movement or double bite, that would tend to indicate that the mark was not caused by the individual whose dentition was provided to you, wouldn't it, doctor?"

"No, I wouldn't agree with that," Mofson countered stubbornly. "It would probably place the mark in a lower category of consistency, a mark that I might say was consistent with that dentition."[522]

Lippman could not believe what he was hearing. Just moments earlier, Mofson said he based his conclusion on his belief that movement during the bite caused the two inconsistent marks. Now, he was telling the jury that even if his belief was untrue, he would still maintain his opinion despite two inconsistencies.

Lippman continued to question the dentist, but Mofson maintained his opinion. Understanding that nothing he said would cause the witness to amend his opinion, Lippman went to a different area of inquiry.

"I know you are somewhat equivocal about this, doctor," the attorney asked, "but you did testify that, in your opinion, the victim was alive when that bruise was caused. Correct?"

"Yes."

"And that bruise could have been there for some period of time prior to death. Isn't that true?"

"I can't speculate as to that," the witness answered. "That is an area you would have to talk to a pathologist about."

"As far as you are concerned," Lippman continued, not letting the matter drop, "it could have been a couple of hours?"

"I have no idea."

"Or a couple of days for that matter?" the attorney pressed.

"It is hard to say. I am not qualified to say."[523]

Lippman paused and looked down at his notes. A moment later, he looked up and asked, "Would this mark be more or less what you would refer to as a hickey-type mark?"

Mofson seemed surprised by the question. "Well, I don't know," he finally answered. "There are hickeys, and then there are hickeys. I think it's a little more bruising than I would tend to expect. Maybe that's a personality issue."[524]

Lippman informed the judge that he was finished. When Kavanagh announced that he had no additional questions, the court excused the witness.

Mofson's testimony had been devastating to the defense. Lippman poked some holes in his opinion, but not enough. Despite very questionable science and an even more questionable assumption, the dentist insisted that Jeff Dawson had bitten Annie Kithcart. If the jury agreed with Mofson, then Dawson's claim of the death being an accident would fall completely apart.

Judge Vogt announced a recess for lunch. When the trial resumed, it would finally be time to hear from Mitchell, the pathologist.

CHAPTER 24 - THE PATHOLOGIST

AFTER LUNCH, DISTRICT ATTORNEY Kavanagh called Dr. Eric Mitchell as his next witness. Mitchell started his testimony by going through his qualifications.[525]

"Now, doctor," Kavanagh asked, moving to the point of his testimony. "Did you have occasion to perform a postmortem examination on the remains of a young girl identified to you by the name of Anna Kithcart?"

"Yes, sir."

"Can you tell us when and where that examination was done?"

"That was done in the medical examiner's office in Onondaga County," he answered. "It commenced in the evening at approximately seven p.m. of July 12, 1988."[526]

Kavanagh had the witness testify that, after the autopsy, he prepared a report of his findings. The prosecutor quickly produced some papers and handed them to Mitchell. The doctor confirmed that it was his report.[527]

Informing the doctor that he could use his report if needed, Kavanagh asked Mitchell to describe his findings on examination to the jury. Mitchell said that he found a severe laceration on the forehead that went right to the bone. In fact, there were scratches on the bone itself. There were significant cuts over the eyebrow and toward the right temple. There was a fracture of the victim's skull and orbital socket of the eye. These injuries were made by at least two strikes to the head.[528]

The victim's nose was broken. There were cuts and abrasions across her lips and some of her teeth were broken. The whites of her eyes were discolored and red, and there were tears and bruising on the right side of her head and on her right ear.[529]

There were bruises on her hands, knees, chest, collarbone, and neck, including one bruise on her neck that resembled a bite. There was a shard of glass sticking in her neck. On her abdomen were scratches that resembled the letter "K," and on each thigh were deep scratches that appeared to spell out "KKK."[530]

"If you know, doctor," Kavanagh continued, "what type of contact could cause the type of injury that you found when you examined the girl's remains?"

"This would require a crushing force with an object, not a mirror flat surface, but with a relatively flat surface," Mitchell explained. "It has to have some sort of coarseness to abrade the skin. It's not absolutely smooth, but overall would tend to be flat."[531]

The prosecutor once again produced the two brick pieces previously identified by Detective Krom. Handing them to the doctor, Kavanagh asked if the bricks could have caused the head injuries to Anna Kithcart.

Mitchell gave a long answer in which he said that the bricks could have been the weapon had they been in one piece when used. The whole piece would also have to have been used at least twice.

Wanting a more concise answer, Kavanagh asked, "But those two pieces are capable of causing that type of injury; is that correct?"

"Yes, sir," Mitchell replied, "the surface has a certain roughness to it that can give you the abrasion of the skin and it has otherwise a basically flat surface that allows it to be used as a tool to compress the face."[532]

Having finished with the pieces of brick, the district attorney next asked the doctor about any cuts or abrasions to the back of Kithcart's head. Mitchell testified that he found no cuts or abrasions anywhere on the rear of her head.[533]

In Jeff Dawson's discussion with the police, he claimed that Kithcart had struck the back of her head when she fell. As he tried to lift her up, he got blood on his hand and panicked. Kavanagh intended to attack this assertion before Dawson could tell it to the jury.

Producing the two sticks that had been found with Kithcart's clothes in the alley a couple of blocks from the crime scene, Kavanagh asked the doctor if either or both of the sticks could have caused the injuries to the side of the girl's face and down her torso. The pathologist conceded that some of the wounds were consistent with these sticks, though he could not state definitively that they had caused them.[534]

Kavanagh now moved to the question of strangulation. Mitchell told the jury that, in addition to the external injuries to the neck, he also discovered internal injuries to the neck as well. The strap muscles of the neck, which function to depress the larynx, or voice box, during speech or swallowing, showed signs of hemorrhage. There was also a fracture to the posterior horn of the larynx itself.

The district attorney asked the doctor if he was able to ascertain the cause of these internal findings. The witness replied grimly, "This is most compatible with manual strangulation."[535]

Under further questioning, Mitchell offered his opinion that the strangulation occurred while the victim was still alive. The hemorrhaging in the strap muscles could only have occurred while the heart was still beating.[536]

He further noted that all of the cuts, wounds, and abrasions were made while Kithcart was still alive with the exception of the insertion of the glass in her neck and some of the letters cut into her legs and torso.[537]

The prosecutor handed his witness two photographs. Mitchell identified them for the jury as photographs of the victim's thighs that showed the "KKK" cut into the skin.

"Do you have an opinion within a reasonable degree of medical certainty," Kavanagh questioned, "as to whether or not any of the injuries that were depicted in those photographs were inflicted after death?"

"Yes, sir," the doctor answered.

"Would you be kind enough to give us the benefit of that opinion, please?"

Mitchell explained to the jury that the cuts on the left thigh showed small blood clots, meaning they were inflicted before death. The cuts on the right thigh were done after death and had no associated bleeding or bruising.[538]

Kavanagh produced an evidence bag containing a piece of slightly curved glass. Mitchell promptly identified it as the same piece of glass he had found sticking in the neck of Anna Kithcart.

"Is that piece of glass that you found in the victim's neck," Kavanagh asked, "capable of causing the marks that you described in the form of the letter K that you found upon this young girl's body?"

"Yes, sir."

The prosecutor asked that the glass be entered into evidence. Lippman objected and asked to briefly question the doctor about it. The judge granted the request and Kavanagh took his seat.

"You are not saying that this piece of glass was actually used to make those lacerations, are you?" Lippman asked.

"I can't prove anything of that nature, no," the doctor admitted. "It is compatible with the object that was used, but I cannot tell you in fact that it did. This piece of glass might have been used or an object with a similar edge."

"In fact," Lippman charged, "those injuries were compatible with having been caused by just about any sharp object?"

"No," Mitchell countered. "There are certain characteristics of those scratches – those incised wounds – that suggests that there be a width to the incising object of approximately that of the glass. So, if you use a razor blade or something of that sort, we would not expect to have that type of injury. So, it is suggestive of an object similar in nature."

"You cannot state, doctor, that this object was used to inflict those incisions, can you?" Lippman persisted.

"That's correct."

Lippman looked to the judge and objected to the glass being formally received. Judge Vogt did not bother waiting for a counter argument. He denied the objection and accepted the glass fragment.[539]

Regardless of whether that specific piece of glass actually caused the cuts on the thighs and abdomen, it was still admissible evidence since it was found inserted into the neck of the victim in a murder. Lippman's attempt to challenge admission of the glass allowed the doctor to add that the wounds were consistent with the size of the glass. It would have been more prudent to concede the point. The defense was not contesting that Kithcart was murdered, but rather that Jeff Dawson was not the one who killed her.

When Lippman returned to his table, the prosecutor stood up and continued his questioning of Mitchell. He only had a few more points to make.

"Can you give an opinion," Kavanagh asked, "as to when these injuries were inflicted in relation to each other?"

"Yes, the injuries appeared to have been caused in a relatively tight time spacing."[540]

Once again, the district attorney was targeting the anticipated defense. Assuming Dawson claimed that another person came along after he left and committed the murder, Kavanagh wanted to narrow the time frame for someone to have done so.

Having made this point, the prosecutor asked Mitchell whether he could offer an opinion as to the cause of death. The doctor replied that the young woman died as the result of both head trauma and strangulation.[541]

Finally, Kavanagh asked about the bite mark on Kithcart's neck and wondered if the doctor was able to tell if she had been bitten before or after death. Based upon the bruising, the pathologist reported that it had definitely been made before death.[542]

"Thank you very much," Kavanagh said politely, before turning toward the judge's bench. "I have no further questions."

Judge Vogt asked the defense attorney if he had any questions. Lippman nodded, knowing that he needed to be careful. This witness had shown during the attorney's brief questioning about the glass fragment that he would not surrender points easily.

Lippman started his questioning by asking whether the bite mark on the victim's neck was consistent with a hickey. Earlier that day, both dentists had deferred to the pathologist when asked a similar question. Ironically, the pathologist announced that he would defer to the dentists.[543]

"With respect to that particular bruise," Lippman continued, "could you estimate the time when that was inflicted or put there?"

"That was a fresh bruise," the doctor said before adding,

"within twenty-four hours of death."

"So that could have happened anytime within one day prior to her death," the attorney asserted. "Is that correct?"

"It would not be possible on pure science alone to place it any more accurately," the doctor replied.

"So, when you testified that all of the wounds occurred within a relatively tight time span, did you mean that they occurred within a period of twenty-four hours of each other?"

Mitchell shook his head as he answered. "The wounds that crushed the face, the bruising that caused the compression of the neck and subsequent fracture of the larynx, and all the other heavy impact injuries all happened in a short time frame."

"As I understand your testimony, doctor," Lippman pressed, unwilling to let the matter drop, "what you meant was that the injuries you consider to have caused death occurred within a relatively short time frame?"

"Yes, sir," the doctor agreed.[544]

Lippman asked if the cut on the right temple in and of itself could have caused death. Mitchell tried avoiding the question by claiming that all the massive trauma to the head made it difficult to be certain. Over the next few minutes, Lippman kept asking whether the cut to the victim's ear was sufficient to cause death, and the doctor avoided answering directly by continually giving long responses about the skull fracture and head wounds.

"Doctor, please just answer the question," Lippman commanded in a tone reflecting his growing frustration. "The tear and bruise of the ear in and of itself could not have caused death, could it?"

Kavanagh stood and objected to the tone of the question, but the judge overruled him and instructed the doctor to answer.

"I would not expect it to cause death in and of itself," Mitchell finally agreed.[545]

"And isn't it possible, doctor," the defense attorney persisted, "that the tear and bruise to the ear occurred prior to any of the other injuries that you observed?"

"Yes, sir," the pathologist responded.

"And isn't it possible, doctor, that the tear and bruise of the ear could have occurred perhaps an hour prior to the injuries which you say caused her death?"

"I guess it's possible."

"It's possible it could have been even more than an hour," Lippman pressed. "Isn't that so?"

"Yes, it could be up to a few hours."[546]

The witness had made Lippman work hard for it, but the attorney had eventually obtained a substantial victory with these concessions. At various points throughout the trial, the prosecutor tried to limit the timeframe of the injuries to blunt Jeff Dawson's possible testimony. Now, Lippman had an admission that the cut to the victim's right ear and temple could have occurred several hours before Kithcart was strangled and bludgeoned.

There was a second and equally important point in this concession. Kavanagh had the pathologist tell the jury that there had been no cuts to the back of Kithcart's head. The purpose of this was to counter the defendant's claim that he felt blood on the back of her head.

However, with a cut to the victim's right ear and right temple, Lippman now had an explanation for blood on the back of the head. The cut on the ear could easily have flowed or dripped onto the back of the girl's head and neck.

In an attempt to further his point, Lippman asked the doctor if a fall could have caused this wound. Mitchell responded that the injury was more likely caused by a blow from an object such as a stick or rod.

Lippman pointed out quite reasonably that the girl could have fallen on a stick and received such a wound. The doctor stubbornly insisted that this was an unlikely fact pattern. However, Lippman eventually forced the doctor to admit that such a scenario was possible.[547]

Leaving this issue behind, the defense attorney asked the pathologist if he had been able to tell if Anna Kithcart had been drinking on the evening of her murder. Mitchell revealed that testing of the victim's blood, urine, and ocular fluid showed that she had an alcohol level over twice the legal limit of intoxication for driving a car.[548]

The attorney asked the doctor to describe some of the physical effects an alcohol level of this nature could cause. The witness once again gave a long answer that talked about various factors such as the drinker's weight, drinking history and so forth. After a little more prodding, Lippman got the doctor to advise the jury that a person with that high an alcohol level would probably have slurred speech, problems with equilibrium and balance, and impairment of judgment.[549]

This was a very solid line of questioning by Lippman. His client told the police that he had pushed Kithcart and she had fallen down and hit her head. If the jury heard this information, either from Jeff Dawson himself or from the tape of his statement to the police, they might find Dawson guilty of manslaughter instead of murder.

However, by introducing the victim's level of alcohol impairment, Lippman was now free to argue to the jury that Dawson's push was minimal and would not have caused her to fall but for the fact that she was drunk. A jury might not come back with a conviction even for manslaughter if they believed this argument.

Lippman was not quite finished with the doctor. He asked

him about the mysterious fluorescent substance found on the legs of the victim that Dr. Harry McNamara had mentioned earlier in the trial. Mitchell confirmed this finding. The doctor told the jury that he had been unable to identify the substance and had no idea if it had been placed on the body before or after death.[550]

Lippman announced to the court that he had no additional questions for this witness. When Kavanagh declined to ask anything further, the doctor was excused.

Judge Vogt informed the jury that the trial was finished for the week. As the coming Monday was Martin Luther King Day, the trial would resume on Tuesday. He cautioned the jurors not to discuss the case and to keep an open mind as more evidence and testimony would be forthcoming.

As the jurors slowly filed out of the courtroom, Lippman felt pretty good about his cross-examination and with some justification. He had done well against a difficult witness and earned some important concessions for his client.

Jeff Dawson had very different thoughts in his mind. He still did not trust his lawyer or the judicial system. He felt the trial was going very poorly and was beginning to realize that he might very well spend the rest of his life in prison.

CHAPTER 25 - BLOOD, HAIR, AND FIBERS

LATE MONDAY EVENING, ROBERT Bruhn, a certified master social worker, met with Jeffrey Dawson inside his cell. Bruhn had been brought in to perform a mental health evaluation.

Earlier that day, Dawson had been found unconscious near his cell. Even though there were no weapons found in the area, guards suspected a possible suicide attempt. Medical personnel were quickly brought in, and the prisoner was revived.

Dawson denied having made any attempt on his own life, but refused to discuss what had actually happened. A doctor cleared Dawson medically. However, given the circumstances, jail officials decided to place their prisoner on suicide watch. This meant that Dawson would have a one-on-one guard watching his every movement.

Dawson was willing to speak with Bruhn even after he learned that it was a psychological exam. Bruhn would later report that, during his interview, Dawson was depressed with a flat affect. A flat affect is a lack of emotional responses to a situation or event that would typically elicit emotion. People with flat affect may appear to be completely unemotional or apathetic.

Dawson maintained that he had not tried to kill himself earlier in the day, but offered that he had made an attempt the previous August. Showing Bruhn a scar on the inside of his right forearm, Dawson admitted that he made the scar with a razor blade in an unsuccessful attempt to slit his wrists.

When asked why he tried killing himself in August, Dawson began talking about his current situation thus offering credence to the belief that he had indeed attempted suicide earlier that day.

"I'm in the middle of a murder trial and it ain't going very well," he said flatly. "I got prior felonies, and the judge is not going to show me any mercy. He's gonna give me the max."[551]

Bruhn tried to get Dawson to talk more about his situation and his feelings, but the prisoner made it clear he was not interested. Given what had transpired earlier in the day, as well as Dawson's admission of a prior suicide attempt, Bruhn had no choice but to recommend a continued suicide watch and a more formal evaluation by a psychiatrist.[552]

When Dawson had spoken out during the investigation and trial, it usually was to profess his innocence or complain about his lawyers and the judicial system. This was the first and only time that he offered any glimpse into his inner thinking. Despite showing no emotion outwardly, the pressure of the trial and the reality of his likely fate was taking its toll.

On Tuesday morning, the trial resumed, and Mike Kavanagh called three witnesses from the New York State Police. The first was Gerald Zoesky, a serologist from the State Police laboratory.

After reviewing his educational qualifications and job-related experiences, Zoesky explained to the jury that a serologist worked to study, identify, and classify bodily fluids such as blood and saliva.[553]

He reported that he performed tests on blood samples

from Anna Kithcart, Jeff Dawson, and Joseph Kiernan. He determined that their blood types were AB, O, and B, respectively.[554]

Kavanagh presented various pieces of evidence one at a time to Zoesky. He examined them and said that he had tested all of them for blood. He determined that there was human blood on the moccasin, washbasin, Styrofoam, and two pieces of brick. He was not able to determine a blood type on any of these samples, as they were too degraded.[555]

He also found human blood on all of the clothing, the white towel, and the sticks found in the alley next to the Royal Grill. He was not able to determine a blood type on any of the objects except for the panties. On those, he determined that the blood was type AB.[556]

He also tested a pair of jeans taken by the police from Jeff Dawson's apartment. On those, he found human blood, but could not determine a type.[557]

Finally, Kavanagh asked the witness about his analysis of the vaginal swab sample taken from the victim. During the autopsy, the pathologist had taken samples of numerous bodily fluids and swabbed various locations and orifices to determine if there were any foreign substances. The witness said he found some human sperm cells during his testing, but they were at least three days old.[558] He did not find seminal fluid, however, and this likely meant that the cells had been deposited at least three days prior, if not more.[559] The finding thus did not appear to be related to the homicide.

Lippman focused on the finding of these sperm cells as he started his questioning.

"Is there any test to your knowledge," he asked, "which can be performed to determine the identity of the person whose sperm that was?"

"Yes."

"What is the name of that test?"

"It's commonly called DNA fingerprinting," Zoesky replied.

"Do you have the equipment to do that test?"

"No," the witness answered, "we do not."[560]

Lippman was disappointed. Had a DNA analysis been done and not showed a match with his client, it would have provided an unknown suspect at whom to point.

He next turned to the jeans found in his client's home and asked the witness to tell the jury how much blood had been found on them. Zoesky answered that he had only found a drop of blood the size of a pinhead.

"Stain the size of a pinhead?" Lippman asked again, feigning surprise.

"That's correct," Zoesky confirmed.

"Considering the amount of blood that you observed on the towel and the clothing and the other items you examined," the attorney pressed, "if you assume that the individual who had committed this crime had in fact been wearing those trousers, wouldn't you expect to find considerably more blood on those trousers?"

Kavanagh immediately objected, and Judge Vogt sustained it. Technically, the judge was correct. The witness was an expert on identifying blood, not an expert on criminology. Either way, Lippman did not care. His question alone made a solid point for the jury to hear. If Dawson had been wearing these jeans when he committed the murder, why were they not completely covered in blood?

As the murmuring reactions to this point continued in the courtroom, Lippman immediately went off in another direction. One of the swabs sent to the State Police lab had been swiped in the victim's nose. Lippman asked Zoesky if that swab had tested positive for cocaine. The witness tried to dodge the question by saying that he had not performed the test himself. It had been done by another technician.[561]

Lippman was not going to let him off the hook. He produced the lab report containing the test results from the nasal swab. After having the witness confirm that the report was an official report from the State Police lab, he asked him to advise the jury of the results of this test. Zoesky relayed that tests had been positive for cocaine.[562]

When Kavanagh was given his chance to again question Zoesky, he produced a lab report concerning analysis of Kithcart's blood. The witness read the report to the jury. Analysis of the victim's blood was negative for cocaine.[563]

This created an odd anomaly. Since no cocaine was in Kithcart's bloodstream, but was present in her nose, there were three possible conclusions. Either she sniffed cocaine just minutes before she was killed or it was inserted into the nose postmortem. The third possibility was that one of the tests was in error calling into question the credibility of the lab. This anomaly has never been resolved to this day.

The defense lawyer had said in front of the jury that more blood than just a pinhead-sized stain should have been present on the defendant's jeans. Kavanagh needed to counter this.

"In your experience as a serologist," the prosecutor asked, "is blood the type of stain that a person can remove from a garment?"

"Yes."

"How?"

"Washing could eliminate a stain," the witness offered.

"If this garment was first put in a swimming pool shortly after the stains were placed on this garment,'" Kavanagh asked in a very leading manner, "would that have an effect on your ability to identify the presence of blood?"

"We would expect it to hinder our identification," Zoesky

said, following the prompt.

"And if it was done within minutes of when the stains were put on the garment, would that impair your ability to locate blood on this garment?"

"Yes."[564]

Kavanagh sat down, confident that he had given the jury a reasonable explanation for the limited amount of blood found on the defendant's jeans.

Lippman rose to ask the witness more questions, but did not inquire about the bloodstains. Instead, he asked Zoesky if he could explain the significance of the positive cocaine findings in the nose, but negative findings in the blood. The serologist responded that he did not have sufficient expertise to answer the question. So, Lippman let it go.

The next witness was a hair and fiber expert named Cathryn Oakes. She testified that she found numerous hairs consistent with Anna Kithcart on the clothes found in the alley.[565] Since the clothes had already been identified as belonging to the victim, this was not really a surprise.

She also said that hair consistent with Kithcart was found on the two bricks previously shown to the jury.[566]

With hair and blood being found on those bricks, along with pathologist Mitchell's testimony, it was becoming quite clear to the jury and all assembled that the bricks were most likely the murder weapons.

Oakes also told the jury that she found hairs on the towel and T-shirts found with the clothes that were consistent with the defendant's chest and head hair.[567] Lippman handled this quite well by having the witness acknowledge that she could not state that it was Jeff Dawson's hair to the exclusion of all others. Rather, it simply meant that the hair came from someone of the same race whose hair was similar.[568]

Of great interest to Lippman was the revelation from the

witness that she found Caucasian hair on the plastic washbasin from the crime scene. Oakes testified that the hair was not consistent with Kiernan's hair samples. She could positively eliminate him as the contributor. She admitted that she had been unable to make any determination as to whose hair it was.[569]

This was another unknown that Lippman could use to his client's advantage. Who else had been there to leave hair on the basin?

Oakes testified that hair was not the only thing she discovered on the evidence. On the jeans and the T-shirt, Oakes found yellow nylon fibers that she felt most likely came from a carpet or rug.[570] She was never provided any carpet samples for comparison, so she could go no further with this area of inquiry. The relevance of this was that the defendant's jeans and the T-shirt found with Kithcart's clothes each had these similar fibers. Therefore, the defendant and the clothes in the alley were definitively connected.

Lippman did not ask many questions about the fibers. His defense was based on his client's statement to the police. In that statement, Dawson admitted he picked up Kithcart's clothes and left them in the alley. To Lippman, the fiber evidence was not contrary to his defense theory.

The last of the State Police lab witnesses was Vincent Rossetti. He testified that he searched for fingerprints on the two brick pieces and the glass fragment found in the victim's neck. He found none, but explained that the surface of bricks is a poor surface for preserving fingerprints.[571]

This testimony really offered nothing against Jeff Dawson one way or the other. Yet, Lippman decided to ask some questions. In a rather clever move, he forced the witness to admit that he had never tested the plastic washbasin for fingerprints, even though plastic is an excellent printing surface.[572]

Unknown hair from a white man or woman had been found on this basin and no attempt to check for prints was undertaken. This was another possible argument for the defense attorney when he made his closing arguments.

With the forensic witnesses done for the day, Kavanagh called Penny DeGroat, the girlfriend of Todd Schleede, to the stand. As she walked to the stand, the expression on her face made it crystal clear that she did not want to testify but had no choice.

Penny DeGroat turned out to be a solid witness for the prosecution. She corroborated much of what Todd Schleede had already told the jury.

She reported that Jeff Dawson, Mark Washington, and her boyfriend were drinking at her home in Ulster Park the evening of July 11. Around 12:30 a.m., Schleede drove the other two back to Kingston and returned about ten to fifteen minutes later. He stayed there the rest of the night.[573]

The next afternoon, she was with Schleede when he picked up Jeff Dawson on Broadway. She confirmed that Dawson had slid down in the back seat when they drove past the police guarding the entrance to the railway bed.[574]

She admitted making an anonymous call to the police to accuse Dawson of murder. She also offered that she had been present in the car when Dawson and Schleede had their fateful conversation on Brewster Street. Unfortunately, she said she was unable to hear what they said.[575]

Lippman started his cross-examination by trying to attack the details of DeGroat's story. The witness responded rather testily, but she maintained her prior testimony. Rather than continue this fruitless strategy, Lippman decided to try to use DeGroat to attack Schleede. He had just the evening before learned something of interest and now planned to use it.

"Are you aware, Miss DeGroat," the defense attorney asked, "that Todd Schleede was arrested and taken into custody by the Ulster County Sheriff's Office on the night before he testified in this case?"

"Yes," she replied. "I don't think he was arrested. They took him, but I never heard a charge. They never gave him his rights or anything like that."

"Were you with him when he was taken into custody?" Lippman continued.

"Yes."

"And isn't it a fact," the attorney alleged, "that he was only released by the Sheriff's Department after a call was made by the District Attorney's Office and the police were directed to release him?"

"I have no way of knowing that," DeGroat replied. "I wasn't home."

"Do you know what he was arrested for?"

"He had too much to drink and was being obnoxious."

"Do you know what the charge was?"

"I never heard him repeat a charge," the witness insisted. "I sat in the car and then I left."

"You don't know what the circumstances were that led to his release that evening?"

"No, I don't. I went home."[576]

Surprisingly, District Attorney Kavanagh never objected during this testimony. Instead, he let the defense attorney make his allegations against his witness and his office. Then, when Lippman was finished, Kavanagh informed the judge that he had no further witnesses planned for the day.

CHAPTER 26 - THE PROSECUTION AND DEFENSE REST

DISTRICT ATTORNEY MIKE KAVANAGH entered the Ulster County Courthouse on Wednesday afternoon knowing this would likely be the final day of his case. He had five witnesses prepared to testify. Four of them would set the foundation for his final exhibit, the audio recording by police of the conversation between Todd Schleede and Jeff Dawson.

The first witness was Mike Jubie, a detective with the Kingston Police Department. He was offered for a slightly different purpose. Jubie was one of the officers who interviewed the defendant prior to his arrest.

Jeff Dawson lied to the police at that first interview about his whereabouts on the night of the murder. He denied ever seeing Anna Kithcart and claimed he had been home with his wife around the time of the crime.

Detective Jubie told the jury about these statements and how he typed them up into a formal statement. The defendant refused to sign the statement, claiming he wanted to speak to a lawyer first.[577]

Kavanagh offered the written statement into evidence, but the judge sustained an objection made by Lippman. Vogt would allow the witness to testify to what he heard, but would not allow an unsigned statement into evidence.[578]

Detective Sergeant Thomas Scarey was the next witness. He explained to the jury how he placed a recording device and transmitter on Schleede in order to record his planned conversation with Dawson.[579]

He testified that there were no signs of tampering with the equipment when he collected the recording later that evening.[580] He then identified the original tape recording so it could be formally entered into evidence.[581]

Kavanagh quickly called two more witnesses: Detective Michael Turck and Investigator Robert Ferrigan. They were necessary witnesses because each at one time or another transported the taped recording. Consequently, this had to be set forth in the record to demonstrate a chain of custody.

Turck had one additional point to make. Over a period of several hours, the detective had listened to the conversation repeatedly and prepared a transcript. Kavanagh entered the transcript into evidence and obtained permission from the judge to allow the jury to read along from it when he played the recording.[582]

Kavanagh's final witness was Christopher Anderson, an audio engineer. He described to the jury how he analyzed and enhanced the original recording from the police. Although he did not change the actual content of the tape, his efforts produced a version that was much easier to hear and understand.[583]

The district attorney offered the enhanced version of the tape into evidence, but Lippman stood to object.

"Your Honor, I'm going to object" the attorney protested. "I don't see any reason why the original can't be produced and played."

Judge Vogt disagreed and granted Kavanagh's request.[584]

Earlier in the afternoon, while the attorneys were meeting with the judge, Anderson set up his equipment to play the taped conversation for the jury. Each juror was provided with an individual headset with extras available for the judge, defendant, and defense attorney.

As Anderson prepared to play both the original and the enhanced versions of the tape, the transcripts prepared by Detective Turck were passed out to the jury.

Judge Vogt took this opportunity to speak with the jury.

"The transcript is merely given to you to assist you in listening to the tape," Vogt said. "If you find a discrepancy between the tape and the transcript, it is the tape that will prevail. The tape is the evidence. The transcript is not evidence in this case."[585]

Satisfied that the jury understood his instructions, the judge turned to Anderson and said, "You may play the tape."

For the next twenty minutes, the men and women of the jury listened to the words of Todd Schleede and Jeff Dawson. A few jurors visibly reacted when they heard Dawson say, "I decided to make it look like…like a psychopath did it."

This was beyond devastating to the defense. Hearing a police officer testify to a defendant's admission is bad. Hearing an admission in the defendant's own voice is much worse.

When the jury finished listening to the tapes and Anderson started collecting the headsets, Mike Kavanagh turned to the judge and said emphatically, "The prosecution rests, Your Honor."[586]

Judge Vogt adjourned court for the day. The defense would start its case at nine thirty the next morning.

Kavanagh's decision to rest his case at that point was interesting. He still had one very significant weapon in his arsenal that he chose not to use, the defendant's recorded statement to the police.

When Dawson spoke to the police after his arrest, he insisted that he had not killed Anna Kithcart. However, he made several significant admissions. He placed himself in the railway bed with Kithcart on the night of the murder. He said he pushed her to the ground causing her to strike her head and become unconscious. He took her clothes and placed them in the alley where they were later found. He wiped blood on his white T-shirt and put it with her clothes.

Had Kavanagh chosen to play this tape to the jury, the defendant's statements would have thoroughly connected him to both crime scenes, as well as to a great deal of the physical evidence. Why had he not done so?

The most likely answer is that the prosecutor was holding it back for rebuttal testimony. In a criminal trial in New York, the prosecution presents its case, and then the defense has the opportunity to present evidence. If the defense chooses to do that, the prosecution is permitted to offer subsequent evidence to rebut.

Based upon Lippman's trial tactics to that point, Kavanagh must have surmised that the defendant planned to testify. Once he did so, the district attorney not only could use the tape for cross-examination, but also could play it during his rebuttal. If this was his strategy, it was not without risk. If Dawson did not testify, Kavanagh would lose his chance to have the jury hear it. It thus seems very clear that the prosecutor fully expected the defendant to testify, as did just about everyone observing the trial.

The next morning, Judge Vogt once again met with the attorneys in chambers before the resumption of testimony. This time, Vogt wanted to discuss the charges he would give to the jury.

At the end of all testimony, a judge will charge the jury. As part of the instructions, the judge states the issues of the case and defines legal terms and concepts for the jury. Both the prosecution and the defense may ask the judge to consider charges or instructions favorable to each side.

Barry Lippman asked Judge Vogt to give the jury the option to consider charges other than murder. The defense attorney suggested manslaughter in the first and second degrees and assault in the third degree.

First-degree manslaughter in New York occurs when a defendant, with intent to cause serious physical injury to another person, causes the death of that person.[587] Basically, to convict on this charge, the jury would have to conclude that Jeff Dawson intended to seriously hurt Kithcart but accidentally went too far and killed her.

Second-degree manslaughter is when a defendant has no intent to kill or injure, but acts recklessly and inadvertently kills someone.[588]

Assault in the third degree is committed when, with intent to cause physical injury to another person, a defendant causes such injury to such person.[589]

By his requests to the court, Barry Lippman was hinting that he intended to argue that his client caused Kithcart's death, but did so accidentally. To effectively make this allegation, however, Lippman would need to have his client testify. Few juries will conclude that a person charged with a brutal murder did not intend to kill without hearing from that person.

Judge Vogt agreed to add both degrees of manslaughter to his jury instructions, but declined to add the assault charge. He did not believe the evidence supported that final request.[590]

When the discussion over jury instructions was completed, Mike Kavanagh informed the others in the judge's chambers that he had something important to disclose.

"Last night," he began, "the Kingston Police Department at ten thirty p.m. received an anonymous telephone call to the effect that Todd Schleede was the person who killed Anna

Kithcart. The police do not know who made the call. The person did not identify themselves, and the person indicated that they had overheard a conversation in which two people, who they did not know and could not name, had in effect made this charge that Schleede was in fact the one who killed Annie Kithcart."[591]

Kavanagh advised that he had a recording of the phone call that he presented to both Lippman and the judge. Although Lippman was given a chance to make any motions once he listened to the tape, all three men understood that nothing would likely come from this without something more.

Before the completion of the conference, Lippman informed the judge that he required guidance from the court. The day before, Lippman had met with Jeff Dawson to discuss additional trial strategy. His client had a witness he wanted presented, but Lippman was not at all certain that this witness would be permitted by the court.

Dawson wanted him to call Jeremiah Flaherty, the first defense attorney assigned to the case. Judge Vogt immediately asked Lippman to explain the relevance of his intended testimony.

"I asked him (Dawson) what information he would have relevant to this case," Lippman answered. "He represented to me that Flaherty had told him that he had been shown some hoods and cloaks at the District Attorney's Office, that had been apparently used by the people responsible for this murder."

Kavanagh groaned audibly upon hearing this allegation. He knew the claim was untrue and had no desire to once again deal with wild racially based conspiracy theories. The Reverend Al Sharpton and his colleagues had not inserted themselves in this case for many weeks, and he wanted to keep it that way.

Before he could voice an objection, Lippman started

speaking again. He said that his client allegedly was further told by Flaherty that the District Attorney's Office had in fact made an unknown deal with Todd Schleede for his testimony.

The district attorney started to object, but was immediately interrupted by defense counsel.

"I spoke with Mr. Flaherty last night," Lippman said, "and he adamantly denied that he ever made such a statement to the defendant and he denied that he was ever given any such information by anyone at the District Attorney's Office."

Seeing Kavanagh relax in his chair, Lippman continued. "On that basis, I don't think it is appropriate for me to call him. I want to get some guidance from the court."

What Lippman was doing was making a record to protect himself in case his client filed a complaint against him. Criminal clients often file complaints against their assigned counsel contending that they either conspired with the district attorney or refused to present a proper defense.

Lippman knew that Flaherty was not a proper witness. Since he already knew that Flaherty would not testify to Dawson's allegations, he would not have a good faith basis to call him to the stand. Moreover, he would be left having to impeach his own witness, and that is rarely, if ever, permitted.[592]

By making his request to the court before attempting to call Flaherty as a witness and obtaining a legal ruling, he could report to his client that he tried to do as instructed, but the judge would not permit it.

Frank Vogt was an experienced trial court judge. He knew exactly what Lippman was doing and understood his ethical dilemma. He ruled that Flaherty would not be permitted to testify.[593]

When the parties returned to court and the jury was seated, Lippman called Detective Junious Harris as the first defense witness. His testimony was extremely brief. Lippman wanted it on the record that his client had requested to speak with a lawyer when he was questioned the first time. Harris conceded the point.[594]

This fact was important due to New York's rule on considering the voluntariness of a defendant's statements. Even though the judge makes a determination that a statement was not taken in violation of an accused's constitutional rights, the question of whether that statement was made voluntarily still is presented to the jury to decide.

Although Kavanagh had not submitted Dawson's partial confession to the jury, Lippman still planned to argue that his client's statements to Todd Schleede, an agent of the police, were involuntary. Dawson's request for a lawyer was a part of his intended argument.

As Detective Harris walked out of the courtroom, Lippman stood as if to call his next witness. However, to the surprise of many, he simply announced, "The defense rests, Your Honor."[595]

The defendant's declining to testify was either a colossal mistake or a "Hail Mary" type of gamble. What is not known is whether this was strategy from the defense lawyer or if Dawson himself refused to testify against the advice of his attorney. It is always the defendant's absolute right to testify. Only the defendant may waive that right, though many rely heavily upon their attorney's advice one way or the other.

In this case, the defendant had to testify, especially if there was any hope at all of the jury convicting on something other than the murder charge. To convict on less than murder, the jury needed to hear from the defendant himself that he never intended to kill.

The pathologist had testified that the strangulation occurred after the victim was severely beaten about the head and neck with bricks and a stick. This allegation presents an image of a cold and heartless murderer, not someone who killed accidentally.

Without hearing the defendant's recorded statement to the police and without hearing from the defendant, the jury had not been presented with a theory of accidental death other than by occasional references by Lippman.

The only possible strategy in not allowing Dawson to testify was to gamble everything on an outright acquittal. Kavanagh had never presented the defendant's recorded statement that linked him to the crime scene, the alley where the clothes were found, and to the victim herself. Without this, the only strong evidence against Dawson was Todd Schleede and the forensic dentist. Perhaps Lippman felt this was simply not enough and convinced his client to roll the dice. Perhaps Dawson just refused to testify. Either way, it was a huge gamble and likely a mistake.

The other question at this point was why Lippman did not call Joseph Kiernan to the stand. He had issued him a subpoena, but decided not to follow through.

Kiernan would certainly have been advised to plead the Fifth Amendment by his attorney and refuse to answer questions about whether he had molested the corpse. While a criminal defendant may refuse to take the stand and answer questions, a witness who has not been charged must take the stand if called. He or she may refuse to answer, citing the Fifth Amendment, but must do so on a question by question basis.

That Kiernan found the body was not something that would incriminate him. This would let the jury know he had been in the railway bed with the body.

Kiernan would have denied committing the murder. That was the one fact he maintained continually without exception. However, the local newspaper contained a statement made by the police chief contending that Kiernan admitted that he had cut up the body.[596] Would Kiernan admit this, deny it, or take the Fifth? No matter which he chose, it would have been a win for the defense.

If he admitted it, then Kiernan placed himself within the narrow time frame for the murder. If he took the Fifth, that would be tantamount to an admission. If he denied it, then he was calling the police chief a liar. If the police falsely claimed that Kiernan made an incriminating statement, then the same argument could be made against any statements the police claimed against Dawson.

The newspapers and the local radio stations had repeated statements from Kiernan wherein he had claimed to be employed as an undercover agent with the CIA. If Kiernan admitted these prior statements or, even better, made this pronouncement to the jury, this would show without question that he was mentally unbalanced.

All of this would have allowed defense counsel to argue to the jury that a mentally disturbed man, with no real alibi, was in the railway bed on the evening/morning of the murder. This same man had made admissions to the police of sexually molesting the corpse. Add in the accusation from Chief James Riggins that Kiernan apparently admitted cutting the body and the chance Kiernan might take the Fifth Amendment on the witness stand, and a juror could have reasonable doubt.

It cannot be said that calling Kiernan would mean an automatic acquittal. Trials are always unpredictable, and juries often surprise. Yet, the potential benefits of Kiernan testifying required that he be called by the defense.

Nevertheless, with no more witnesses to be called by either side, Judge Vogt advised, "I'll take the closing arguments."[597]

CHAPTER 27 - SUMMATIONS

IN A CRIMINAL TRIAL, the defense gives its closing argument first. Many consider this to be blatantly unfair. The prosecution gives the initial opening statement and gets to close out the trial with its closing summation. They get the first and final word.

If there is any advantage for the accused in a trial, it is that the district attorney bears the entire burden of proof. A defendant does not have to prove anything, and is presumed to be completely innocent unless and until the prosecution proves guilt beyond a reasonable doubt. If there is even one reasonable doubt, the defendant must be found not guilty.

Defense attorney Barry Lippman focused on this important point right from the start of his summation. He also told the jury that they could not hold it against the defendant that he did not testify. He promised the jurors that they would receive the same instructions from the judge.[598]

This was not a prediction. Trial judges are required by law to include these instructions in their jury charge. Defense attorneys always include this language in their presentations. They start with it in jury selection and keep referring to it whenever they can.

When he finished discussing the presumption of innocence, Lippman told the jury that the case was actually quite simple. In fact, the defense conceded a great deal of the evidence.

"We don't dispute that a murder was committed," he continued. "We don't dispute that it took place somewhere in the area behind the Kingston Hospital. We don't dispute what caused the death."[599]

Lippman then announced that there would be no dispute to the findings of the medical examiner, or that a nurse called the police, or that a security guard patrolled the path earlier in the evening.

"The only issue in this case," the defense attorney told the jurors, "is who committed this murder. Who is the person, or who are the persons, who committed this crime? And when you address yourself to that issue, you will see that the prosecution's case rises and falls with Todd Schleede."[600]

With this brief statement, Lippman's strategy became crystal clear. He may have asked the judge for lesser charges of manslaughter, but he had no intention of arguing that. It had been a ruse. Instead, he was going for a full acquittal. To get it, he planned to destroy Todd Schleede.

"Well, what do we know about Todd Schleede?" Lippman asked reflectively.

He paused momentarily for effect before continuing. "Todd Schleede is a convicted felon. He has been convicted for the sale of drugs. He has been convicted of burglary. He has been convicted of other crimes. He told you he lived off his parents. He lived off his girlfriend. He was on parole. He wasn't working at the time of this crime."[601]

Lippman continued ripping into Schleede for several minutes, making various references to his prison record. He then moved to Schleede's girlfriend, Penny DeGroat. He accused her and Schleede of making up a story together to get Jeff Dawson out of their lives.

"It's very clear that Todd Schleede and Penelope DeGroat didn't like Jeff Dawson and didn't want him around,"

Lippman accused. He speculated that DeGroat wanted Dawson and Schleede's other friends out of the picture, so she could have the man she loved all to herself.[602]

The defense attorney pointed out to the jurors that neither Schleede nor DeGroat contacted the police on the day Dawson supposedly admitted to murder. They did not report it on the second day, the third day, or even the fourth day; it was not reported until the fifth day, Lippman told them. Even then, he noted, it was done with an anonymous phone call.[603]

Lippman did an effective job assailing Schleede's credibility and his first conversation with Dawson. The second conversation was more problematic because it was on tape. This did not stop the defense counsel from continuing to blame Schleede.

"Bear in mind," Lippman said, "if you listen to the statement, Todd Schleede is the one that does all the talking on this tape."[604]

He further assaulted the credibility of the conversation by pointing out that Dawson's only words in the conversation about the murder were inconsistent with the scientific evidence. On the tape, Dawson was heard to say that Annie Kithcart fell, hit the back of her head, and died. The medical examiner had told the jury that Annie died from strangulation and wounds on the front of her head. There were no wounds on the back of her head.

"If Jeffrey Dawson confided in Todd Schleede that he committed a murder, wouldn't he have told him how he actually did it?" Lippman asked.[605]

This was a shrewd argument. Lippman was not asking the jury to ignore his client's words. Instead, he wanted them to find that his client's statement was not credible. Dawson was not admitting to a murder. He was telling Todd Schleede what he thought Schleede wanted to hear to make him go away. It was perhaps the only way to get around his client's recorded words.

"You know, there are many, many questions that I would like to go into here," Lippman said starting to wrap things up, "but I am not going to into everything. There are some questions that you really have to ask yourselves."[606]

The first question Lippman posed was why Jeff Dawson's fingerprints were not found anywhere in or around the crime scene. Experts processed the bricks and pieces of glass. Dawson's prints were not found.[607]

The attorney wondered aloud why the washbasin was never processed for prints. He questioned why the sperm sample found in the vaginal swab was not tested for DNA to identify the contributor.[608]

Some hair samples found were considered consistent with Jeff Dawson's hair. Why, Lippman questioned, were they never compared with Todd Schleede, who, like Dawson, was also African-American?[609]

Lippman was throwing question after question at the jury hoping that just one of them would refuse to convict with so much unknown about the murder. He had still more points for them to consider.

"We know that cocaine was found in the nose and yet no cocaine was found in the blood test," the attorney asserted. "How is cocaine usually taken? The witness testified that it is usually taken in through the nose and it would then go into the bloodstream."

"Could he explain the inconsistency?" Lippman asked philosophically before answering his own by question by sarcastically noting that this question had been beyond the expertise of the witness.[610]

He then asked about the unknown fluorescent substance found on the victim's thighs during the autopsy. "This was never explored in terms of the investigation of this case," Lippman noted. "It was never explained by the prosecution in this case." Why was more not done to explain this odd finding, he asked.[611]

The next point was motive. Lippman reminded everyone that District Attorney Mike Kavanagh started the trial by admitting that he could not prove a motive. However, Lippman argued that the real motive was obvious.

"Anna Kithcart was wearing a necklace. Anna Kithcart was wearing a pin," he reminded the jury. "They are missing. They were taken and were never recovered. This was a robbery."[612]

Lippman accused the prosecution of ignoring this obvious motive. He pointed out that the railway bed was a known hangout for bums, drug addicts, and other menaces to society. Robbery was a real theory that had been ignored.

Finally, Lippman brought up Joseph Kiernan. He only mentioned him briefly. "He was there at six forty-five a.m.," he said. "Was he there at three forty-five a.m.? Could he have been there a couple of hours before and then come back? What contact did he have?"[613]

This was a good start, but Lippman said nothing more about the disturbed vagrant. Frankly, Kiernan should have been the main focus of his closing argument. He was not called as a witness, but he was still a major issue worthy of further discussion. Trial observers had been expecting Lippman to accuse Kiernan of being the murderer. The fact that he was a mentally unbalanced derelict accused of doing terrible things to the victim's body and that he had no alibi made him the perfect straw man to attack. Lippman chose not to do so.

"I am sure," the attorney continued, "you have questions of your own about the evidence that creates reasonable doubts. If you consider this fairly and honestly, I think you will find there is more than a reasonable doubt in this case. I ask that you return a verdict of not guilty. Thank you."

Lippman walked back to the defense table and sat down. He turned to his client, but Jeff Dawson refused to even look at him. For the past few days, Dawson had become sullen and extremely quiet. His wife frequently tried to talk to him during the breaks, but court security had not permitted her to get near her husband.

At the prosecution table, Kavanagh stood and walked toward the jury. Even though Lippman had not discussed the possible manslaughter charges, Kavanagh was not taking any chances. After a brief introduction where he thanked the jurors for their service and attention, Kavanagh wasted no time announcing he wanted the jury to convict Dawson of murder.

"Mr. Lippman in his summation candidly indicated to you that they have no quarrel with the fact that this girl was murdered. Murder, plain and simple," Kavanagh noted. "The condition of this girl's body was laid out to you in sordid detail. Dr. Mitchell testified to an exhaustive examination of her remains. He described to you the injuries found on this girl."

"He told you that she had been struck violently and forcibly with a crushing blow from a hard object to the forehead, and it may have happened more than once. It was a devastating, deadly blow that caused catastrophic injury to this girl."[614]

Kavanagh picked up the two pieces of brick found at the scene and showed them to the jury. "This cinder block was found covered in blood and covered with Anna Kithcart's head hair," he charged. "Is there any doubt that this is what was used to smash and crush her skull?"[615]

Setting the bricks down, Kavanagh continued his gory description. "Whoever did this to this girl wasn't satisfied with maiming, mutilating, and crushing her skull. He [Dr.

Mitchell] told you that she was also smashed in the face with a violent devastating blow that loosened her jaw, broke her nose, and loosened her teeth, and caused her to bleed profusely from the face."[616]

The prosecutor reminded the jury that the pathologist testified that all of these injuries were inflicted while she was still alive. He also referred to Mitchell's opinion that Annie Kithcart had been choked while she was alive, but after the beating to her skull.

"Whoever did this was not satisfied with maiming her, mutilating her, or assaulting her," Kavanagh thundered. "He then took her with his hands and crushed her larynx by strangling her to death."[617]

Kavanagh's purpose was clear. These horrible injuries were not done for any purpose other than cold-blooded murder. He continued his point by describing the letters KKK cut into her thighs. It was started while the victim was still alive and continued after her death.[618]

Referring for the first time to Todd Schleede, Kavanagh cited his testimony and Dawson's words on the recorded conversation that these wounds were done to make it look like a psychopath was the culprit.

"Where he is wrong," Kavanagh countered, "is that it wasn't done to look like a psychopath. It was done by a psychopath. As a result of what he did, a nineteen-year-old girl lies dead, the victim of a brutal, horrible murder."[619]

The district attorney was seeking a murder conviction and only a murder conviction. His vivid recounting of the terrible injuries suffered by Kithcart likely ended any possibility of the jury considering manslaughter. He and Lippman were both in agreement. The verdict would be either murder or a full acquittal.

Next, Kavanagh addressed the subject of Joseph Kiernan.

Lippman had made a passing reference to Kiernan possibly being the killer. Though he had not pushed this accusation hard, Kavanagh decided to push back.

"It was put forth before you in this trial that Joseph Kiernan admitted to the Kingston Police Department that he sodomized the girl's corpse," the prosecutor said somberly. "There is no question that he did an unspeakable, horrible thing, and he will be prosecuted for that. But, the evidence in this case established beyond question that Joseph Kiernan didn't kill this poor soul."[620]

To support his claim, Kavanagh pointed out that Kiernan's clothes had been tested for blood and hairs consistent with Kithcart, but none were found. He suggested to the jury that, had Kiernan committed the murder, there would have been a substantial amount of blood found. The man had stayed in the area after reporting his grisly find and never had the chance to change clothes.[621]

The district attorney further argued that Kiernan was also eliminated as a suspect by Mofson, the forensic dentist. Mofson testified to a bite on Kithcart's neck. Kiernan could not have made this bite, as he had almost no teeth.[622]

Switching to the defendant, Kavanagh made careful note of Mofson's opinion that Jeff Dawson was the one who made the bite. Referring to the pathologist's opinion that all of the wounds had been made within a short period of time, the prosecutor claimed the bite proved Dawson was the killer.[623]

Satisfied that he had explained away Kiernan, Kavanagh next addressed the allegations made by defense counsel against Todd Schleede. Lippman had called him a felon, criminal, and parolee. The prosecutor did not deny any of it.

"We told you he is a convicted felon, a thief, a burglar, and a person whose word has to evaluated very carefully and scrutinized very carefully," Kavanagh explained, "not someone upon whom you should rely to make an important decision."[624]

"I tell you now," he continued, "that if it was simply Todd Schleede's word and no other evidence in this case, you could not convict any person of any crime. You could not base an important decision simply upon what that man said. That is why the Kingston Police wired Todd Schleede."[625]

It was the tape, Kavanagh argued, that made Schleede's testimony credible. He stressed that the jury should listen to the tape and hear Dawson tell them in his own words how he took a knife and made it look like a psychopath did it.

Kavanagh's argument seemed sound. The police wired Schleede to get a statement from Dawson because without it, Schleede's word was just not enough. Then, the prosecutor went further in an attempt to convince the jury that Todd Schleede's entire testimony should be believed. He told them they should believe him because he was on parole.

"Do you honestly believe that a parolee, a person with so much at stake in terms of his personal freedom, would at that point in his life, intentionally mislead the Police Department in a major investigation?" Kavanagh asked.

For several minutes, the prosecutor repeatedly suggested Schleede would not risk going back to prison just to frame Dawson. He would not risk lying to the police. It was almost comical to hear a district attorney argue that a person on parole would never lie to the police.

"Ladies and gentlemen of the jury, ask yourselves, does that make any sense? Would a parolee lie? Would he get on the stand under those circumstances and lie when it would be so easy to verify?" Kavanagh asked, "No. Schleede didn't lie to you."[626]

He insisted that Schleede told the truth about his contacts with Dawson, but not because he was concerned about the community or wanted to see justice done. Instead, he asserted that Schleede was honest because he had no choice. He was forced to wear the wire, cooperate, and be honest. He also contended that the testimony of his girlfriend, Penny DeGroat, supported and confirmed his account.[627]

When Kavanagh finished his long discussion about Schleede, he turned to the forensic evidence from the railway bed. He discussed the blood, fiber, and hair evidence. He referred to the bricks and the blood and hair found on them.[628]

He talked about the bloodstained clothing found in the alley a few blocks away. These were identified by Kithcart's mother as the clothes the victim wore on the night she was killed. Also found in the pile of clothes was a man's white T-shirt that was covered in blood. Kavanagh held up the bloody T-shirt for the jury to see.

"Now this shirt was worn by the person who murdered Anna Kithcart," he announced. "This shirt contains heavy traces of blood all over."[629]

Kavanagh reminded the jury that Dawson's wife testified that her husband had been wearing a white T-shirt on the evening of the murder. However, when he came home, he had no shirt at all. The prosecutor suggested to the jury that Dawson, covered in blood after bludgeoning and strangling the young girl, removed his shirt and left it with his victim's clothes. To cement his point, he highlighted the testimony of Cathy Oakes. She said she found hairs on that shirt consistent with Jeff Dawson's chest hairs.[630] Just as he promised in his opening statement, Kavanagh was demonstrating that the T-shirt was Jeff Dawson's shirt.

When finished with the forensics, Kavanagh started his final point. While the police were recovering the clothing in the alley, Jeff Dawson and his wife were at the police station giving a statement. However, he noted, the statements were lies.

"Why would they lie about what he was doing that night?"

the district attorney asked the jury. "Why would he lie about any contact he had with Anna Kithcart?"[631]

Kavanagh answered his own question. He told the jurors that Rose Dawson lied to protect her husband. As for Jeff Dawson, he lied because he brutally murdered Kithcart, hid her clothes in an alley, and rinsed off her blood in his neighbor's pool.

"If you look at everything that we have established regarding what this man did," he continued, "while this investigation was going on every step of the way, he comported and carried himself like a killer, like a man who had something to hide. Every step of the way, his effort was to hide evidence, to hide involvement, and to cover up any contact he had with Anna Kithcart. And but for the tape recording and but for the outstanding work of the Kingston Police Department and Medical Examiner's Office, he may very well have succeeded."[632]

"Ladies and gentlemen of the jury," Kavanagh said, starting to wrap up his remarks, "it is not Todd Schleede who convicted this defendant of murder. It is not the chemist who convicted this defendant of murder. It is not the Kingston Police Department who convicted this defendant of murder. It is the defendant in his very own words uttered to a person who was being monitored by the Kingston Police Department."

"He was wrong in only one respect, when he told Todd Schleede, 'I did it because I wanted to make it look like a psychopath,'" Kavanagh said, his voice starting to rise with emotion. "It didn't look like a psychopath did it. It was the product of a psychopath's acts. What he did to this girl was what a psychopath would do to a nineteen-year-old girl under those circumstances."[633]

After thanking the jury for their attention, Kavanagh asked the jury to identify Jeff Dawson as Annie Kithcart's killer and to convict him of murder.[634]

Both attorneys offered effective presentations and scored points with the jury. They also made some questionable decisions on what to argue and what not to argue. While Judge Vogt started his lengthy jury instructions, each attorney sat quietly hoping he had done enough to win.

CHAPTER 28 – THE DECISION

IT WAS APPROXIMATELY 11:00 p.m. on Thursday, January 19, 1989, and all parties were back in court to hear the jury's unanimous verdict. The jurors had been deliberating off and on for nearly eight and a half hours.

On three prior occasions, the court clerk called the attorneys back to court. Each time, the jury had sent a note to Judge Vogt seeking clarifications and readback of testimony. Whenever this happens, the prosecution, defense, and courtroom observers all try to read the tea leaves and speculate exactly what the jurors are thinking and how they are leaning.

The first note was believed to be positive for the defense. The jury wanted to hear both the original and enhanced recordings of the conversation between the defendant and Todd Schleede.[635]

During his summation, Barry Lippman sought to convince the jurors that the entire case against Dawson was the credibility of Schleede. He wanted them to focus exclusively on this point. The jury's note caused many to assume that he might well have succeeded.

After a nearly twenty-minute delay caused by the necessity of setting up the necessary equipment, both tapes were played in their entirety. When finished, Judge Vogt asked if the jury was satisfied and ready to resume its deliberation.

"I believe so, Your Honor" the jury's foreman replied

before surprisingly adding, "We do have two more requests, please."[636]

Judge Vogt asked that the requests be made in writing to properly preserve them for the official record. The foreman quickly complied.

The first request was for a chalkboard and chalk. This was granted without further comment.

The second request was for a further explanation of the charges against the defendant with use of layman's terms. Judge Vogt explained that he was obligated to stay with the statutory language. If he varied too far from it, he might possibly convey the wrong impression.

The judge offered to again read the charges and legal explanations. This seemed to satisfy the jurors.[637]

About an hour after deliberations resumed, the court received another note. This note again asked for clarification of the law, but specified that they wanted to hear only about intentional murder.[638]

This seemed to support the positions set forth by both legal counsel. The verdict was either going to be guilty of murder or a full acquittal. There would be no middle ground.

Judge Vogt reread the law on intentional murder. When done, he looked up from his papers and asked, "Now, does that answer the juror's question?"

The foreman, speaking for the jury, replied, "I believe so, sir."

"All right," the judge said, looking up at the clock. "I think we'll send you out to dinner. So, why don't you take a break for a few minutes."

Several of the jurors mouthed, "Thank you" at the offer.

Before leaving the bench, Vogt said. "I trust the clerk has made all the necessary arrangements. If you don't like your dinner, you can blame it on him."[639]

At 9:20 p.m., approximately two hours after the jury finished eating and resumed deliberations, a third note appeared. This time, the jury wanted to hear the recorded conversation again. They also asked to have another readback of Schleede's testimony. Specifically, they wanted only the portion of his testimony in which he described the first conversation he had with Dawson.[640]

When the stenographer finished reading the requested testimony, the technicians stood to play the tape. Judge Vogt waved them off. Rather than have the tape played for the third time, he ordered a cassette player brought to jury room. He instructed the jurors that they would be free to listen to the conversation in the jury room as many times as needed.

Whether or not Judge Vogt was being as accommodating as possible for the jury, or was just sick and tired of hearing the same tape replayed is not known. Regardless, there were no other notes from the jury until they announced at nearly 11:00 p.m. that they had reached a verdict.

There was palpable tension as the jurors slowly took their seats. The prosecutor and defense counsel sat on the very front edge of their seats, anxious to learn the result of their hard work. The families of both the victim and the defendant were clearly tense as Judge Vogt started the proceedings. Rose Dawson, the defendant's wife, sat in the front row against the rail, directly behind her husband. Throughout the trial, she sat as close to Jeff as the court officers would allow. She was visibly shaking.

Only Jeff Dawson seemed calm. His face was expressionless.

The strained silence was broken by the court clerk. He loudly asked the jury if they had reached a verdict.

The foreman stood and replied, "We have."

As had been explained by the judge earlier that day, the jury could only reach the lesser included charges of manslaughter if they acquitted the defendant of intentional murder and then acquitted him of murder based on reckless disregard for human life. Once they found the defendant guilty of any charge, they would go no further. So, the court clerk moved to the first count of the indictment.

"How do you find the defendant with respect to the first count of this indictment, murder in the second degree?"

The foreman cleared his throat before saying, "Guilty."[641]

There were audible gasps in the courtroom. Some pumped their fists in approval while others started crying. Rose Dawson initially said nothing. She slowly leaned forward on the wooden courtroom bench and buried her head in her hands as the tears came.[642]

Jeff Dawson offered no outward reaction other than to turn his head slightly to the left. He maintained a stoic expression and said nothing.[643]

Barry Lippman stood and asked the court to poll the jury. Customarily, after a guilty verdict, the defense attorney requests that each juror be required to give his or verdict aloud. The hope is that one juror might have second thoughts. This almost never happens, though the defense has nothing to lose by trying. All twelve members of the jury maintained their guilty verdicts.

The jury was excused and left the courtroom. When they were out of the room, Judge Vogt scheduled sentencing for February 25 and adjourned. The sheriff's deputies stepped forward and began shackling Dawson for his trip back to the jail. The defendant's sister, Joyce Dawson, tried to hug her brother, but the guards prevented her. The deputies completed their work and escorted their prisoner out the door.

"Jeffrey," Joyce called after her brother, "I love you, and we're going to fight for an appeal." Dawson looked back and just quietly shook his head.[644]

The family of Anna Kithcart declined to answer any questions as they left the courtroom. Though they were pleased that her killer had been convicted, it still would not bring her back to them.

Outside the courtroom, members of the media scrambled for quotes. Barry Lippman offered very little other than to say, "All we ever asked for was a fair trial, and I think we received it."[645]

Mike Kavanagh stopped in front of a group of reporters saying, "I think the case against this fellow was overwhelming and the evidence was devastating. It is just a reflection of outstanding police work by the Kingston Police Department."[646]

As for the Police Department, Chief James Riggins summed up their collective feelings, as well as the feelings of many Kingstonians, when he said, "I'm truly glad it's over."[647]

Thirty-seven days later, on February 25, Jeff Dawson stood with his attorney before Judge Frank Vogt for his sentencing. The judge wasted little time getting straight to business.

"Is the defendant ready for sentencing?"

"Your Honor," Barry Lippman replied as he stood, "Mr. Dawson has indicated to me that he would like a one-week adjournment."

"Why?" Vogt asked, a quizzical look on his face.

"He wishes to review many of his papers and listen to the tapes."

"Denied," the judge responded immediately. "Any other reason to show why sentence should not be pronounced?"

"No, Your Honor," Lippman replied quietly.

Judge Vogt turned in his chair toward District Attorney Mike Kavanagh. It is customary for both sides to make a statement before imposition of sentence. Kavanagh stood ready with his presentation.

"Your Honor, as the court is well aware, this defendant has what can only be described as an atrocious prior criminal record. He has had numerous and substantial contact with the criminal justice system. I only mention that to point out that, in our opinion, there's absolutely no hope for redemption or rehabilitation here, even forgetting what he has done in this particular instance. This defendant quite frankly is a career criminal.

"This was one of the most brutal and savage killings I have ever been exposed to in the eighteen years I have been in the business. The court has seen the photographs of Anna Kithcart's remains. They are startling and vivid proof as to the measure of violence this defendant inflicted upon her. Not being satisfied with simply crushing her skull and strangling her to death, the defendant defaced her remains with those obscene markings on her thighs and abdomen.

"In light of his prior history and in light of the heinous nature of the crime for which he stands convicted, it is our recommendation to the court most respectfully that the maximum period of confinement of twenty-five years to life be imposed as a sentence."[648]

When Kavanagh completed his remarks, Judge Vogt swiveled his chair back to the defense table. "Mr. Lippman, is there anything you care to say?"

The attorney stood and cleared his throat before addressing the court. "I would just point out to Your Honor that, as I reviewed the presentence report, and I do not quarrel with the facts that are set forth therein, but I notice an absence in that report of any reference to the facts and circumstances giving rise to this particular incident. Perhaps we will never know exactly how this happened, but I think…"

"The defendant refused to be interviewed by the person

preparing this report, right?" Judge Vogt interrupted.

"Apparently, Your Honor," Lippman replied, showing just a hint of annoyance. Lippman waited for a second to make sure the judge had nothing further to offer. Then, he continued his statement.[649]

"Your Honor, the evidence at trial indicated that the defendant had been drinking that evening. The victim had a very high degree of alcohol in her system. There was evidence of cocaine having been inhaled or in the nasal cavities. The tape indicated that the defendant had 'bugged out,' or whatever the expression was.

"It would seem to suggest some question of the state of mind of the defendant at the time. He was perhaps high on alcohol. Both parties perhaps suffered the effects of drugs and alcohol. That is the evidence in this case, Your Honor.

"It does raise some questions as to the state of mind of the defendant at the time of this incident and certainly should be considered by the court in imposing sentence."[650]

Vogt now directed his attention to the defendant. "Mr. Dawson," the judge asked, "is there anything you care to say prior to the imposition of sentence?"

For the first time in the entire trial, Jeff Dawson spoke. "You are not going to give me a postponement? I need a postponement because I just got my paperwork and stuff today. I haven't had a chance to go over them. I haven't had a chance to go over the case. I won't get a chance unless you give me a postponement."

"I see no reason why I should give you a postponement, Mr. Dawson," Vogt replied. "You have had a month to do these things."

"I had a month?" Dawson asked incredulously. "I wrote you a letter. I gave you a letter when I was here last. I didn't get the papers until today. I wrote you."

The judge was not convinced. "I don't see how that would in any way affect the sentence which I am about to impose, Mr. Dawson. I assume you want this matter for appellate purposes. Anything else you care to say?"

Dawson glared at the judge for a moment before speaking. "I got nothing to say," he offered glumly.

Judge Vogt straightened himself in his chair and pronounced the sentence of the court.

"The incident leading to this indictment is an extremely brutal murder of a young woman. There is absolutely no explanation as to why this happened. There was never any evidence introduced with respect to motive, and, to be perfectly frank, in light of the brutality here, I think this is a situation that calls for the maximum. There are certainly no mitigating circumstances here whatsoever.

"Granted, I don't know what caused Mr. Dawson to do this. I am certainly satisfied in light of the overwhelming proof elicited during the course of the trial that he did it. There is no question in my mind about that. Why he did it, I don't know. I don't know that he had been drinking that night. I don't know that he was using drugs. All I know is that a young lady was assaulted brutally, about as brutal a thing as I have seen in my thirty years in this business.

"Also, his [Dawson's] record is atrocious, and I agree with the district attorney when he describes this man as a career criminal. Most of his life has been spent in some correctional institution. Why that happened might be of interest to a sociologist, but as far as I'm concerned, he represents a clear and present danger to this community when he's walking around free. That is what I have to contend with.

"So, in light of the brutality of this homicide and the atrocious record on the part of the defendant, it is the judgment of this court, Mr. Dawson, that you be sentenced to an indeterminate period of imprisonment, the maximum of which shall be the rest of your natural life, the minimum of which shall be twenty-five years."[651]

With a quick bang of the gavel, court was adjourned and the proceedings concluded. As the defendant was led out of the courtroom, a reporter asked him if he felt he got a fair trial.

Dawson looked up and said, "If you really want to know, come up to the jail and see me."[652] He would later decline two requests filed with the jail for an interview.

The courtroom emptied quickly. Reporters scrambled to follow the defendant and the attorneys hoping for great quotes for the evening edition. The last person to leave the courtroom was the defendant's sister, Joyce. She was the only member of Dawson's family who attended that day. In fact, she had not missed a single day of the trial.

She had not said a word or even reacted when the judge imposed sentence, choosing instead to try to keep a brave face for her brother. As she walked out alone, her emotions burst out of her, unable to be contained. As tears streamed across her face, she said more to herself than anyone else, "My baby brother didn't do it."[653]

CHAPTER 29 - KIERNAN'S FATE

A FEW DAYS AFTER Jeff Dawson received his sentence, Joseph Kiernan was back in Kingston City Court. His case was scheduled once again for a hearing on whether his alleged statement to the police was given voluntarily or if it should be suppressed.

There was just one minor problem. For the fifth consecutive time, Kiernan's attorney, Alton Maddox, did not show up. Judge Mike Bruhn, upon taking the bench, noted that he had been informed that Maddox was on call for a trial in Brooklyn and thus could not attend.

Indeed, Alton Maddox did have a case in Brooklyn that day. His client was the Reverend Al Sharpton. Sharpton had been charged with disorderly conduct related to a December 21, 1987, "Day of Outrage" demonstration during the racially charged trial of white teenagers in the killing of a black man. The march by hundreds of protesters snarled subways and partially closed the Brooklyn Bridge.[654]

As it turned out, Maddox's case that day ended up being adjourned due to the absence of Sharpton. Sharpton also had a very valid excuse for not being in court as he had surrendered himself to authorities in Albany, New York, to finish serving a sentence for obstructing traffic during a demonstration for Tawana Brawley.[655]

Judge Bruhn was frustrated, but he noted for the record that defense counsel was legitimately tied up in another court.

He adjourned the case until March 9.

Reporters asked several questions of Joseph Kiernan as he left. They hoped for another one of his colorful remarks. To their disappointment, Kiernan said nothing.

When March 9, arrived, Judge Bruhn again took the bench. He noted the presence of Assistant District Attorney Joan Zooper. He also observed that Alton Maddox had finally returned to Kingston City Court.

However, the proceedings still could not continue. For the previous five court appearances, Joseph Kiernan had stood before the bench, but without legal counsel. Now, his lawyer was present, but Kiernan was missing.

"Where is your client, Mr. Maddox?" Bruhn inquired.

Maddox told the court that his client was currently somewhere in Arizona. When the judge gave him a look of fury, Maddox offered a more detailed explanation. After Kiernan was freed on bail, he decided to travel to California. Once there, he ran out of money and had been unable to get back to Kingston for his hearing.

"He knows his obligation, and he is not trying to shirk it," Maddox offered. "He has an economic problem, not a criminal problem."[656]

Judge Bruhn demanded to know whether Maddox could reach his client. The attorney advised that he did not know Kiernan's current whereabouts. He also had no updated phone number for him, though his client called him periodically.

As Judge Bruhn shook his head in utter disbelief, Maddox stated for the record that Kiernan made all previous court appearances and there were no provisions on his bail prohibiting him from traveling. This was technically true.

Judge Bruhn once again continued the case, not expecting that he would ever see Joseph Kiernan again. The judge could issue a bench warrant. However, this was just a misdemeanor charge and it was highly unlikely that authorities would seek Kiernan's extradition. In all probability, Kiernan would never return to Kingston. Effectively, the case was over.

Just before adjourning the case, Judge Bruhn looked at Alton Maddox and asked, "Why did Kiernan go to California?"

Maddox merely shrugged. Then, with an absolutely straight face, he replied, "He's a man of the world."[657]

CHAPTER 30 - EPILOGUE

NEARLY THIRTY YEARS AFTER this horrible murder, many questions remain. Some may never be answered, though the evidence does allow for an educated guess.

1. Did Jeffrey Dawson kill Anna Kithcart?

I do not think there can be much doubt that he did. By his own admission, he was with Annie in the railway bed on the night of her murder. His claim to the police that someone else came along after Annie was accidentally knocked out and killed her, stripped her, and cut her body is perhaps theoretically possible, but extraordinarily unlikely.

The path along the old railroad tracks was heavily overgrown. Large trees and bushes overhead made it dark, even in the brightest sunshine. At night, visibility would have been no more than a foot or two. Had another person come along that night, it is unlikely he would have seen an unconscious Annie lying on the side of the pathway unless he practically tripped over her.

Furthermore, Jeff Dawson's behavior after Annie's death was the behavior of a guilty man. He hid her clothes and his own shirt in the alley a few blocks away. He washed off blood in a pool. He hid from the police. When asked about that night, he and his wife both lied to the police and created a false alibi.

Lastly, the recorded conversation between Todd Schleede

and Jeff Dawson leaves little doubt. While there is no question that Schleede did most of the talking, Dawson made a clear admission. He said:

> "She started bugging out man, just bugging me, man. She fell and cut her head and shit. She had a big gash. She's dead. I knew she was, and that's when I took the knife. I decided to make it look like…like a psychopath did it."

Based on his admissions, the physical evidence, and the extreme unreasonableness of his claim that a third person showed up out of the darkness and committed the murder, I conclude that Jeffrey Dawson killed Annie Kithcart.

2. Did the killer or Kiernan make the "KKK" marks on the body?

This question is answered definitively. Both the pathologist and county coroner concluded that the "K" on the abdomen and the "KKK" on the left thigh were cut while Kithcart was still alive. On the other hand, the "KKK" cut into the right thigh occurred after death.

Further, both doctors agreed that all of these wounds occurred in relative proximity to one another. This means that the killer and the person who sliced into the body were one and the same. This person was Jeff Dawson.

3. Why did he kill her? What was his motive?

This is perhaps the most difficult question of the entire case. There was no known history of animosity between Jeff and Annie. The evidence also does not suggest a premeditated murder.

The evidence supports two possible conclusions. The first is a crime of passion and anger, as alleged by the police. The second is a crime of accidental death and panic.

The prosecution maintained that there was an argument between them, possibly over cocaine, alcohol, or perhaps the rejection of a sexual overture. They contended that Dawson, in a fit of rage, beat his victim over the head, neck, and shoulders with a brick, and then with a stick after the brick broke into two pieces. Then, in an act of total and complete savagery, the killer picked up his victim and strangled her with his bare hands. The rage continued as the killer desecrated his victim by stripping off her clothes and carving "KKK" into her thighs.

This theory is supported by the testimony of Dr. Eric Mitchell, the pathologist, but contradicted by the conclusions of Dr. Harry McNamara, the county coroner. McNamara testified that the victim was choked first and bludgeoned afterwards.

Moreover, Jeff Dawson did not have a history of violence. He was a thief and a burglar, with multiple convictions for both. He had one charge of assault from an incident in which he punched someone in the face. That charge was later reduced and pleaded out. He was not a violent man. He was a man who took shortcuts in life and stole anything he could. He was not a cold-blooded murderer.

It is therefore the second theory, an accidental death and panicked cover-up, that makes the most sense. This theory also fits partially with the defendant's statement to the police and his recorded conversation with Schleede. The following is what I believe likely happened.

Dawson and Kithcart walked behind the hospital with Annie asking Jeff to do something with her. All of the witnesses who saw Annie that evening reported that she was asking people to hang out with her and drink or possibly get some cocaine. While she wanted to get high, she seemed to want company just as much.

Dawson refused, but she kept at him, probably charged up from all of the alcohol she drank that evening. She got on Dawson's nerves and he pushed her away. Kithcart became angry, started yelling at him, and may have struck him. (This would explain the slight bruise noticed by Schleede.)

Dawson grabbed her in a choke hold, not intending to kill her, but instead to control her and calm her down. When a choke hold is applied correctly across the carotid artery, unconsciousness can often occur quickly, sometimes even in seconds. Dawson was very strong and the added adrenaline and alcohol in his system caused him to squeeze harder than he otherwise planned. This caused the fracture of the horn of the larynx and rendered Annie unconscious.

Thinking she was faking, he flung her away and she fell to the ground landing on a nearby stick causing the cut on her face and ear, the blood flow of which streamed toward the back of head and neck.

Still thinking she was not really unconscious or hurt, Dawson reached down and started to lift her head. His hand got wet and when he brought it back to his face, he saw his hand was bloody.

Fear started tingling through his body. He bent down and checked for a pulse. His own heart was pounding and racing from fear. He could not feel any sign of a pulse. Panic overtook him. The girl was dead. He was on parole and had multiple prior felonies. Nobody would believe him that the whole thing was an accident.

The next few seconds must have seemed like forever as he weighed his options. He decided to make it appear that Annie was killed by a psychopathic maniac. He stripped off her clothes and dragged her a short distance off the main part of the path. As he dragged her, one of her shoes came off and Dawson could not find it in the darkness, if he even noticed it was missing.

Next to where he placed Annie was a brick. He took it and smashed down on Annie's face two or three times. The last time caused the brick to break. Her blood splattered all over his hands, face, and white T-shirt he was wearing.

He stripped off Annie's clothes, which included the white towel around her waist, and wrapped them into a ball. Then, he took a piece of glass lying nearby and started cutting her skin. He chose to cut "KKK" into her skin because he thought police would never suspect a black man of doing so.

The bite mark (if it was even a bite mark at all) was probably inflicted as part of Dawson's efforts to create a scene of a psychopath's frenzy. It is possible it happened during the chokehold as well. It may even have happened sometime prior and was thus unrelated to the murder.

When finished, Dawson stuck the glass fragment into Annie's neck, took her clothes, and went out of the railway bed onto Foxhall Avenue. He avoided Broadway so as not to risk being seen. Instead, he chose to walk down Jansen Avenue, a smaller and much quieter street.

He turned down the alley between Cheap Charlies and the Royal Grill. About halfway down the alley, he decided to dump the clothes. The lighting there was better, and he could see all of the blood on his shirt and hands. He took off his shirt, wiped his hands on it, and placed the shirt with the other clothes. There was also blood on his pants. He could be seen walking without his shirt on a warm summer evening, but walking without his pants would certainly have drawn attention.

He walked out of the alley onto Broadway and went two and a half blocks to his home. He quietly climbed into his neighbor's pool while still wearing his pants and rinsed off the blood. This was enough to block the forensic technology of 1988 and 1989 from finding more than a spot of blood on his pants. (Forensic technique of today would have revealed much more.)

Assuming this theory is correct, and Dawson never intended to kill her, it is important to note that Annie was still alive, albeit unconscious after being choked. Only a few hundred yards away was the Kingston Hospital emergency room. Had Dawson picked her up and carried her there, Annie Kithcart would probably have lived.

Dawson would have almost certainly gone to prison for assaulting her and violating his parole. The ironic thing is that Annie Kithcart might very well have asked the court to be merciful on Dawson. That was the type of person she was.

4. Was Joseph Kiernan guilty of molesting Annie Kithcart's corpse?

After extensive questioning by the police and a lie detector test, Kiernan admitted the crime. However, despite this admission, the answer is no. He was not guilty.

Contained within the official case file of the Ulster County District Attorney's Office for the case of the *People of the State of New York v. Jeffrey A. Dawson* are records revealing that evidence swabs were taken at the autopsy of Anna Kithcart. These swab samples were taken from the thighs, vagina, and external pubic area. Each and every one of the samples was tested and found negative for saliva.

Joseph Kiernan was mentally disturbed. He often made outrageous statements with no basis in fact or reality. Despite his claims, he was not a secret agent for the CIA and he did not lick the corpse that he found that morning. Had he been pressed hard enough by the police, he might well have confessed to almost any crime. Kiernan was just a man in serious need of mental health treatment who was in the wrong place at the wrong time.

5. What happened to Sharpton, Maddox, and Mason after making their unfounded accusations in this case?

Al Sharpton went on to run for president in 2004. He became a political commentator and the host of shows on television and radio. He is considered a significant civil rights activist.

Although Joseph Kiernan was not working for federal government as he claimed, it was later claimed that Al Sharpton was. A website known as The Smoking Gun claims that Sharpton worked as a confidential informant for the FBI during the 1980s.[658]

In the article, The Smoking Gun wrote that the "account of Sharpton's secret life as 'CI-7' is based on hundreds of pages of confidential FBI affidavits, documents released by the bureau in response to Freedom of Information Act requests, court records, and extensive interviews with law enforcement officials to whom the activist provided assistance. Like almost every other FBI informant, Sharpton was solely an information source. The parameters of his cooperation did not include Sharpton ever surfacing publicly or testifying on a witness stand."[659]

The Smoking Gun interviewed Sharpton. He denied working as a confidential informant. Instead, he claimed that his prior cooperation was "limited to efforts to prompt investigations of drug dealing in minority communities, as well as the swindling of black artists in the recording industry."[660]

Sharpton denied that he was "flipped" by federal agents in the course of an undercover operation. However, when asked specifically about his alleged recording of a member of the Gambino crime family, Sharpton was noncommittal, saying, "I'm not saying yes, I'm not saying no."[661]

In a later interview with the *New York Daily News*, Sharpton acknowledged assisting the FBI beginning in 1983, but denied he was an informant.[662]

Sharpton, Maddox, and Mason, as well as Tawana Brawley herself, were later sued for slander and libel by Stephen Pagones, the former assistant district attorney whom they all accused of being involved in the alleged attack on Brawley.

After a lengthy and extraordinarily emotional trial, the jury found Sharpton liable for making seven defamatory statements about Pagones. They found Maddox liable for two and Mason for one defamatory statement. Maddox was found liable for $97,000, Mason for $188,000, and Sharpton for $66,000. The jury also found against Tawana Brawley, ordering her to pay $190,000.

Brawley's judgment remains unpaid, though there have been some payments and garnishment of her wages. Pagones claims he will drop the rest of the judgment (now over $400,000 with the accumulation of interest), if Brawley publicly recants her allegations. She has thus far declined to do so.

The judgments against Sharpton, Maddox, and Mason were paid, though not by them. The money was paid by celebrity lawyer Johnnie Cochran and other benefactors.[663]

Maddox did not fare as well as Sharpton. In 1990, after complaints of professional misconduct were filed against him by the New York Attorney General's Office, the matter was reviewed by the Second Department of the Appellate Division of the New York Supreme Court.

In its decision, the court noted, "Although the respondent was advised that his unexcused failure to answer the Attorney General's complaint would constitute professional misconduct, his response did not address the substance of that complaint, but instead accused the Grievance Committee of racial discrimination, invidious bias, and open hostility toward him, and asked that the matter be transferred to the Appellate Division, First Department."[664]

The court suspended Maddox indefinitely from the practice of law, but allowed him to finish a trial he was working on at the time.[665] His client in that trial was Sharpton.

In 1994, Maddox was again suspended from the practice of law. This time the suspension was for a period of at least five years. The court further ruled that Maddox could apply for reinstatement no sooner than six months prior to the expiration of the period of five years. Reinstatement would be contingent upon Maddox furnishing satisfactory proof that during the suspension he refrained from practicing or attempting to practice law, he fully complied with the terms and provisions of the written rules governing the conduct of disbarred, suspended, and resigned attorneys, and that he "otherwise properly conducted himself."[666]

A substantial basis cited by the court in both cases was the refusal of Maddox to cooperate in any of the investigations. Although Maddox was suspended, he has the right to apply for reinstatement. As of June 2017, he was still listed as suspended by the New York Unified Court System.

Mason fared even worse than Maddox. In 1995, a decision by a five-judge panel of the First Judicial District in Manhattan found:

> A review of the evidence presented to the Hearing Panel indicates that there is ample support for the Hearing Panel's findings that respondent is guilty of 66 instances of professional misconduct involving 20 different clients. Respondent's misconduct includes repeated neglect of client matters, many of which concerned criminal cases where a client's liberty was at stake; misrepresentations to clients; refusal to refund the unearned portion of fees; and multiple instances in which respondent improperly facilitated the practice of law by an otherwise unqualified layperson or unadmitted attorney.[667]

Mason was "disbarred, with his name to be stricken from the roll of attorneys."[668] Mason would later claim that he had not received a fair hearing from the court disciplinary committee. Although the decision was based on completely different allegations, Mason claimed that the decision was actually based on an intent to punish him for the Brawley case.

"It was an all-white panel," he said. "They rubber-stamped it."[669]

   6. Why were there no statements after the trial from Anna Kithcart's family?

Her family was present throughout the trial. Although there were one or two comments right after her death, the family refused to speak with the media thereafter.

The Kithcarts were intensely private people. Their loss was great, and certainly not something they would easily get over. Like many who have lost a loved one, each day followed the last, and not one went by without thoughts of their Annie. You never get over it. You just try to move on.

Annie's life was stolen from her before she really had a chance to live. The victim of a beating and senseless murder, she never had the opportunity to discover what her future held. She was a girl with a sunny disposition and a bubbly personality, who enjoyed being with her friends and having a good time.

Ironically, at a time when racial issues were being stirred up by opportunists like Sharpton, Annie herself was never a part of the turmoil. She saw herself as neither black nor white. She was a unique blend. The impact of her brief life was felt by all.

PHOTOS

This is a photo of the entrance from Foxhall Avenue to the old railway bed taken on the morning after the murder. The small circular light seen toward top of the photograph is the exit on to East O'Reilly Street.

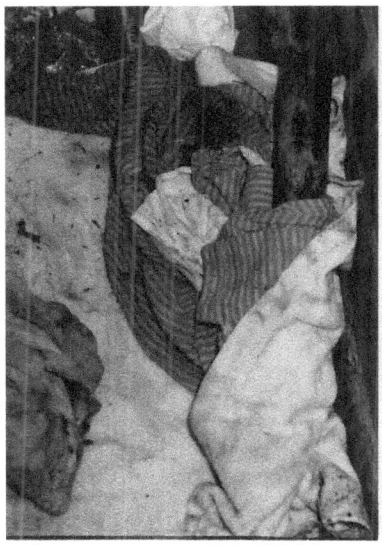

This is a photo of the bloody clothing found in the alley between Cheap Charlies and the Royal Grill. Note the large stick that the clothing was wrapped around.

This is a close up of the rear entrance to the alley.

This is the alley between Cheap Charlies and the Royal Grill as seen from Jansen Avenue.

One of Annie Kithcart's moccasin's as it was found in the railway bed.

The orange plastic washbasin covered with blood
found near Annie Kithcart's body.

The front entrance to the alley from Broadway. The building on the left is Cheap Charlies and the building on the right is the Royal Grill.

An aerial photograph of the wooded area where the body of Anna Kithcart was found. The building on the far right is Kingston Hospital.

Anna Kithcart. It is her Senior Picture from the 1988 Kingston High Yearbook.

This is a portion of a map of the streets of Kingston, New York from the files of the Ulster County District Attorney. The area where the murder occurred is noted as "#1". The alley where the bloody clothing was found is noted as "#2", and boxes have been added there to indicate the locations of building and thus create the actual alley on the map.

Another aerial photograph of the wooded area where the body of Anna Kithcart was found, but from the opposite side. The building on the left is Kingston Hospital. The middle building is the Kingston City Lab. The building to the right is what was then Old City Hall. Though it was an abandoned building at the time of the murder, it was later refurbished and reopened in 2000 once again as City Hall.

Chief James Riggins

Booking photo of Jeff Dawson

Alton Maddox Jr. speaking to reporters at the Ulster County Jail.
Note the cake on the table with the words "Happy Birthday Joseph"
Photo courtesy of the Daily Freeman, Kingston, New York.

Al Sharpton speaks to reporters. *Photo courtesy of the Daily Freeman, Kingston, New York.*

Al Sharpton answers a question from a reporter from WKIP Radio. *Photo courtesy of the Daily Freeman, Kingston, New York.*

Al Sharpton and Alton Maddox putting on badges while visiting the Ulster County Jail. *Photo courtesy of the Daily Freeman, Kingston, New York.*

Alton Maddox in Kingston City Court waiting for his client, Joseph Kiernan. *Photo courtesy of the Daily Freeman, Kingston, New York.*

Anna Kithcart. *Photo courtesy of the Daily Freeman, Kingston, New York.*

Jeff Dawson reacts to the jury's verdict. *Photo courtesy of the Daily Freeman, Kingston, New York.*

Jeff Dawson appears in Kingston City Court before Judge Mike Bruhn. *Photo courtesy of the Daily Freeman, Kingston, New York.*

Dr. Eric Mitchell, the forensic pathologist testifying at trial and showing the container with the shard of glass found in the victim's neck. *Photo courtesy of the Daily Freeman, Kingston, New York.*

Joseph Kiernan being taken back to the Ulster County Jail.
Photo courtesy of the Daily Freeman, Kingston, New York.

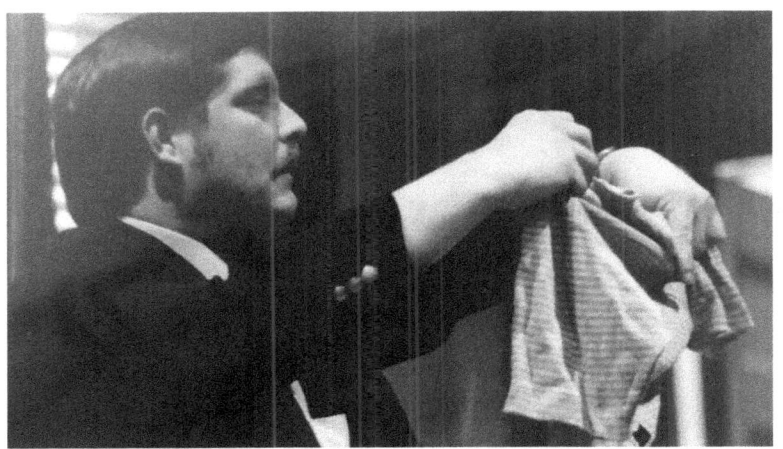

Detective Richard Krom testifying at trial and showing the jury an article of clothing worn by the victim when murdered. *Photo courtesy of the Daily Freeman, Kingston, New York.*

Defense counsel, Barry Lippman, makes a point at trial while Jeff Dawson looks on. *Photo courtesy of the Daily Freeman, Kingston, New York.*

Police Chief Jim Riggins and District Attorney Mike Kavanagh at a press conference. *Photo courtesy of the Daily Freeman, Kingston, New York.*

Barry Lippman and Jeff Dawson at trial. *Photo courtesy of the Daily Freeman, Kingston, New York.*

Jeff Dawson. *Photo courtesy of the Daily Freeman, Kingston, New York.*

ACKNOWLEDGEMENTS

THIS BOOK WOULD NOT have been possible without the assistance of numerous people.

I must first offer thanks to my good friend Don Ryan. Don worked with many of the police officers and members of the Ulster County District Attorney's Office involved in the investigation of Anna Kithcart's murder and the prosecution of Jeff Dawson. He provided me with insight into their personalities, as well as internal police procedure from the 1980s. He also arranged for my interview of retired detectives Paul Watzka and Junious Harris.

The *Daily Freeman* graciously permitted me to review their treasure trove of original photographs from their coverage of the investigation and trial. Further, the Ulster County District Attorney's Office allowed me full access to their original file with the exception of those documents, such as grand jury minutes, that cannot be released per New York law.

This book also could not have been completed without Steve Jackson, Michael Cordova, Ashley Butler, and the entire staff at WildBlue Press, including Mary Kay Wayman, my copy editor.

On a personal note, my family deserves tremendous thanks. My wife, Laura, was continually patient with all the time needed for research, writing, and editing. My mother, Margaret, used her skills as a retired schoolteacher to edit the original manuscript, and she and my sister, Julie, served as a sounding board. I cannot thank them enough.

For More News About Richard T. Cahill Jr., Signup For Our Newsletter:

http://wbp.bz/newsletter

Word-of-mouth is critical to an author's long-term success. If you appreciated this book please leave a review on the Amazon sales page:

http://wbp.bz/sidetrackeda

ENDNOTES

[1] Robert McFadden, *Outrage: The Story Behind the Tawana Brawley Hoax* (New York: Bantam 1990), pages 16-18.

[2] Ibid., 17.

[3] Ibid., 18.

[4] Ibid., 19.

[5] Ibid., 41.

[6] Ibid., 44-45.

[7] Ibid., 50-51.

[8] Ibid., 52. McFadden writes that Broderick specifically called WCBS-TV in New York City.

[9] Newburgh is a small city in New York located about eighteen miles south of Poughkeepsie.

[10] McFadden, *Outrage*, 62-63.

[11] Ibid., 61.

[12] Todd S. Purdom, "Lawyer Asserts Queens Victim Would Aid U.S.," *New York Times*, January 2, 1987.

[13] Ronald Smothers, "Hynes Is Selected to Be Prosecutor in Queens Attack," *New York Times*, January 14, 1987.

[14] James Barron, "Brawley Lawyer Urged as Prosecutor," *New York Times*, February 28, 1988.

[15] Ibid.

[16] McFadden, *Outrage*, 254-255.

[17] William Glaberson, "The Brawley Ruling: The Overview; Sharpton Liable for Defamation in Brawley Case," *New York Times*, July 14, 1998.

[18] Vernon Mason was also named in the defamation suit filed by Steven Pagones. At Harvard Law School in March of 1989, Mason said, "I want to repeat to everyone within the sound of my voice that Steven Pagones, Scott Patterson, and Harry Crist, amongst others, raped, kidnapped and sodomized Tawana Brawley."

[19] John J. Goldman, "Former Aide to Tawana Brawley Advisor

Labels Teenager's Charges 'A pack of Lies,'" *Los Angeles Times*, June 16, 1988, and; Craig Wolff, "Former Worker With Sharpton Testifies To Jury," *New York Times*, June 17, 1988.

[20] Ibid.

[21] Goldman, "Former Aide to Tawana Brawley Advisor Labels Teenager's Charges 'A pack of Lies.'"

[22] Joseph Kiernan, written statement to Kingston Police Department, dated July 12, 1988.

[23] Erik Nelson, "Slaying Could Be Racial," *Daily Freeman,* July 7, 1988.

[24] Carl Korn, "Brawley Advisers Back Transient Charged With Carving 'KKK' on Dead Teenager," United Press International, July 16, 1988.

[25] At one time, Hasbrouck Avenue continued straight through, but had been closed off some time before and used as a storage area for the Board of Public Works. It was still used by people as a short cut.

[26] Kiernan, police statement.

[27] Dorothy "Dottie" Clarke and Deborah Stewart, written statements to police, July 13, 1988.

[28] Stewart's statement uses the word "mannequin," but Clarke's statement says Kiernan used the word "dummy."

[29] The victim was actually of mixed heritage, having an African-American parent and a white parent. Her skin was light enough that Clarke reported in her statement that the body was of a white woman.

[30] Stewart initially reported that a white T-shirt was around the victim's neck.

[31] Stewart, police statement.

[32] Clarke and Stewart, police statements.

[33] Matthew Felton, written statement to police, July 12, 1988.

[34] Robert Lunan, written statement to police, July 13, 1988.

[35] Felton, written statement to police.

[36] Though there were numerous officers on scene, the notes of Detective Richard Krom were the best-organized and most-detailed. For this reason, Krom's notes concerning the scene are the best source of information concerning the condition of the crime scene.

[37] Handwritten crime scene notes of Detective Richard Krom, July

12, 1988.

[38] Ibid.

[39] Ibid.

[40] Krom's description of the "KKK" marks on the victim's thighs and abdomen are taken from his testimony at trial. *People of the State of New York v. Jeffrey A. Dawson*, trial transcript, page 389.

[41] Krom, notes. Krom measured the distance from the victim's head to the washbasin at eight feet, nine inches.

[42] Krom, notes. Krom measured the distance from the body's head to the Styrofoam at nine feet, four inches and to the brick at seven feet, ten inches. The leaf was found right next to the brick.

[43] Krom, notes.

[44] Lieutenant Detective Paul Watzka and Detective Junious Harris (both now retired from the Kingston Police Department), interview with author, August 6, 2016. Watzka and Harris stated emphatically that while there were obviously concerns about the racial angle of the case, all of the detectives working on the murder were perfectly comfortable focusing solely on the investigation and letting Chief James Riggins handle the media and public relations. This also speaks strongly on the respect the men had for their chief, even twenty-eight years later.

[45] Tom Wakeman, "A Friendly Face Is Gone From Streets of Rondout," *Daily Freeman*, July 14, 1988.

[46] Tom Wakeman and Joe Ostoyich, "Friends of 'Street Smart' Anna Never Believed Racial Theory," *Daily Freeman*, July 18, 1988.

[47] Erik Nelson, "Slaying Could Be Racial," *Daily Freeman*, July 15, 1988.

[48] Wakeman, "A Friendly Face Is Gone From Streets of Rondout."

[49] Nelson, "Slaying Could Be Racial."

[50] Wakeman and Ostoyich, "Friends of 'Street Smart' Anna Never Believed Racial Theory."

[51] Wakeman, "A Friendly Face Is Gone From Streets of Rondout."

[52] Ibid.

[53] Ibid.

[54] Denise Noonan, statement to Kingston Police Department, July 12, 1988.

[55] Ibid.

[56] Ibid.

[57] Scott Mayer, statement to police, July 12, 1988.

[58] Ibid.

[59] Ibid.

[60] Ibid.

[61] Annie Kithcart's actions from the Convenient Mart until she reached the Royal Grill are based on the statement to police of Joseph Misasi, July 14, 1988. Annie could have used a different path to get to the Royal Grill. I chose the most direct route primarily because it is easier to explain to someone who never has been to Kingston, New York, during the late 1980s. Additionally, I chose the same route Annie and Joseph used when they went back to get the beer.

[62] Joseph Misasi, statement to police, July 14, 1988.

[63] Jeffrey Dawson, statement to police, July 12, 1988.

[64] Misasi, statement.

[65] Ibid.

[66] Ibid.

[67] Ibid.

[68] Ibid.

[69] Kathleen Bentley, statement to police, July 12, 1988. Bentley said Annie entered the Royal Grill at 12:15, while the statements to police of Geraldine Jones, Linda Appolonia, and Chanise Evans, all dated July 12, 1988, report the time as 12:30 a.m.

[70] William Charles Davis, statement to police, July 12, 1988.

[71] Jacqueline Bradford, statement to police, July 12, 1988.

[72] There is a statement from a witness named Ann Williams, dated July 12, 1988, claiming that Annie was with Scott Mayer and Denise Noonan in the parking lot in front of the Broadway East complex from 1:30 a.m. to 2:00 a.m. on July 12, 1988. However, this statement cannot be confirmed and is contrary to all other statements taken by the police.

[73] Alonia Williams Jr., statement to police, July 12, 1988.

[74] Arrest record card for Joseph Kiernan maintained by Kingston Police Department.

[75] Ibid.

[76] Detective Michael Turck, report, July 16, 1988.

[77] There is no transcript of the actual interrogation of Joseph Kiernan. There are only some handwritten notes.

[78] Detective Richard Krom, report, July 13, 1988.

[79] Ibid.

[80] Detective Junious Harris, report, July 13, 1988.

[81] Krom, report.

[82] Detective Michael Turck, supplemental report, July 13, 1988.

[83] The entire lie detector test and the circumstances surrounding it are taken from handwritten police notes. The actual polygraph papers are not within the files maintained by the Kingston Police Department or Ulster County District Attorney's Office.

[84] *United States v. Scheffer*, 523 U.S. 303 (decided March 31, 1998).

[85] From the handwritten notes from the Kiernan polygraph exam. No formal report is in the files of the Kingston Police Department or Ulster County District Attorney's Office.

[86] Ibid. The notes are somewhat cryptic and do not always identify which officer asked the specific questions. However, the questions and the answers are noted in detail.

[87] Watzka and Harris, interview with author.

[88] Detective Junious Harris, report, July 21, 1988, and Detective Richard Krom, intelligence report, July 18, 1988.

[89] District Attorney Mike Kavanagh actually met with Annie's mother and Aunt Anna first. Shortly after, they had a second nearly identical meeting with Annie's father and sister, Gina.

[90] Mike Kavanagh, memorandum, July 14, 1988.

[91] Nelson, "Slaying Could Be Racial."

[92] Ibid.

[93] Ulster County District Attorney's Office, press release, July 14, 1988.

[94] Dr. Eric Mitchell's credentials are taken from his trial testimony. Trial transcript, pages 615-616.

[95] The doctor's preliminary findings are taken from a File Memorandum of Donald A. Williams, dated July 13, 1988.

[96] Nelson, "Slaying Could Be Racial."

[97] Ibid.

[98] Tom Wakeman, "Case 'Like a Nightmare Come True,'" *Daily Freeman*, July 15, 1988.

[99] Nelson, "Slaying Could Be Racial."

[100] Wakeman, "Case 'Like a Nightmare Come True.'"

[101] Nelson, "Slaying Could Be Racial."

[102] Wakeman, "Case 'Like a Nightmare Come True.'"

[103] Ibid.

[104] Nelson, "Slaying Could Be Racial," and Wakeman, "Case 'Like a Nightmare Come True.'"

[105] Ibid.

[106] Ibid.

[107] Ibid.

[108] John J. Goldman, "N.Y. Girl's Death Likened to Brawley Case," *Los Angeles Times*, July 15, 1988.

[109] Ibid.

[110] Ibid.

[111] Erik Nelson, "Kingston Man Charged With Killing Anna Kithcart," *Daily Freeman,* July 17, 1988, and Billy House and Tracy Dell'Angela, "Brawley Advisers Visit Suspect in Ulster Jail," *Poughkeepsie Journal*, July 16, 1988.

[112] Nelson, "Kingston Man Charged With Killing Anna Kithcart."

[113] Ibid.

[114] Korn, "Brawley Advisers Back Transient Charged With Carving 'KKK' on Dead Teenager."

[115] Carl Korn, "Two civil rights activists charged Friday that an upstate...," United Press International, July 15, 1988.

[116] House and Dell'Angela, "Brawley Advisers Visit Suspect in Ulster Jail."

[117] Korn, "Two civil rights activists charged Friday that an upstate...."

[118] Nelson, "Kingston Man Charged With Killing Anna Kithcart.".

[119] Ibid.

[120] Lieutenant Douglas Gaston and Detective Wayne Freer, report, July 16, 1988.

[121] Ibid.

[122] Ibid. The exact conversation is not recorded. The words are taken from the nature and tone of the officers' notes.

[123] Jeffrey Dawson, statement to police, July 12, 1988.

[124] The exact words of the phone call are taken from the trial testimony of Penelope DeGroat, page 782.

[125] Jeffrey A. Dawson, unsigned statement to police, July 13, 1988.

[126] Rose Dawson, statement to police, July 13, 1988.

[127] Testimony of Detective Junious Harris, trial transcript, page 950.

[128] Ibid.

[129] Todd Schleede, statement to police, July 16, 1988.

[130] Ibid.

[131] The Old City Hall building was abandoned in 1972. As of July 1988, it was still vacant.

[132] Schleede, statement.

[133] Ibid.

[134] Ibid.

[135] Ibid.

[136] Ibid.

[137] Ibid.

[138] Ibid.

[139] Penelope DeGroat, statement to police, July 16, 1988.

[140] Ibid.

[141] Detective Michael Turck, report, July 17, 1988.

[142] The team consisted of Lieutenants Gaston and Watzka, Detectives Freer, Harris, Turck, Wallace, and Kron, Sergeants Dunn and Scarey, and Officers Spetalieri and Maisenhelder.

[143] Turck, report.

[144] Ibid.

[145] Transcript of wire recording by police of conversation between Todd Schleede and Jeffrey A. Dawson, page 3.

[146] Ibid.

[147] Ibid., 4.

[148] Ibid., 5-6.

[149] Ibid, 7.

[150] Ibid.

[151] Ibid., 7-8.

[152] Ibid., 8. The actual conversation has Schleede saying "yeah" and "huh" a few times while Dawson spoke. They were removed from clarity and more easy reading.

[153] Ibid. This would become a highly debated response. The quality of the tape is poor and even when attempts were made to enhance the quality, Dawson's actual response was still unclear. The official transcript still contains the reply "Nah."

[154] It must have been just a regular patrol that came by. There is no logic whatsoever for a marked car to come by and disrupt the conversation. Either the arrest team did not advise other cars to stay clear from the area or someone had not followed the directive. Either way, the entire operation was now compromised.

[155] Transcript of wire recording, page 9. Dawson was comfortable using racial language since Schleede was also African-American.

[156] Ibid.

[157] Ibid., 11-12.

[158] Turck, report.

[159] Detective Junious Harris, statement, July 16, 1988.

[160] Stenographic transcription of the taped statement to police of Jeffrey Alan Dawson, July 16, 1988 (certified August 31, 1988).

[161] Dawson's version of events come directly from pages 3 through 5 of the stenographic transcription of his recorded statement from July 16, 1988.

[162] Ibid., 6-7.

[163] Ibid., 8.

[164] Ibid., 8-9.

[165] Ibid., 9.

[166] Ibid., 9-10.

[167] Ibid.

[168] Ibid., 11-12.

[169] Ibid., 12.

[170] Ibid., 14.

[171] Ibid., 14-15.

[172] Ibid., 15-16.

[173] Ibid.

[174] *Frazier v. Cupp*, 394 US 731 (1969).

[175] For example, *Oregon v Mathiason*, 429 US 492 (1977), in which the court upheld the legality of police lying to a suspect that his fingerprints were found at the scene of a burglary.

[176] Stenographic transcription of the taped statement of Dawson, 16-17.

[177] Ibid., 17-18.

[178] Second audio recording of the police interrogation of Jeffrey A. Dawson.

[179] Ibid.

[180] Ibid.

[181] Ibid.

[182] Ibid.

[183] Ibid.

[184] Ibid.

[185] Erik Nelson, "Police: Kithcart Killing Was the Result of Argument," *Daily Freeman*, July 18, 1988.

[186] Under New York state law, a City Court judge is without power to grant bail on a murder charge. Applications for bail must go to the County or Supreme Court.

[187] In New York, whenever the Public Defender is conflicted out of a case, the judge has a list of attorneys to choose from. The list is known as the Assigned Counsel list or the 18b list, named after the section of New York law allowing for assignment of counsel.

[188] Nelson, "Police: Kithcart Killing Was the Result of Argument."

[189] Ibid.

[190] Ibid.

[191] Erik Nelson, "Kithcart Killing Goes Before County Jury," *Daily Freeman*, July 19, 1988.

[192] Judy Charnow, "Vagrant: I Didn't Abuse Body of Anna Kithcart," *Daily Freeman*, July 18, 1988. In the official files maintained by the Ulster County District Attorney's Office and Kingston Police Department, I have been unable to find any statements, recordings, or officer notes where Kiernan made this admission. There are notes concerning his admission to necrophilia, but not that he "carved up the body."

[193] Nelson, "Kingston Man Charged With Killing Anna Kithcart."

[194] Nelson, "Police: Kithcart Killing Was the Result of Argument."

[195] Mark Uhlig, "Acquaintance Is Charged in Kingston Woman's Death," *New York Times*, July 18, 1988.

[196] "Brawley Departs for Convention to Seek Dukakis' Aid," United Press International, July 17, 1988.

[197] "The Democrats in Atlanta: Sharpton and 50 Followers Confront New York Delegates," *New York Times*, July 20, 1988.

[198] John Chattin, "Clergymen Target Drugs Over Racism in Slaying," *Daily Freeman*, July 19, 1988.

[199] The audio of this interview no longer exists. As such, Kiernan's statements are taken from two different sources of reports on the interview: Charnow, "Vagrant: I Didn't Abuse Body of Anna Kithcart," and Korn, "Two civil rights activists charged Friday that an upstate...."

[200] Ibid.

[201] NewYork Criminal Procedure Law, § 180.80.

[202] Transcript of preliminary hearing, Ulster County Court, July 20, 1988, pages 2-3.

[203] Transcript of preliminary hearing, July 20, 1988, pages 3-5. The actual comments from Williams were much longer. However, his original comments have been shortened, somewhat ironically, in the interest of brevity.

[204] Ibid., 5.

[205] Ibid., 6.

[206] Ibid., 8-9.

[207] Ibid., 9.

[208] Ibid., 10. The actual answer was interrupted with an objection. The doctor's complete answer is presented together without the interruption.

[209] Ibid., 10-11.

[210] Ibid., 11-12.

[211] Ibid., 12-13.

[212] New York Criminal Procedure Law §60.50 provides: A person may not be convicted of any offense solely upon evidence of a confession or admission made by him or her without additional proof that the offense charged has been committed.

[213] Transcript of preliminary hearing, July 20, 1988, pages 13-14.

[214] Ibid., 14-15.

[215] Ibid., 15-16.

[216] Ibid., 17. The actual answer was longer, but has been shortened. The doctor just added some very technical medical jargon to support his answer.

[217] Ibid., 17-18.

[218] Ibid., 19-20. The term "surplusage" is a legal term that generally refers to language in a legal pleading that is not relevant to the cause of action. Williams was basically contending that the answer of the doctor went beyond the question.

[219] Transcript of preliminary hearing, July 20, 1988, page 23.

[220] Ibid., 24.

[221] Ibid., 24-25.

[222] Ibid., 25-26.

[223] Ibid., 26-27.

[224] Ibid., 27-28.

[225] Ibid., 28-29.

[226] Ibid., 30-31.

[227] Ibid., 31.

[228] Ibid., 31-32.

[229] Ibid., 32-33.

[230] Ibid., 33.

[231] Ibid., 34.

[232] Ibid., 34-41.

[233] Ibid., 40.

[234] Ibid., 41-50.

[235] Ibid., 51-52.

[236] Ibid., 52-53.

[237] Ibid., 55-56.

[238] Ibid., 56.

[239] Ibid., 57-58.

[240] Ibid., 62-63.

[241] Vincent Bradley was a New York State Supreme Court judge.

[242] Transcript of preliminary hearing, July 20, 1988, page 64.

[243] Ibid., 68.

[244] Tom Wakeman, "Judge Halves Kiernan's Bail," *Daily Freeman*, July 22, 1988.

[245] Tom Wakeman, "Kithcart Probe Nearing an End," *Daily Freeman*, July 24, 1988.

[246] Ibid.

[247] Ibid. The television station was Fox Channel Five News in New York City.

[248] Ibid.

[249] Ibid.

[250] Ibid.

[251] Ibid.

[252] *Upjohn Co. v. United States*, 449 US 483 (1981). The chief justice cited numerous cases as precedent including *Trammel v. United States*, 445 U. S. 40 (1980); *Fisher v. United States*, 425 U. S. 391 (1976); and *Hunt v. Blackburn*, 128 U. S. 464 (1888).

[253] Wakeman, "Kithcart Probe Nearing an End."

[254] This charge is under New York Penal Law section 125.25 (1).

[255] This charge is under New York Penal Law section 125.25 (2).

[256] This description comes generally from the New York State Court of Appeals in the case of *People v. Register*, 60 NY2d 273, 469 NYS2d 599 (1983).

[257] *People v. Lewie*, 17 NY3d 348, 359 (2011).

[258] Criminal negligent homicide is defined under New York Penal Law section 125.10 as when, with criminal negligence, a person causes

the death of another person. Manslaughter in the second degree is defined under New York Penal Law section 125.15 as when, a person recklessly causes the death of another person. It is different from reckless endangerment murder as that section requires a higher level of recklessness.

[259] Tom Wakeman, "Dawson Facing Two Counts of Murder," *Daily Freeman,* July 28, 1988.

[260] Ibid.

[261] Steven J. Stark, "Vagrant's Lawyer Aims to Free Him," *Daily Freeman* July 29, 1988.

[262] Ibid.

[263] Ibid.

[264] Nelson, "Kingston Man Charged With Killing Anna Kithcart."

[265] Korn "Brawley Advisers Back Transient Charged With Carving 'KKK' on Dead Teenager."

[266] Stark, "Vagrant's Lawyer Aims to Free Him."

[267] Ibid.

[268] Steven J. Stark, "Judge Frees Kiernan But Kithcart Murder Suspect Still Held in County Jail," *Daily Freeman,* July 31, 1988.

[269] Ibid.

[270] Ibid.

[271] Ibid.

[272] Lizabeth Martin, "Kithcart Pals March Against Drugs," *Daily Freeman,* August 1, 1988.

[273] Ibid.

[274] Ibid.

[275] Tom Wakeman, "Family Discusses Tragedy and Talks of a Cautious Teen," *Daily Freeman,* July 17, 1988.

[276] Wakeman, "A Friendly Face Is Gone From Streets of Rondout."

[277] Wakeman, "Family Discusses Tragedy and Talks of a Cautious Teen."

[278] Erik Nelson, "Kithcart Slay Case Lawyer Bows Out," *Daily Freeman,* August 7, 1988.

[279] Stewart's Shops is a U.S. chain of convenience stores located primarily in eastern Upstate New York and southwestern Vermont,

owned by the Dake family.

[280] Ulster County District Attorney's Office, trial memo, dated March 31, 1988.

[281] Not his real name. Since this person became a police snitch and his identity was never made public, I have chosen not to identify him.

[282] Ulster County District Attorney's Office, trial memo.

[283] Ibid.

[284] Ibid.

[285] Ibid.

[286] Ulster County District Attorney's Office, file memorandum, dated June 27, 1988.

[287] New York Penal Law section 40.10 (3).

[288] Erik Nelson, "Slay Suspect Assigned New Lawyer," *Daily Freeman*, August 14, 1988.

[289] The title of the hearing comes from the case of *People v. Huntley*, 15 N.Y.2d 72 (1965). This case was New York state's application of *Jackson v. Denno* (378 US 368), a 1964 United States Supreme Court case holding that the state court must hold a pretrial hearing upon request of a defendant to determine whether said statement was voluntarily made and not the result of improper coercion. Previously, many of these determinations were left to the state jury or a federal *habeas corpus* proceeding.

[290] Steven J. Stark, "Activist Attorney Stands Up Client," *Daily Freeman*, August 31, 1988.

[291] Ibid.

[292] Ibid.

[293] Ibid.

[294] Ibid.

[295] Steven J. Stark, "Dawson's Lawyer Seeks Discharge," *Daily Freeman*, September 23, 1988.

[296] Ibid.

[297] Steven J. Stark, "Dawson in Court; Kiernan on Hold," *Daily Freeman*, September 27, 1988.

[298] Ibid.

[299] McFadden, *Outrage,* pages 367–368.

[300] Ibid., 368.

[301] New York Attorney General Robert Abrams was reading from page 88 of the Report of the Grand Jury of the Supreme Court of Dutchess County.

[302] McFadden, *Outrage,* page 367.

[303] Report of the Grand Jury of the Supreme Court of Dutchess County, page 87.

[304] Associated Press, "Report Brands Tawana a Liar," October 7, 1988.

[305] McFadden, *Outrage,* page 368.

[306] Associated Press, "Abrams Wants Mason, Maddox Prosecuted," October 7, 1988.

[307] In 1988, this rule was set forth in 7-102 (A) (5) of the Disciplinary Rules of the Code of Professional Responsibility.

[308] October 6, 1988, letters to Grievance Committee for the 2nd and 11th Judicial Districts and the disciplinary committee of the First Judicial Department, pages 2-4.

[309] In 1988, this rule was codified in 7-102 (A) (7) of the Disciplinary Rules of the Code of Professional Responsibility.

[310] October 6, 1988, letters to Grievance Committee for the 2nd and 11th Judicial Districts and the disciplinary committee of the First Judicial Department, page 6.

[311] Abrams needed to send his letter to different legal bodies because Alton H. Maddox Jr. was admitted in the 2nd Judicial District while C. Vernon Mason was admitted in the 1st Judicial Department.

[312] Associated Press, "Abrams Wants Mason, Maddox Prosecuted."

[313] Ibid.

[314] Associated Press, "Brawley Standing by Her Story," October 9, 1988.

[315] Ibid.

[316] Associated Press, "Assistant Dutchess DA to Sue Tawana, Advisors," October 12, 1988.

[317] Ibid.

[318] Ibid.

[319] Ibid.

[320] Ibid.

[321] Ibid.

[322] Ibid.

[323] Erik Nelson, "11 Sworn in for Dawson Jury," *Daily Freeman*, January 10, 1989.

[324] Jacqueline Sergeant, "Dawson Denise Killing, Says Lawyer Pushing Plea," *Daily Freeman* January 6, 1989.

[325] Ibid.

[326] Ibid.

[327] Ibid.

[328] Trial transcript, January 10, 1989, page 230.

[329] Ibid.

[330] Ibid.

[331] Ibid., 231.

[332] Ibid., 232.

[333] Ibid.

[334] Ibid., 233.

[335] Ibid., 234.

[336] Ibid., 235.

[337] Ibid.

[338] Ibid., 236.

[339] Ibid.

[340] Ibid., 237-238.

[341] Ibid., 238.

[342] Trial transcript, pages 239-240.

[343] Ibid., 240.

[344] Ibid., 240-241.

[345] Ibid., 242-243.

[346] Ibid., 243-244.

[347] Ibid., 244-245.

[348] Ibid., 245-246.

[349] Ibid., 246-249.

[350] Ibid., 250-251.

[351] Ibid., 252.

[352] Ibid., 255.

[353] Ibid., 260.

[354] Ibid., 260.

[355] Ibid., 262.

[356] Ibid., 262-263.

[357] Ibid., 263-266.

[358] Ibid., 266-267.

[359] Ibid., 267.

[360] Ibid., 267-268.

[361] Ibid., 268-269.

[362] There are exceptions such as showing a common plan or scheme. For example, a serial murderer who uses a specific modus operandi could have the prior murder convictions used against him. These exceptions are uncommon.

[363] In New York, the hearing to examine prior convictions is called a Sandoval Hearing, while the hearing for prior bad acts without convictions is called a Molyneaux/Vertimiglia Hearing.

[364] Trial transcript, pages 269-270.

[365] Ibid., 270.

[366] Ibid., 273.

[367] Ibid., 273.

[368] Ibid., 274.

[369] Ibid., 275.

[370] Ibid., 278-279.

[371] Trial transcript, pages 281-282.

[372] Ibid., 282.

[373] Ibid., 283-287. The photograph was entered into evidence as People's Exhibit "1."

[374] Ibid., 288.

[375] Ibid., 289-290.

[376] Ibid., 292.

[377] Ibid., 293.

[378] Lincoln was able to overcome this mistake when the witness insisted he saw everything by the light of the full moon, and Lincoln pulled out a copy of the Farmer's Almanac, which revealed that there was no moon on the evening of the crime

[379] Trial transcript at 298-300.

[380] Ibid., 301-302.

[381] Dorothy Clarke, police statement, dated July 13, 1988

[382] Trial transcript at 304-305.

[383] Ibid., 306-307.

[384] Ibid., 307.

[385] Ibid., 307-309. The photographs were entered collectively as People's Exhibit "2," though the individual photographs were labeled 2A, 2B, 2C, 2D, 2E, and 2F to distinguish them.

[386] Ibid., 310-311.

[387] Ibid., 311.

[388] Ibid., 311-312.

[389] Ibid., 312-313.

[390] Ibid., 314.

[391] Ibid., 314-315.

[392] Ibid.,316-317.

[393] Ibid., 317-318.

[394] Trial transcript, page 336-337.

[395] Ibid., 337-338.

[396] Ibid., 338-339.

[397] The photographs were entered as People's Exhibit "4," though each photo was given its own letter designation from "A" to "H."

[398] Trial transcript, pages 339-342. This type of testimony is needed to establish the required legal foundation to enter photographs into evidence

[399] Trial transcript, pages 342-343. I have slightly changed the actual answer only insofar as grammar is concerned for easier reading and understanding. The doctor initially forgot to mention the scratches on the abdomen and he added that information directly in the middle of his answer creating a grammatical mess.

[400] Ibid., 343-344.
[401] Ibid., 344.
[402] Ibid., 345.
[403] Ibid., 345-346.
[404] Ibid., 346.
[405] Ibid., 347-350.
[406] Ibid., 352-356.
[407] Ibid., 366-367.
[408] Ibid., 369.
[409] Ibid., 370-371.
[410] Ibid., 371-372.
[411] Ibid., 374-375.
[412] Ibid., 373. The order of the questions and answers has been changed slightly. In the actual cross examination, Lippman jumped around from topic to topic. The content of the questions and answers has not been changed. Only the order has been altered to make it more readable.
[413] Ibid., 375.
[414] Ibid., 376-377.
[415] Ibid., 377-378.
[416] Ibid., 381-382.
[417] Ibid., 382.
[418] Ibid., 382-383.
[419] Ibid., 383. I have condensed the question without changing its meaning. That actual question in the transcript was very long and difficult to follow.
[420] Ibid., 384.
[421] Ibid., 385.
[422] Trial transcript, page 387.
[423] Ibid., 387-388.
[424] Ibid., 388-389
[425] Ibid., 394. The actual answer has been abridged and corrected for grammar. The relevant content, however, has not been changed

[426] Ibid., 395

[427] Ibid., 397-398. The washbasin was People's Exhibit "20," and the photograph was People's Exhibit "5."

[428] Ibid., 398-399.

[429] Ibid., 399-400.

[430] Ibid., 404-405.

[431] Ibid., 406-407.

[432] Ibid., 407.

[433] Ibid., 408.

[434] Ibid., 409.

[435] Ibid., 410-411.

[436] Ibid., 411.

[437] Ibid., 413-414.

[438] Ibid., 424-429.

[439] Ibid., 429-431.

[440] Ibid., 432.

[441] Ibid., 433-434.

[442] Ibid., 442.

[443] Erik Nelson, "Dawson Unhappy With Lawyer, Doubts He'll Be Given Fair Trial," *Daily Freeman,* January 12, 1989.

[444] Ibid.

[445] Ibid.

[446] Trial transcript, page 454.

[447] Ibid., 455.

[448] Ibid., 455-456.

[449] Ibid., 456

[450] Ibid., 456-457

[451] Ibid., 458

[452] Ibid., 462-463

[453] Ibid., 464-465

[454] Ibid., 469-469

[455] Trial transcript, page 472-473

[456] Ibid., 473

[457] Ibid., 474-475

[458] Ibid., 476-478

[459] Ibid., 479-480

[460] Civil Practice Laws and Rules 4502 (b). This rule has been applied to criminal cases. See, e.g. *People v. Wilson*, 64 NY2d 634 (1984)

[461] Trial transcript, pages 481-482

[462] Ibid., 482-483. This ruling was later affirmed by the Appellate Division. See, *People v. Dawson*, 166 Ad2d 808 (3rd Dept 1990)

[463] Ibid., 484-485

[464] Ibid., 486-487

[465] Ibid., 488-489

[466] Ibid., 490.

[467] Ibid., 491-492.

[468] Ibid., 493-494.

[469] *People v. Hobson*, 39 NY2d 479 (1976).

[470] *Miranda v. Arizona*, 384 US 436 (1966).

[471] Suppression hearing transcript, December 14, 1988, pages 116-121.

[472] Trial transcript, pages 495-501.

[473] Ibid., 502-503.

[474] Ibid., 507-508.

[475] Ibid., 512.

[476] Ibid., 515.

[477] Ibid., 516.

[478] Trial transcript, pages 521-523.

[479] Ibid., 525-526. The jeans were People's Exhibit "44," and the hat was People's Exhibit "45."

[480] Ibid., 526-528.

[481] Ibid., 528-530.

[482] Exactly what was said at the bench is not known. The conversation was off the record, and the official transcript only mentions

generically that a conference took place.

[483] Trial transcript, pages 530-531.

[484] Ibid., 531. "Tommy Harris" was not the actual name used. It is a fake name created to hide the actual person's identity.

[485] Ibid., 531.

[486] Ibid., 532-533.

[487] Ibid., 535-538.

[488] Ibid., 542-544.

[489] Ibid., 546.

[490] Ibid., 548.

[491] Ibid., 549.

[492] Ibid., 550-551. Lippman's actual statements regarding Kiernan were much longer. They have been condensed without taking away from the merit of his request.

[493] Ibid., 552-553. After later reviewing the lie detector notes, Judge Vogt ruled that they did not have to be disclosed.

[494] Trial transcript, pages 562-563. He obtained his Doctor of Medicine in Dentistry degree (DMD) from the University of Pennsylvania and received further training in forensic dentistry while serving in the United States Air Force. The DDS (Doctor of Dental Surgery) and DMD (Doctor of Dental Medicine) are the same degrees. They are awarded upon graduation from dental school to become a General Dentist. Most dental schools award the DDS degree, but the degrees are essentially the same.

[495] Ibid., 564.

[496] Ibid.

[497] Ibid., 555-567.

[498] Ibid., 568-571.

[499] Ibid., 567-568.

[500] Ibid., 572-573.

[501] Ibid., 574.

[502] Radley Balco, "Incredibly, Prosecutors are Still Defending Bite Mark Evidence," *Washington Post,* January 30, 2017.

[503] Radley Balco, "Man Wrongly Convicted With Bite Mark Evidence Confronts Bite Mark Analysts," *Washington Post,* February

16, 2017.

[504] Trial transcript, pages 583-586. Dr. Mofson told the jury that he graduated from New York University's College of Dentistry in 1972. He took many post-graduate courses through annual meetings of the American Academy of Forensic Science, and consulted on several criminal cases for both the prosecution and defense.

[505] Ibid., 586.

[506] Ibid., 586-587. The content of the questions and answers are the same though the author has slightly changed the grammar to make them more easily read.

[507] Ibid., 587-589.

[508] Ibid., 589. The photograph was People's Exhibit "48."

[509] Ibid., 589-590.

[510] Ibid., 590.

[511] Ibid., 591.

[512] Ibid., 592.

[513] Ibid., 593.

[514] Ibid., 594-595.

[515] American Dental Association "Current Dental Terminology Third Edition (CDT-3)" 1999.

[516] Trial transcript, page 598.

[517] Ibid., 598-599.

[518] Ibid., 600.

[519] Ibid., 606-607.

[520] Ibid., 607-608.

[521] Ibid., 608-609.

[522] Ibid., 609-610.

[523] Ibid., 611-612.

[524] Ibid., 612.

[525] Trial transcript, 614-615. He graduated in 1976 from the Upstate Medical Center followed by a specialty program in anatomic clinical and forensic pathology. As a result, he obtained board certification in this specialty. Thereafter, he worked in Chapel Hill, North Carolina, as an assistant medical examiner. He later served as a medical examiner in Miami, Florida, before being hired as medical examiner for Onondaga

County, New York.

[526] Ibid., 618.

[527] Ibid., 619. The autopsy report was marked as People's Exhibit "49."

[528] Ibid., 621.

[529] Ibid., 622.

[530] Ibid., 622-624.

[531] Ibid., 625.

[532] Ibid., 626.

[533] Ibid., 626-627.

[534] Ibid., 627-628.

[535] Ibid., 632-633.

[536] Ibid.

[537] Ibid.

[538] Ibid., 634-635.

[539] Ibid., 637-638.

[540] Ibid., 640-641. Kavanagh actually used three or four verbose questions to bring this out. The author has condensed these without changing the ultimate content or intent of the questions and answers.

[541] Ibid., 642.

[542] Ibid., 643-644.

[543] Ibid., 644.

[544] Ibid., 645-646.

[545] Ibid., 649-652.

[546] Ibid., 652.

[547] Ibid., 652-653.

[548] Ibid., 654-655. The actual findings were 0.19 grams per deciliter for the blood, 0.21 grams per deciliter for the urine, and 0.23 grams per deciliter for the ocular fluid. The legal limit in New York in 1988 was 0.10 grams per deciliter, though it was since reduced to 0.08 grams.

[549] Ibid., 654-658.

[550] Ibid., 659 to 662.

[551] The entire suicide attempt and the conversation between

Dawson and Bruhn is based upon the January 16, 1989, handwritten note from Robert L. Bruhn. The quote from Dawson was constructed based upon these notes.

[552]   Ibid. There are no records of any follow up by a psychiatrist.
[553]   Ibid., 667-668.
[554]   Ibid., 675-676.
[555]   Ibid., 679-683.
[556]   Ibid., 683-687.
[557]   Ibid., 689-690.
[558]   Ibid., 693-694.
[559]   Ibid., 694-695.
[560]   Ibid., 696.
[561]   Ibid., 698-699.
[562]   Ibid., 699-702.
[563]   Ibid., 705-706.
[564]   Ibid., 707-708.
[565]   Ibid., 716-722.
[566]   Ibid., 719.
[567]   Ibid., 726-727.
[568]   Ibid., 744-745.
[569]   Ibid., 741-742.
[570]   Ibid., 734-735.
[571]   Ibid., 764-765.
[572]   Ibid.,769.
[573]   Trial transcript, pages 772-774.
[574]   Ibid., 775-776.
[575]   Ibid., 781-785.
[576]   Ibid., 805-806.
[577]   Trial transcript, pages 835-839.
[578]   Ibid., 840-841.
[579]   Ibid., 849-850.
[580]   Ibid., 859.

[581] Ibid., 866. The tape was People's Exhibit "57."
[582] Ibid., 887-888.
[583] Ibid., 916-922.
[584] Ibid., 922.
[585] Ibid., 926-927.
[586] Ibid., 934.
[587] New York Penal Code Section 125.20.
[588] New York Penal Code Section 125.15.
[589] New York Penal Code Section 120.00 (1).
[590] Trial transcript, pages 937-938.
[591] Ibid., 941.
[592] *Hanrahan v. New York Edison Co.*, 238 N.Y. 194 (1924).
[593] Trial transcript, page 943.
[594] Ibid., 947-948.
[595] Ibid., 951.
[596] Charnow, "Vagrant: I Didn't Abuse Body of Anna Kithcart."
[597] Trial transcript, page 953.
[598] Ibid., 954-957.
[599] Ibid., 957.
[600] Ibid., 957-958.
[601] Ibid., 958.
[602] Ibid., 960-961.
[603] Ibid., 961-962.
[604] Ibid., 963.
[605] Ibid., 964.
[606] Ibid., 966.
[607] Ibid., 967.
[608] Ibid., 967-968.
[609] Ibid., 968-969.
[610] Ibid., 969.
[611] Ibid., 971-972.

[612] Ibid., 972.

[613] Ibid., 974.

[614] Ibid., 981-982.

[615] Kavanagh seems to have interchanged the words "brick" and "cinder block." They are very different. The actual items were building bricks, not cinder blocks.

[616] Trial transcript, page 982. There are some minor grammatical changes to Kavanagh's actual words.

[617] Ibid., 983.

[618] Ibid., 985.

[619] Ibid.

[620] Ibid., 986.

[621] Ibid., 986-987.

[622] Ibid., 987.

[623] Ibid.

[624] Ibid., 989.

[625] Ibid.

[626] Ibid., 993.

[627] Ibid., 993-994.

[628] Ibid., 999-1000.

[629] Ibid., 1000.

[630] Ibid., 1001-1002.

[631] Ibid., 1003-1004.

[632] Ibid., 1004-1005.

[633] Ibid., 1008.

[634] Ibid., 1009.

[635] Ibid., 1058.

[636] Ibid., 1062.

[637] Ibid., 1062-1063.

[638] Ibid., 1077.

[639] Ibid., 1080.

[640] Ibid., 1082.

[641] Ibid., 1090.

[642] Erik Nelson, "Dawson Guilty," *Daily Freeman*, January 20, 1989.

[643] Ibid.

[644] Ibid.

[645] Erik Nelson, "Investigators, Prosecutors Glad Dawson Trial Is Over," *Daily Freeman*, January 22, 1989.

[646] Nelson, "Dawson Guilty."

[647] Nelson, "Investigators, Prosecutors Glad Dawson Trial Is Over."

[648] Sentencing transcript, pages 3-4. There have been slight changes of grammar to the actual statement of the prosecutor.

[649] Ibid., 4.

[650] Ibid., 4-5.

[651] Ibid., 5-7.

[652] Erik Nelson, "Anna Kithcart's Killer Draws 25 Years to Life," *Daily Freeman*, February 26, 1989.

[653] Ibid.

[654] Erik Nelson, "Where's Alton Maddox? No-show Lawyer Misses Fifth City Court Date," *Daily Freeman*.

[655] Ibid.

[656] Tom Wakeman, "Maddox Here: Now Where's Client, Kiernan?," *Daily Freeman*, March 9, 1989.

[657] Ibid.

[658] http://www.thesmokinggun.com/documents/investigation/al-sharpton-764312

[659] Ibid.

[660] Ibid.

[661] Ibid.

[662] Erin Durkin, "Rev. Al Sharpton Worked as FBI Informant, Taping Conversations With Mob Pals to Help Bring Down Genovese Crime Family: Report," *New York Daily News*, April 8, 2014.

[663] Michael Gartland, "Pay-up time for Brawley: '87 rape-hoaxer finally shells out for slander," *New York Post*, August 4, 2013.

[664] Matter of Alton H. Maddox (Admitted as Alton H. Maddox, Jr.),

an Attorney, Respondent. Grievance Committee for the 2nd and 11th Judicial Districts, Petitioner, 157 A.D.2d 244 (1990).

[665] Ibid.

[666] Matter of Alton H. Maddox (Admitted as Alton H. Maddox, Jr.), a Suspended Attorney, Respondent. Grievance Committee for the Second and Eleventh Judicial Districts, Petitioner, 201 A.D.2d 24 (1994).

[667] Matter of Mason, 208 A.D.2d 1 (1995).

[668] Ibid.

[669] Frank Bruni, "Defendant Becomes an Issue in Slander Case," *New York Times*, December 10, 1997.

Also Available From WildBlue Press

When her missing boyfriend is found murdered, his body encased in cement inside a watering trough and dumped in a cattle field, a local sheriff is arrested and charged with his murder. But as an investigative journalist digs in, the truth leads to questions about her guilt. In his first full-length, original true-crime book for WildBlue Press, M. William Phelps delivers a hard-hitting, unique reading experience, immersing readers in the life of the first female deputy in Oglethorpe County, Georgia, who claims a sexual harassment suit she filed against the sheriff led to a murder charge. Is Tracy Fortson guilty or innocent? Read TARGETED and decide.

Read More: **http://wbp.bz/targeted**

Another Great True Crime Read From WildBlue Press

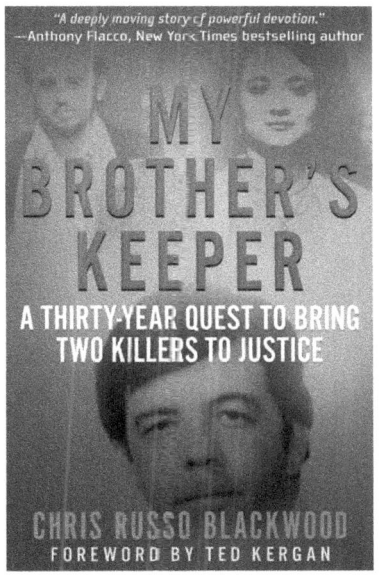

The moment he found out his brother was missing, Ted Kergan launched a relentless effort to bring two suspected killers—a teenaged-prostitute and her much older grifter boyfriend—to justice and find Gary Kergan's remains. Little did he know his quest would consume a fortune and take thirty years to reach a dramatic conclusion. MY BROTHER'S KEEPER is "a tremendous story of love and murder, faith and tenacity." (Steve Jackson, New York Times bestselling author of No Stone Unturned)

Read More: http://wbp.bz/mbk

See even more at:
http://wbp.bz/tc

More True Crime You'll Love From WildBlue Press

RAW DEAL by Gil Valle

RAW DEAL: The Untold Story of the NYPD's "Cannibal Cop" is the memoir of Gil Valle, written with co-author Brian Whitney. It is part of the controversial saga of a man who was imprisoned for "thought crimes," and a look into an online world of dark sexuality and violence that most people don't know exists, except maybe in their nightmares.

wbp.bz/rawdeal

BETRAYAL IN BLUE by Burl Barer & Frank C. Girardot Jr.

Adapted from Ken Eurell's shocking personal memoir, plus hundreds of hours of exclusive interviews with the major players, including former international drug lord, Adam Diaz, and Dori Eurell, revealing the truth behind what you won't see in the hit documentary THE SEVEN FIVE.

wbp.bz/bib

THE POLITICS OF MURDER by Margo Nash

"A chilling story about corruption, political power and a stacked judicial system in Massachusetts."–John Ferak, bestselling author of FAILURE OF JUSTICE.

wbp.bz/pom

FAILURE OF JUSTICE by John Ferak

If the dubious efforts of law enforcement that led to the case behind MAKING A MURDERER made you cringe, your skin will crawl at the injustice portrayed in FAILURE OF JUSTICE: A Brutal Murder, An Obsessed Cop, Six Wrongful Convictions. Award-winning journalist and bestselling author John Ferak pursued the story of the Beatrice 6 who were wrongfully accused of the brutal, ritualistic rape and murder of an elderly widow in Beatrice, Nebraska, and then railroaded by law enforcement into prison for a crime they did not commit.

wbp.bz/foj

www.ingramcontent.com/pod-product-compliance
Lightning Source LLC
Chambersburg PA
CBHW051526020426
42333CB00016B/1793